D1333385

WE WISH TO INFORM YOU

THAT TOMORROW

WE WILL BE KILLED

WITH OUR FAMILIES

WE WISH TO INFORM YOU

THAT TOMORROW

WE WILL BE KILLED

WITH OUR FAMILIES

STORIES FROM RWANDA

PHILIP GOUREVITCH

PICADOR

First published 1998 by Farrar, Straus & Giroux, New York

This edition published 1999 by Picador
an imprint of Macmillan Publishers Ltd
25 Eccleston Place, London SW1W 9NF
Basingstoke and Oxford
Associated companies throughout the world
www.macmillan.co.uk

ISBN 0 330 37120 7

9 8 7 6 5 4 3

A CIP catalogue record for this book is available from
the British Library.

Printed and bound in Great Britain by
Mackays of Chatham plc, Chatham, Kent

for my parents

WE WISH TO INFORM YOU

THAT TOMORROW

WE WILL BE KILLED

WITH OUR FAMILIES

Decimation means the killing of every tenth person in a population, and in the spring and early summer of 1994 a program of massacres decimated the Republic of Rwanda. Although the killing was low-tech—performed largely by machete—it was carried out at dazzling speed: of an original population of about seven and a half million, at least eight hundred thousand people were killed in just a hundred days. Rwandans often speak of a million deaths, and they may be right. The dead of Rwanda accumulated at nearly three times the rate of Jewish dead during the Holocaust. It was the most efficient mass killing since the atomic bombings of Hiroshima and Nagasaki.

IN THE SOUTHERN hill town of Gikongoro, the electricity had failed for the night; the Guest House bar was lit by a half dozen candles, and the eyes of the three soldiers who invited me to drink glowed the color of blood oranges. A single glass of beer was passed, from which I was the last to sip—a ritual signifying that I was not to be poisoned. The soldiers were too drunk for conversation, but a civilian among their party, a man in a shiny black training suit, appeared determined to demonstrate his sobriety. He sat stiffly straight with his arms folded over his chest and his eyes fixed in a hard squint, aloof and appraising. He asked my name in stern, robotic English, each syllable precise and abrupt. I told him, "Philip."

"Ah." He clutched my hand. "Like in Charles Dickens."

"That's Pip," I said.

"*Great Expectations*," he pronounced. He dropped my hand. His lips bunched up tightly, and he considered me with his humorless stare. Then he said, "I am a pygmy from the jungle. But I learned English from an Anglican bishop."

He didn't say his name. The soldier beside me, who had been leaning forward, propped on the upturned barrel of his machine gun, fell suddenly into his own lap, asleep, then jerked awake and smiled and drank some more. The pygmy took no notice. "I have a principle," he announced. "I believe in the principle of *Homo sapiens*. You get me?"

I took a guess. "You mean that all humanity is one?"

"That is my theory," the pygmy said. "That is my principle. But I have a problem. I must marry a white woman."

"Why not?" I said. Then, after a moment, I said, "But why, if we're all the same? Who cares what color your wife is?"

"She *must* be a white woman," the pygmy said. "Only a white woman can understand my universal principle of *Homo sapiens*. I must not marry a Negro." The unalloyed disgust with which he spoke this last word inclined me to agree, for the future wife's sake. "This is my problem," he went on. "How am I to attain this goal? You have the opportunity. I have not." He looked around the dark, nearly empty room and held out an empty hand. A sour look came over him, an atmosphere of accustomed disappointment, and he said, "How am I to meet the white woman? How do I find the white wife?"

The question was not entirely rhetorical. I had entered the bar with a Dutch woman, then lost track of her—she had gone to bed—but she had made an impression; I believe the pygmy wanted me to fix him up. "I have an idea," he said. "The Netherlands. The bishop, my teacher, had traveled through all the world. To me, the Netherlands is just imagination. But it is real to me."

I'M TELLING YOU this here, at the outset, because this is a book about how people imagine themselves and one another—a book about how we imagine our world. In Rwanda, a year before I met the pygmy, the government had adopted a new policy, according to which everyone in the country's Hutu majority group was called upon to murder everyone in the Tutsi minority. The government, and an astounding number of its subjects, imagined that by exterminating the Tutsi people they could make the world a better place, and the mass killing had followed.

All at once, as it seemed, something we could have only imagined was upon us—and we could still only imagine it. This is what fascinates me most in existence: the peculiar necessity of imagining what is, in fact, real. During the months of killing in 1994, as I followed the news from Rwanda, and later, when I read that the United Nations had decided, for the first time in its history, that it needed to use the word "genocide" to describe what had happened, I was repeatedly reminded of the moment, near the end of Conrad's *Heart of Darkness*, when the narrator Marlow is back in Europe, and his aunt, finding him depleted, fusses over his health. "It was not my strength that needed nursing," Marlow says, "it was my imagination that wanted soothing."

I took Marlow's condition on returning from Africa as my point of departure. I wanted to know how Rwandans understood what had happened in their country, and how they were getting on in the aftermath. The word "genocide" and the images of the nameless and numberless dead left too much to the imagination.

I BEGAN VISITING Rwanda in May of 1995, and I hadn't been there long before I met the pygmy in Gikongoro. I wouldn't have guessed that he was a pygmy: he was nearly five and a half feet tall. By declaring himself, he seemed to be setting himself apart from the matter of Hutu and Tutsi, and relating to me as a fellow outsider—an observer at large. Still, although he never said a word about the genocide, I came away with the impression that that was the true subject of our exchange. It may have been possible to talk of something else in Rwanda, but I never had a conversation of substance there in which the genocide did not figure, at least quietly, as the point of reference from which all other understandings and misunderstandings stemmed.

So the pygmy spoke of *Homo sapiens*, and I heard a subtext. Pygmies were Rwanda's first inhabitants, a forest people, who were generally looked down upon by Hutu and Tutsi alike as a vestigial, aboriginal lot. In the precolonial monarchy, pygmies served as court jesters, and because Rwanda's kings were Tutsis, the memory of this ancestral role meant that during the genocide pygmies were sometimes put to death as royalist tools, while elsewhere they were enlisted by Hutu militias as rapists—to add an extra dash of tribal mockery to the violation of Tutsi women.

Quite likely, the Anglican bishop who had instructed the man I met in the Guest House bar would have regarded the education of such an original savage as a special trophy challenge to the missionary dogma that we are all God's children. But perhaps the pygmy had learned his lessons too well. Clearly, in his experience, the oneness of humanity was not a fact but, as he kept saying, a theory, a principle—a proposition of the white priest. He had taken this proposition to heart as an invitation, only to discover that it had forbidding limits. In the name of universalism, he had learned to despise the people and the jungle he came from, and to love himself for disdaining that inheritance. Now he had conceived that a white wife was the missing link required to prove his theory, and the improbability of such a match was sorely testing his faith.

I sought to ease the pygmy's frustration by suggesting that even for white men surrounded by white women—even in the Netherlands—finding a sympathetic mate can prove a great challenge. "I am talking about the African," he said. "The African is sick." He managed, for the first time, a twisted little smile.

"There is a novel," he went on. "The book is *Wuthering Heights*. You get me? This is my larger theory. It doesn't matter if you are white or yellow or green or a black African Negro. The concept is *Homo sapiens*. The European is at an advanced technological stage, and the African is at a stage of technology that is more primitive. But all humanity must unite together in the struggle against nature. This is the principle of *Wuthering Heights*. This is the mission of *Homo sapiens*. Do you agree?"

I said, "I hear you."

"Humanity's struggle to conquer nature," the pygmy said

fondly. "It is the only hope. It is the only way for peace and reconciliation—all humanity one against nature."

He sat back in his chair, with his arms crossed over his chest, and went silent. After a while, I said, "But humanity is part of nature, too."

"Exactly," the pygmy said. "That is exactly the problem."

Part One

Leontius, the son of Aglaion, was coming up from the Peiraeus, close to the outer side of the north wall, when he saw some dead bodies lying near the executioner, and he felt a desire to look at them, and at the same time felt disgust at the thought, and tried to turn aside. For some time he fought with himself and put his hand over his eyes, but in the end the desire got the better of him, and opening his eyes wide with his fingers he ran forward to the bodies, saying, "There you are, curse you, have your fill of the lovely spectacle."

—PLATO, *The Republic*

1

IN THE PROVINCE of Kibungo, in eastern Rwanda, in the swamp- and pastureland near the Tanzanian border, there's a rocky hill called Nyarubuye with a church where many Tutsis were slaughtered in mid-April of 1994. A year after the killing I went to Nyarubuye with two Canadian military officers. We flew in a United Nations helicopter, traveling low over the hills in the morning mists, with the banana trees like green starbursts dense over the slopes. The uncut grass blew back as we dropped into the center of the parish schoolyard. A lone soldier materialized with his Kalashnikov, and shook our hands with stiff, shy formality. The Canadians presented the paperwork for our visit, and I stepped up into the open doorway of a classroom.

At least fifty mostly decomposed cadavers covered the floor, wadded in clothing, their belongings strewn about and smashed. Macheted skulls had rolled here and there.

The dead looked like pictures of the dead. They did not smell. They did not buzz with flies. They had been killed thirteen months earlier, and they hadn't been moved. Skin stuck here and there over the bones, many of which lay scattered away from the bodies, dismembered by the killers, or by scavengers—birds, dogs, bugs. The more complete figures looked a lot like people, which they were once. A woman in a cloth wrap printed with flowers lay near the door. Her fleshless hip bones were high and her legs slightly spread, and a child's skeleton extended between them. Her torso was hollowed out. Her ribs and spinal column poked through the rotting cloth. Her head was tipped back and her mouth was open: a strange image—half agony, half repose.

I had never been among the dead before. What to do? Look? Yes. I wanted to see them, I suppose; I had come to see them— the dead had been left unburied at Nyarubuye for memorial purposes—and there they were, so intimately exposed. I didn't need to see them. I already knew, and believed, what had happened in Rwanda. Yet looking at the buildings and the bodies, and hearing the silence of the place, with the grand Italianate basilica standing there deserted, and beds of exquisite, decadent, death-fertilized flowers blooming over the corpses, it was still strangely unimaginable. I mean one still had to imagine it.

Those dead Rwandans will be with me forever, I expect. That was why I had felt compelled to come to Nyarubuye: to be stuck with them—not with their experience, but with the experience of looking at them. They had been killed there, and they were dead there. What else could you really see at first? The Bible bloated with rain lying on top of one corpse or, littered about, the little woven wreaths of thatch which Rwandan women wear as crowns to balance the enormous loads they carry on their heads, and the water gourds, and the Converse tennis sneaker stuck somehow in a pelvis.

The soldier with the Kalashnikov—Sergeant Francis of the Rwandese Patriotic Army, a Tutsi whose parents had fled to Uganda with him when he was a boy, after similar but less extensive massacres in the early 1960s, and who had fought his way home in 1994 and found it like this—said that the dead in this room were mostly women who had been raped before being murdered. Sergeant Francis had high, rolling girlish hips, and he walked and stood with his butt stuck out behind him, an oddly purposeful posture, tipped forward, driven. He was, at once, candid and briskly official. His English had the punctilious clip of military drill, and after he told me what I was looking at I looked instead at my feet. The rusty head of a hatchet lay beside them in the dirt.

A few weeks earlier, in Bukavu, Zaire, in the giant market of a refugee camp that was home to many Rwandan Hutu militiamen, I had watched a man butchering a cow with a machete. He was quite expert at his work, taking big precise strokes that made a sharp hacking noise. The rallying cry to the killers during the genocide was "Do your work!" And I saw that it *was* work, this butchery; hard work. It took many hacks—two, three, four, five hard hacks—to chop through the cow's leg. How many hacks to dismember a person?

Considering the enormity of the task, it is tempting to play with theories of collective madness, mob mania, a fever of hatred erupted into a mass crime of passion, and to imagine the blind orgy of the mob, with each member killing one or two people. But at Nyarubuye, and at thousands of other sites in this tiny country, on the same days of a few months in 1994, hundreds of thousands of Hutus had worked as killers in regular shifts. There was always the next victim, and the next. What sustained them, beyond the frenzy of the first attack, through the plain physical exhaustion and mess of it?

The pygmy in Gikongoro said that humanity is part of nature and that we must go against nature to get along and have peace. But mass violence, too, must be organized; it does not occur aimlessly. Even mobs and riots have a design, and great and sustained destruction requires great ambition. It must be conceived as the means toward achieving a new order, and although the idea behind that new order may be criminal and objectively very stupid, it must also be compellingly simple and at the same time absolute. The ideology of genocide is all of those things, and in Rwanda it went by the bald name of Hutu Power. For those who set about systematically exterminating an entire people—even a fairly small and

17

unresisting subpopulation of perhaps a million and a quarter men, women, and children, like the Tutsis in Rwanda—blood lust surely helps. But the engineers and perpetrators of a slaughter like the one just inside the door where I stood need not enjoy killing, and they may even find it unpleasant. What is required above all is that they want their victims dead. They have to want it so badly that they consider it a necessity.

So I still had much to imagine as I entered the classroom and stepped carefully between the remains. These dead and their killers had been neighbors, schoolmates, colleagues, sometimes friends, even in-laws. The dead had seen their killers training as militias in the weeks before the end, and it was well known that they were training to kill Tutsis; it was announced on the radio, it was in the newspapers, people spoke of it openly. The week before the massacre at Nyarubuye, the killing began in Rwanda's capital, Kigali. Hutus who opposed the Hutu Power ideology were publicly denounced as "accomplices" of the Tutsis and were among the first to be killed as the extermination got under way. In Nyarubuye, when Tutsis asked the Hutu Power mayor how they might be spared, he suggested that they seek sanctuary at the church. They did, and a few days later the mayor came to kill them. He came at the head of a pack of soldiers, policemen, militiamen, and villagers; he gave out arms and orders to complete the job well. No more was required of the mayor, but he also was said to have killed a few Tutsis himself.

The killers killed all day at Nyarubuye. At night they cut the Achilles tendons of survivors and went off to feast behind the church, roasting cattle looted from their victims in big fires, and drinking beer. (Bottled beer, banana beer—Rwandans may not drink more beer than other Africans, but they drink prodigious quantities of it around the clock.) And, in the morning, still drunk after whatever sleep they could find beneath the cries of their prey, the killers at Nyarubuye went back and killed again. Day after day, minute to minute, Tutsi by Tutsi: all across Rwanda, they worked like that. "It was a process," Sergeant Francis said. I can see that it happened, I can be told how, and after nearly three years of looking around Rwanda and listening to Rwandans, I can tell you how, and I will. But the horror of it—the idiocy, the waste, the sheer wrongness—remains uncircumscribable.

Like Leontius, the young Athenian in Plato, I presume that you are reading this because you desire a closer look, and that you, too, are properly disturbed by your curiosity. Perhaps, in examining this extremity with me, you hope for some understanding, some insight, some flicker of self-knowledge—a moral, or a lesson, or a clue about how to behave in this world: some such information. I don't discount the possibility, but when it comes to genocide, you already know right from wrong. The best reason I have come up with for looking closely into Rwanda's stories is that ignoring them makes me even more uncomfortable about existence and my place in it. The horror, as horror, interests me only insofar as a precise memory of the offense is necessary to understand its legacy.

The dead at Nyarubuye were, I'm afraid, beautiful. There was no getting around it. The skeleton is a beautiful thing. The randomness of the fallen forms, the strange tranquillity of their rude exposure, the skull here, the arm bent in some uninterpretable gesture there—these things were beautiful, and their beauty only added to the affront of the place. I couldn't settle on any meaningful response: revulsion, alarm, sorrow, grief, shame, incomprehension, sure, but nothing truly meaningful. I just looked, and I took photographs, because I wondered whether I could really see what I was seeing while I saw it, and I wanted also an excuse to look a bit more closely.

We went on through the first room and out the far side. There was another room and another and another and another. They were all full of bodies, and more bodies were scattered in the grass, and there were stray skulls in the grass, which was thick and wonderfully green. Standing outside, I heard a crunch. The old Canadian colonel stumbled in front of me, and I saw, though he did not notice, that his foot had rolled on a skull and broken it. For the first time at Nyarubuye my feelings focused, and what I felt was a small but keen anger at this man. Then I heard another crunch, and felt a vibration underfoot. I had stepped on one, too.

RWANDA IS SPECTACULAR to behold. Throughout its center, a winding succession of steep, tightly terraced slopes radiates out from small roadside settlements and solitary compounds. Gashes of red clay and black loam mark fresh hoe work; eucalyptus trees flash silver against brilliant green tea plantations; banana trees are everywhere. On the theme of hills, Rwanda produces countless variations: jagged rain forests, round-shouldered buttes, undulating moors, broad swells of savanna, volcanic peaks sharp as filed teeth. During the rainy season, the clouds are huge and low and fast, mists cling in highland hollows, lightning flickers through the nights, and by day the land is lustrous. After the rains, the skies lift, the terrain takes on a ragged look beneath the flat unvarying haze of the dry season, and in the savannas of the Akagera Park wildfire blackens the hills.

One day, when I was returning to Kigali from the south, the car mounted a rise between two winding valleys, the windshield filled with purple-bellied clouds, and I asked Joseph, the man who was giving me a ride, whether Rwandans realize what a beautiful country they have. "Beautiful?" he said. "You think so? After the things that happened here? The people aren't good. If the people were good, the country might be OK." Joseph told me that his brother and sister had been killed, and he made a soft hissing click with his tongue against his teeth. "The country is empty," he said. "Empty!"

It was not just the dead who were missing. The genocide had been brought to a halt by the Rwandese Patriotic Front, a rebel army led by Tutsi refugees from past persecutions, and as the RPF advanced through the country in the summer of 1994, some two million Hutus had fled into exile at the behest of the same leaders who had urged them to kill. Yet except in some rural areas in the south, where the desertion of Hutus had left nothing but bush to reclaim the fields around crumbling adobe houses, I, as a newcomer, could not see the emptiness that blinded Joseph to Rwanda's beauty. Yes, there were grenade-flattened buildings, burnt homesteads, shot-up facades, and mortar-pitted roads. But these were the ravages of war, not of genocide, and by the summer of 1995, most of the dead had been buried. Fifteen months earlier, Rwanda had been the most densely populated country in Africa. Now the work of the killers looked just as they had intended: invisible.

From time to time, mass graves were discovered and excavated, and the remains would be transferred to new, properly consecrated mass graves. Yet even the occasionally exposed bones, the conspicuous number of amputees and people with deforming scars, and the superabundance of packed orphanages could not be taken as evidence that what had happened to Rwanda was an attempt to eliminate a people. There were only people's stories.

"Every survivor wonders why he is alive," Abbé Modeste, a priest at the cathedral in Butare, Rwanda's second-largest city, told me. Abbé Modeste had hidden for weeks in his sacristy, eating communion wafers, before moving under the desk in his study, and finally into the rafters at the home of some neighboring nuns. The obvious explanation of his survival was that the RPF had come to the rescue. But the RPF didn't reach Butare till early July, and roughly seventy-five percent of the Tutsis in Rwanda had been killed by early May. In this regard, at least, the genocide had been entirely successful: to those who were targeted, it was not death but life that seemed an accident of fate.

"I had eighteen people killed at my house," said Etienne Niyonzima, a former businessman who had become a deputy in the National Assembly. "Everything was totally destroyed—a place of fifty-five meters by fifty meters. In my neighborhood they killed six hundred and forty-seven people. They tortured them, too. You had to see how they killed them. They had the number of everyone's house, and they went through with red paint and marked the homes of all the Tutsis and of the Hutu moderates. My wife was at a friend's, shot with two bullets. She is still alive, only"— he fell quiet for a moment—"she has no arms. The others with her were killed. The militia left her for dead. Her whole family of sixty-five in Gitarama were killed." Niyonzima was in hiding at the time. Only after he had been separated from his wife for three months did he learn that she and four of their children had survived. "Well," he said, "one son was cut in the head with a machete. I don't know where he went." His voice weakened, and caught. "He disappeared." Niyonzima clicked his tongue, and said, "But the others are still alive. Quite honestly, I don't understand at all how I was saved."

Laurent Nkongoli attributed his survival to "Providence, and also good neighbors, an old woman who said, 'Run away, we don't want to see your corpse.' " Nkongoli, a lawyer, who had become the vice president of the National Assembly after the genocide, was a robust man, with a taste for double-breasted suit jackets and lively ties, and he moved, as he spoke, with a brisk determination. But before taking his neighbor's advice, and fleeing Kigali in late April of 1994, he said, "I had accepted death. At a certain moment this happens. One hopes not to die cruelly, but one expects to die anyway. Not death by machete, one hopes, but with a bullet. If you were willing to pay for it, you could often ask for a bullet. Death was more or less normal, a resignation. You lose the will to fight. There were four thousand Tutsis killed here at Kacyiru"— a neighborhood of Kigali. "The soldiers brought them here, and told them to sit down because they were going to throw grenades. And they sat.

"Rwandan culture is a culture of fear," Nkongoli went on. "I remember what people said." He adopted a pipey voice, and his face took on a look of disgust: " 'Just let us pray, then kill us,' or

'I don't want to die in the street, I want to die at home.' " He resumed his normal voice. "When you're that resigned and oppressed you're already dead. It shows the genocide was prepared for too long. I detest this fear. These victims of genocide had been psychologically prepared to expect death just for being Tutsi. They were being killed for so long that they were already dead."

I reminded Nkongoli that, for all his hatred of fear, he had himself accepted death before his neighbor urged him to run away. "Yes," he said. "I got tired in the genocide. You struggle so long, then you get tired."

Every Rwandan I spoke with seemed to have a favorite, unanswerable question. For Nkongoli, it was how so many Tutsis had allowed themselves to be killed. For François Xavier Nkurunziza, a Kigali lawyer, whose father was Hutu and whose mother and wife were Tutsi, the question was how so many Hutus had allowed themselves to kill. Nkurunziza had escaped death only by chance as he moved around the country from one hiding place to another, and he had lost many family members. "Conformity is very deep, very developed here," he told me. "In Rwandan history, everyone obeys authority. People revere power, and there isn't enough education. You take a poor, ignorant population, and give them arms, and say, 'It's yours. Kill.' They'll obey. The peasants, who were paid or forced to kill, were looking up to people of higher socio-economic standing to see how to behave. So the people of influence, or the big financiers, are often the big men in the genocide. They may think that they didn't kill because they didn't take life with their own hands, but the people were looking to them for their orders. And, in Rwanda, an order can be given very quietly."

As I traveled around the country, collecting accounts of the killing, it almost seemed as if, with the machete, the *masu*—a club studded with nails—a few well-placed grenades, and a few bursts of automatic-rifle fire, the quiet orders of Hutu Power had made the neutron bomb obsolete.

"Everyone was called to hunt the enemy," said Theodore Nyi-linkwaya, a survivor of the massacres in his home village of Kimbogo, in the southwestern province of Cyangugu. "But let's say someone is reluctant. Say that guy comes with a stick. They tell him, 'No, get a *masu*.' So, OK, he does, and he runs along with the rest, but he doesn't kill. They say, 'Hey, he might denounce us later. He must kill. Everyone must help to kill at least one person.' So this person who is not a killer is made to do it. And the next day it's become a game for him. You don't need to keep pushing him."

At Nyarubuye, even the little terracotta votive statues in the sacristy had been methodically decapitated. "They were associated with Tutsis," Sergeant Francis explained.

2

IF YOU COULD walk due west from the massacre memorial at Nyarubuye, straight across Rwanda from one end to the other, over the hills and through the marshes, lakes, and rivers to the province of Kibuye, then, just before you fell into the great inland sea of Lake Kivu, you would come to another hilltop village. This hill is called Mugonero, and it, too, is crowned by a big church. While Rwanda is overwhelmingly Catholic, Protestants evangelized much of Kibuye, and Mugonero is the headquarters of the Seventh-Day Adventist mission. The place resembles the brick campus of an American community college more than an African village; tidy tree-lined footpaths connect the big church with a smaller chapel, a nursing school, an infirmary, and a hospital complex that enjoyed a reputation for giving excellent medical care. It was in the hospital that Samuel Ndagijimana sought refuge during the killings, and although one of the first things he said to me was "I forget bit by bit," it quickly became clear that he hadn't forgotten as much as he might have liked.

Samuel worked as a medical orderly in the hospital. He had landed the job in 1991, when he was twenty-five. I asked him about his life in that time that Rwandans call "Before." He said, "We were simple Christians." That was all. I might have been asking about someone else, whom he had met only in passing, and

25

who didn't interest him. It was as if his first real memory was of the early days in April of 1994 when he saw Hutu militiamen conducting public exercises outside the government offices in Mugonero. "We watched young people going out every night, and people spoke of it on the radio," Samuel said. "It was only members of Hutu Power parties who went out, and those who weren't participants were called 'enemies.' "

On April 6, a few nights after this activity began, Rwanda's long-standing Hutu dictator, President Juvénal Habyarimana, was assassinated in Kigali, and a clique of Hutu Power leaders from the military high command seized power. "The radio announced that people shouldn't move," Samuel said. "We began to see groups of people gathering that same night, and when we went to work in the morning, we saw these groups with the local leaders of Hutu Power organizing the population. You didn't know exactly what was happening, just that there was something coming."

At work, Samuel observed "a change of climate." He said that "one didn't talk to anyone anymore," and many of his co-workers spent all their time in meetings with a certain Dr. Gerard, who made no secret of his support for Hutu Power. Samuel found this shocking, because Dr. Gerard had been trained in the United States, and he was the son of the president of the Adventist church in Kibuye, so he was seen as a figure of great authority, a community leader—one who sets the example.

After a few days, when Samuel looked south across the valley from Mugonero, he saw houses burning in villages along the lakefront. He decided to stay in the church hospital until the troubles were over, and Tutsi families from Mugonero and surrounding areas soon began arriving with the same idea. This was a tradition in Rwanda. "When there were problems, people always went to the church," Samuel said. "The pastors were Christians. One trusted that nothing would happen at their place." In fact, many people at Mugonero told me that Dr. Gerard's father, the church president, Pastor Elizaphan Ntakirutimana, was personally instructing Tutsis to gather at the Adventist complex.

Wounded Tutsis converged on Mugonero from up and down the lake. They came through the bush, trying to avoid the countless militia checkpoints along the road, and they brought stories. Some told how a few miles to the north, in Gishyita, the mayor had been so frantic in his impatience to kill Tutsis that thousands had been slaughtered even as he herded them to the church, where the remainder were massacred. Others told how a few miles to the south, in Rwamatamu, more than ten thousand Tutsis had taken refuge in the town hall, and the mayor had brought in truckloads of policemen and soldiers and militia with guns and grenades to surround the place; behind them he had arranged villagers with machetes in case anyone escaped when the shooting began—and, in fact, there had been very few escapees from Rwamatamu. An Adventist pastor and his son were said to have worked closely with the mayor in organizing the slaughter at Rwamatamu. But perhaps Samuel did not hear about that from the wounded he met, who came "having been shot at, and had grenades thrown, missing an arm, or a leg." He still imagined that Mugonero could be spared.

By April 12, the hospital was packed with as many as two thousand refugees, and the water lines were cut. Nobody could leave; militiamen and members of the Presidential Guard had cordoned off the complex. But when Dr. Gerard learned that several dozen Hutus were among the refugees, he arranged for them to be evacuated. He also locked up the pharmacy, refusing treatment to the wounded and sick—"because they were Tutsi," Samuel said. Peering out from their confines, the refugees at the hospital watched Dr. Gerard and his father, Pastor Ntakirutimana, driving around with militiamen and members of the Presidential Guard. The refugees wondered whether these men had forgotten their God.

Among the Tutsis at the Mugonero church and hospital complex were seven Adventist pastors who quickly assumed their accustomed role as leaders of the flock. When two policemen turned up at the hospital, and announced that their job was to protect the refugees, the Tutsi pastors took up a collection, and raised almost four hundred dollars for the policemen. For several days, all was calm. Then, toward evening on April 15, the policemen said they had to leave because the hospital was to be attacked the next morning. They drove away in a car with Dr. Gerard, and the seven pastors in the hospital advised their fellow refugees to expect the end. Then the pastors sat down together and wrote letters to the mayor and to their boss, Pastor Elizaphan Ntakirutimana, Dr. Gerard's father, asking them in the name of the Lord to intercede on their behalf.

"And the response came," Samuel said. "It was Dr. Gerard who announced it: 'Saturday, the sixteenth, at exactly nine o'clock in the morning, you will be attacked.'" But it was Pastor Ntakirutimana's response that crushed Samuel's spirit, and he repeated the church president's words twice over, slowly: "Your problem has already found a solution. You must die." One of Samuel's colleagues, Manase Bimenyimana, remembered Ntakirutimana's response slightly differently. He told me that the pastor's words were "You must be eliminated. God no longer wants you."

In his capacity as a hospital orderly, Manase served as the household domestic for one of the doctors, and he had remained at the doctor's house after installing his wife and children—for safety—among the refugees at the hospital. Around nine o'clock on the morning of Saturday, April 16, he was feeding the doctor's dogs. He saw Dr. Gerard drive toward the hospital with a carload of armed men. Then he heard shooting and grenades exploding. "When the dogs heard the cries of the people," he told me, "they too began to howl."

Manase managed to make his way to the hospital—foolishly, perhaps, but he felt exposed and wanted to be with his family. He found the Tutsi pastors instructing the refugees to prepare for death. "I was very disappointed," Manase said. "I expected to die, and we started looking for anything to defend ourselves with— stones, broken bricks, sticks. But they were useless. The people were weak. They had nothing to eat. The shooting started, and people were falling down and dying."

There were many attackers, Samuel recalled, and they came from all sides—"from the church, from behind, from the north and south. We heard shots and cries and they chanted the slogan 'Eliminate the Tutsis.' They began shooting at us, and we threw stones at them because we had nothing else, not even a machete. We were hungry, tired, we hadn't had water for more than a day. There were people who had their arms cut off. There were dead. They killed the people at the chapel and the school and then the hospital. I saw Dr. Gerard, and I saw his father's car pass the hospital and stop near his office. Around noon, we went into a basement. I was with some family members. Others had been killed already. The attackers began to break down the doors and to kill, shooting and throwing grenades. The two policemen who had been our protectors were now attackers. The local citizenry also helped. Those who had no guns had machetes or *masus*. In the evening, around eight or nine o'clock, they began firing tear gas. People who were still alive cried. That way the attackers knew where people were, and they could kill them directly."

ON THE NATIONAL average, Tutsis made up a bit less than fifteen percent of Rwanda's population, but in the province of Kibuye the balance between Hutus and Tutsis was close to fifty-fifty. On April 6, 1994, about a quarter million Tutsis lived in Kibuye and a month later more than two hundred thousand of them had been killed. In many of Kibuye's villages, no Tutsi survived.

Manase told me that he was surprised when he heard that "only a million people" were killed in Rwanda. "Look at how many died just here, and how many were eaten by birds," he said. It was true that the dead of the genocide had been a great boon to Rwanda's birds, but the birds had also been helpful to the living. Just as birds of prey and carrion will form a front in the air before the advancing wall of a forest fire to feast on the parade of animals fleeing the inferno, so in Rwanda during the months of extermination the kettles of buzzards, kites, and crows that boiled over massacre sites marked a national map against the sky, flagging the "no-go" zones for people like Samuel and Manase, who took to the bush to survive.

Sometime before midnight on April 16, the killers at the Mugonero Adventist complex, unable to discover anybody left there to kill, went off to loot the homes of the dead, and Samuel in his basement, and Manase hiding with his murdered wife and children, found themselves unaccountably alive. Manase left immediately. He made his way to the nearby village of Murambi, where he joined up with a small band of survivors from other massacres who had once more taken shelter in an Adventist church. For nearly twenty-four hours, he said, they had peace. Then Dr. Gerard came with a convoy of militia. Again there was shooting, and Manase escaped. This time, he fled high up into the mountains, to a place called Bisesero, where the rock is steep and craggy, full of caves and often swaddled in cloud. Bisesero was the only place in Rwanda where thousands of Tutsi civilians mounted a defense against the Hutus who were trying to kill them. "Looking at how many people there were in Bisesero, we were convinced we could not die," Manase told me. And at first, he said, "only women and children were killed, because the men were fighting." But in time tens of thousands of men fell there, too.

Down in the corpse-crowded villages of Kibuye, live Tutsis had become extremely hard to find. But the killers never gave up. The hunt was in Bisesero, and the hunters came by truck and bus. "When they saw how strong the resistance was, they called militias from far away," Manase said. "And they did not kill simply. When we were weak, they saved bullets and killed us with bamboo spears. They cut Achilles tendons and necks, but not completely, and then they left the victims to spend a long time crying until they died. Cats and dogs were there, just eating people."

Samuel, too, had found his way to Bisesero. He had lingered in the Mugonero hospital, "full of dead," until one in the morning. Then he crept out of the basement and, carrying "one who had lost his feet," he proceeded slowly into the mountains. Samuel's account of his ordeal following the slaughter at his workplace was as telegraphic as his description of life in Mugonero before the genocide. Unlike Manase, he found little comfort at Bisesero, where the defenders' only advantage was the terrain. He had concluded that to be a Tutsi in Rwanda meant death. "After a month," he said, "I went to Zaire." To get there he had to descend through settled areas to Lake Kivu, and to cross the water at night in a pirogue—an outrageously risky journey, but Samuel didn't mention it.

Manase remained in Bisesero. During the fighting, he told me, "we got so used to running that when one wasn't running one didn't feel right." Fighting and running gave Manase spirit, a sense of belonging to a purpose greater than his own existence. Then he got shot in the thigh, and life once again became about little more than staying alive. He found a cavern, "a rock where a stream went underground, and came out below," and made it his home. "By day, I was alone," he said. "There were only dead people. The bodies fell down in the stream, and I used those bodies as a bridge to cross the water and join the other people in the evenings." In this way, Manase survived.

3

RWANDA HAS GOOD roads—the best in central Africa. But even the roads tell a story of Rwanda's affliction. The network of proper two-lane tarmac that spokes out from Kigali, stitching a tidy web among nine of the country's ten provincial capitals, excludes Kibuye. The road to Kibuye is an unpaved mess, a slalom course of steep hairpin switchbacks, whose surface alternates between bone-rattling rocks and red dirt that turns to deep, slurping clay in the rain, then bakes to stone-hard ruts and ridges in the sun. That the Kibuye road is in this condition is no accident. In the old order—"Before"—Tutsis were known in Rwanda as *inyenzi*, which means cockroaches, and, as you know, Kibuye was teeming with them. In the 1980s, when the government hired road builders from China, the Kibuye road was last on the list for a makeover, and when its turn finally came, the millions of dollars set aside for the job had vanished. So beautiful Kibuye, pinned east and west between mountains and lake, hemmed in north and south by swaths of primeval forest, remained (with a hotel full of idle Chinese road builders) a sort of equatorial Siberia.

The seventy-mile trip from Kigali to Kibuye town could normally be accomplished in three to four hours, but it took my convoy of four-wheel-drives twelve. A downpour began just after we started, around three in the afternoon, and by six, when the slick, shin-deep mud of a mountain pass sucked the first of our vehicles into the ditch, we had made only half the journey. Night fell and clouds of rippling mist closed in, amplifying the darkness. We didn't see the soldiers—a dozen men with Kalashnikovs, in slouch hats, trench coats, and rubber Wellington boots, picking their way through the mud with long wooden staffs—until they tapped on our windows. So it was no comfort when they informed us that we should shut off our lights, gather in one vehicle, and keep quiet, while we waited for rescue. This was in early September of 1996, more than two years after the genocide, and Hutu militiamen were still terrorizing Kibuye almost nightly.

On one side of the road, the mountain formed a wall, and on the other side, it plunged into an apparently vertical banana plantation. The rain dwindled to a beady mist, and I stood outside the designated vehicle, listening to the arrhythmic plink and plonk of water globules bouncing among the banana leaves. Unseen birds clucked fitfully. The night was a sort of xylophone, and I stood keenly alert. "You make a nice target," one of the soldiers had told us. But, so long as our periphery held, I was glad to be out there, on an impassable road in an often impossible-seeming country, hearing and smelling—and feeling my skin tighten against— the sort of dank, drifting midnight that every Rwandan must know and I had never experienced so unprotectedly.

An hour passed. Then a woman down in the valley began to scream. It was a wild and terrible sound, like the war whoop of a Hollywood Indian flapping his hand over his mouth. Silence followed for as long as it takes to fill lungs with air, and the ululating alarm rang out again, higher now and faster, more frantic. This time, before the woman's breath broke, other voices joined in. The whooping radiated out through the nether darkness. I took it that we were under attack, and did nothing because I had no idea what to do.

Within moments, three or four soldiers materialized on the road, and went over the shoulder, pitching down through the banana trees. The continuous whooping knotted around a focal point, reached a peak of volume, and began to subside into shouting, in which the voice of the original woman stood out with magnificently adamant fury. Soon the valley fell quiet, except for the old plink and plonk among the banana leaves. Another hour elapsed. Then, just as cars arrived from Kibuye to escort my halted party to our predawn beds, the soldiers climbed back onto the road, leading a half dozen ragged peasants who carried sticks and machetes. In their midst walked a roughed-up, hang-dog-looking prisoner.

A Rwandan in my convoy made inquiries and announced, "This fellow was wanting to rape the woman who cried." He explained that the whooping we'd heard was a conventional distress signal and that it carried an obligation. "You hear it, you do it, too. And you come running," he said. "No choice. You must. If you ignored this crying, you would have questions to answer. This is how Rwandans live in the hills." He held his hands up flat, and tipped them against each other this way and that, shuffling them around to indicate a patchwork, which is the way the land is parceled up, plot by plot, each household well set off from the next within its patch. "The people are living separately together," he said. "So there is responsibility. I cry, you cry. You cry, I cry. We all come running, and the one that stays quiet, the one that stays home, must explain. Is he in league with the criminals? Is he a coward? And what would he expect when he cries? This is simple. This is normal. This is community."

It struck me as an enviable arrangement. If you cry out, where you live, can you expect to be heard? If you hear a cry of alarm, do you add your voice and come running? Are rapes often averted, and rapists captured, in this way in your place? I was deeply impressed. But what if this system of communal obligation is turned on its head, so that murder and rape become the rule? What if innocence becomes a crime and the person who protects his neighbor is counted as an "accomplice"? Does it then become normal for tear gas to be used to make people in dark hiding places cry so that they can be killed? Later, when I visited Mugonero, and Samuel told me about the tear gas, I remembered the woman's cry in the valley.

IN MID-JULY of 1994, three months after the massacre at the Mugonero Adventist complex, the church president, Pastor Elizaphan Ntakirutimana, fled with his wife to Zaire, then to Zambia, and from there to Laredo, Texas. It wasn't easy for Rwandans to get American visas after the genocide, but the Ntakirutimanas had a son named Eliel in Laredo, a cardiac anesthesiologist who had been a naturalized United States citizen for more than a decade. So the pastor and his wife were granted green cards—"permanent resident alien" status—and settled in Laredo. Shortly after they arrived, a group of Tutsis who lived in the Midwest sent a letter to the White House, asking that Pastor Ntakirutimana be brought to justice for his conduct during the Mugonero massacre. "After several months," one of the letter's signers told me, "an answer came from Thomas E. Donilon, Assistant Secretary of State for Public Affairs, expressing sympathy for what happened and then just stating the terms of all the foreign aid America was giving to Rwanda. We were saying, here are one million people killed, and here's one man—so we were kind of upset."

On the second anniversary of the Mugonero massacre, a small group of Tutsis descended on Laredo to march and wave signs outside the Ntakirutimanas' residence. They hoped to attract press coverage, and the story *was* sensational: a preacher accused of presiding over the slaughter of hundreds in his congregation. Serbs suspected of much less extensive crimes in the former Yugoslavia—men with no hope of American green cards—were receiving daily international coverage, but aside from a few scattered news briefs, the pastor had been spared such unpleasantness.

Yet, when I returned to New York in September of 1996, a week after my visit to Mugonero, I learned that the FBI was preparing to arrest Elizaphan Ntakirutimana in Laredo. The United Nations' International Criminal Tribunal for Rwanda, sitting in Arusha, Tanzania, had issued an indictment against him, charging him with three counts of genocide and three counts of crimes against humanity. The indictment, which made the same charges against Dr. Gerard Ntakirutimana, as well as the mayor, Charles Sikubwabo, and a local businessman, told the same story that survivors had told me: the pastor had "instructed" Tutsis to take refuge at the Adventist complex; Dr. Gerard had helped to extricate "non-Tutsis" from among the refugees; father and son had arrived at the complex on the morning of April 16, 1994, in a convoy of attackers; and "during the months that followed" both men were held to have "searched for and attacked Tutsi survivors and others, killing or causing serious bodily or mental harm to them."

The indictment was a secret, as were the FBI's plans for an arrest. Laredo, a hot, flat town, tucked into one of the southernmost bends of the Rio Grande, overlooks Mexico, and the pastor had a record of flight.

THE ADDRESS I had for Dr. Eliel Ntakirutimana in Laredo was 313 Potrero Court—a suburban brick ranch house at the end of a drab cul-de-sac. A dog growled when I rang the bell, but nobody answered. I found a pay phone and called the local Adventist church, but I don't speak Spanish, and the man who answered didn't speak English. I had a tip that Pastor Ntakirutimana was working at a health-food store, but after making the rounds of a few places with names like Casa Ginseng and Fiesta Natural that seemed to specialize in herbal remedies for constipation and impotence, I went back to Potrero Court. There was still nobody at 313. Down the street I found a man spraying his driveway with a garden hose. I told him I was looking for a family of Rwandans, and indicated the house. He said, "I don't know about that. I only know the people next door here a little." I thanked him, and he said, "Where'd you say these people were from?" Rwanda, I said. He hesitated a moment, then said, "Colored people?" I said, "They're from Africa." He pointed to 313, and told me, "That's the house. Fancy cars they drive. They moved out about a month ago."

Eliel Ntakirutimana's new phone number was unlisted, but late at night I got hold of an operator who gave me his address, and in the morning I drove there. The house was on Estate Drive, in an expensive-looking new private community, designed, as in Rwanda, with each home set within a walled compound. An electronic gate controlled access to the subdivision, where most of the plots were still empty prairie. The few houses were wild, vaguely Mediterranean fantasias, whose only common attribute was immensity. The Ntakirutimanas' stood at the end of the road behind another electronic security fence. A barefoot Rwandan maid led me past an open garage that housed a white Corvette convertible and into a vast kitchen area. She phoned Dr. Ntaki—he had chopped down his name as a professional courtesy to American tongues—and I told him I was hoping to meet his father. He asked how I'd found the house. I told him that, too, and he gave me an appointment in the afternoon at a hospital called Mercy.

While I was still on the phone, the doctor's wife, Genny, a handsome woman with an easy manner, came home from taking her kids to school. She offered me a cup of coffee—"From Rwanda," she said proudly. We sat on huge leather couches beside a gigantic television in an alcove of the kitchen, with a view over a patio, a barbecue pavilion, and, on the far shore of a tiled swimming pool, a patch of garden. The distant voices of the Rwandan maid and a Mexican nanny echoed off the marble floors and lofty ceilings of further rooms, and Genny said, "With my father-in-law, we were the last ones to hear anything. He was in Zaire, he was in Zambia, a refugee, and an old man—more than seventy years old. His one great wish was retirement and old age in Rwanda. Then he comes here and suddenly they say he killed people. You know Rwandans. Rwandans go crazy with jealousy. Rwandans don't like if you are rich or in good health."

Genny's own father was a Hutu who had been involved in politics and was killed by rivals in 1973. Her mother was a Tutsi who was saved by chance on the brink of being killed in 1994, and who still lived in Rwanda. "We mixed people don't hate Tutsi or Hutu," Genny said. This was an inaccurate generalization—many people of mixed parentage had killed as Hutus, or been killed as Tutsis—but Genny had been living in exile, and she explained, "Most Rwandans who are here in America like my husband have been here so long that they all take positions according to their families. If they say your brother killed, then you take his side." She did not seem to have her own mind entirely made up about her father-in-law, the pastor. She said, "This is a man who can't stand to see blood even when you kill a chicken. But anything is possible."

Just before noon, Dr. Ntaki called with a new plan: we would lunch at the Laredo Country Club. Then the family lawyer, Lazaro Gorza-Gongora, showed up. He was dapper and mild-mannered and very direct. He said that he wasn't prepared to let the pastor speak to me. "The accusations are outrageous, monstrous, and completely destructive," he said with disarming tranquillity. "People say whatever they want, and an old man's last years are in jeopardy."

Dr. Ntaki was a round, loquacious man with strikingly bulging eyes. He wore a malachite-faced Rolex watch and a white dress shirt with a boldly hand-stitched collar. As he drove Gorza-Gongora and me to the country club in a Chevrolet Suburban that had been customized to feel like a living room, complete with a television set, he spoke with great interest about Russian President Boris Yeltsin's preparations for open-heart surgery. Dr. Ntaki himself presided over the intravenous drips of open-heart patients, and he shared his wife's view that any charges against his father were the product of typical Rwandan class envy and spite. "They see us as rich and well educated," he said. "They can't take it." He told me that his family owned a spread of five hundred acres in Kibuye—kingly proportions in Rwanda—with coffee and banana plantations, many cattle, "and all those good Rwandan things." He said, "Here's a father with three sons who are doctors and two other children who work in international finance. This is in a country that didn't have a single person with a bachelor's degree in 1960. Of course everyone resents him and wants to destroy him."

We ate overlooking the golf course. Dr. Ntaki held forth on Rwandan politics. He didn't use the word "genocide"; he spoke of "chaos, chaos, chaos," with every man for himself just trying to save his own skin. And Tutsis had started it, he said, by killing the President. I reminded him that there was no evidence linking Tutsis to the assassination; that, in fact, the genocide had been meticulously planned by the Hutu extremists who set it in motion within an hour of the President's death. Dr. Ntaki ignored me. "If President Kennedy had been assassinated in this country by a black man," he said, "the American population would have most certainly killed all the blacks."

Gorza-Gongora watched me writing this absurd statement in my notebook and broke his silence. "You say 'extermination,' you say 'systematic,' you say 'genocide,' " he said to me. "That's just a theory, and I think you've come all the way to Laredo to hold up my client as a clever proof of this theory."

No, I said, I had come because a man of God was accused of having ordained the murder of half his flock, co-religionists, simply because they had been born as something called Tutsi.

"What's the evidence?" Gorza-Gongora said. "Eyewitnesses?" He chuckled. "Anybody can say they saw anything."

Dr. Ntaki went further; he detected a conspiracy: "The witnesses are all government tools. If they don't say what the new government wants, they'll be killed."

Still, Dr. Ntaki said that despite his lawyer's counsel, his father was concerned for his honor and wished to speak to me.

"The pastor thinks silence looks like guilt," Gorza-Gongora said. "Silence is peace."

Leaving the country club, I asked Dr. Ntaki if he ever had doubts about his father's innocence. He said, "Of course, but—" and, after a second, "Do you have a father? I will defend him with everything I have."

PASTOR ELIZAPHAN NTAKIRUTIMANA was a man of stern composure. He sat in a wing chair in the doctor's parlor, clutching a manila folder in his lap, and wearing a gray cap over his gray hair, a gray shirt, black suspenders, black pants, black square-toed shoes, and squarish wire-rimmed glasses. He spoke in Kinyarwanda, the language of his country, and his son translated. He said, "They are saying I killed people. Eight thousand people." The number was about four times higher than any I had previously heard. The pastor's voice was full of angry disbelief. "It is all one hundred percent pure lies. I did not kill any people. I never told anybody to kill any people. I could not do such things."

When the "chaos" began in Kigali, the pastor explained, he didn't think it would reach Mugonero, and when Tutsis began going to the hospital, he claimed he had to ask them why. After about a week, he said, there were so many refugees that "things started turning a little weird." So the pastor and his son Gerard held a meeting to address the question "What are we going to do?" But at that moment two policemen showed up to guard the hospital, and he said, "We didn't have the meeting, because they had done it without our asking."

Then, on Saturday, April 16, at seven in the morning, the two policemen from the hospital came to Pastor Ntakirutimana's house. "They gave me letters from the Tutsi pastors there," he said. "One was addressed to me, another to the mayor. I read mine. The letter they gave me said, 'You understand they are plotting, they are trying to kill us, can you go to the mayor and ask him to protect us?'" Ntakirutimana read this, then went to the mayor, Charles Sikubwabo. "I told him what my message from the Tutsi pastors said, and gave him his letter. The mayor told me, 'Pastor, there's no government. I have no power. I can do nothing.'

"I was surprised," Ntakirutimana went on. "I returned to Mugonero, and I told the policemen to go with a message to the pastors to tell them, 'Nothing can be done, and the mayor, too, said he can do nothing.'" Then Pastor Ntakirutimana took his wife and some others who "wanted to hide" and drove out of town—to Gishyita, which is where Mayor Sikubwabo lived, and where many of the injured refugees at Mugonero had received their wounds. "Gishyita," he explained, "had killed its people already, so there was peace."

Pastor Ntakirutimana said that he hadn't returned to Mugonero until April 27. "Everybody was buried," he told me, "I never saw anything." After that, he said, "I never went anywhere. I stayed at my office. Only, one day I went to Rwamatamu because I heard that pastors had also died there, and I wanted to see if I could find even a kid of theirs to save. But I found nothing to save. They were Tutsis."

The pastor made himself out as a great patron of Tutsis. He said he had given them jobs and shelter, and promoted them within the Adventist hierarchy. He lifted his chin and said, "As long as I live, in my whole life, there is nobody I tried to help more than Tutsis." He could not understand how Tutsis could be so ungrateful as to make accusations against him. "It looks as if there is no justice anymore," he said.

The name Ntakirutimana means "nothing is greater than God," and the pastor told me, "I think I'm closer to God than I have ever been in my life." He said, "When I see what happened in Rwanda, I'm very sad about it because politics is bad. A lot of people died." He didn't sound sad; he sounded tired, harassed, indignant. "Hatred is the result of sin, and when Jesus Christ comes, he's the only one who's going to take it away," he said, and once more, he added, "Everything was chaos."

"They say you organized it," I reminded him.

He said, "Never, never, never, never."

I asked him whether he remembered the precise language of the letter addressed to him by the seven Tutsi pastors who were killed at Mugonero. He opened the folder in his lap. "Here," he said, and held out the handwritten original and a translation. His daughter-in-law, Genny, took the documents to make me copies on the fax machine. Dr. Ntaki wanted a drink, and fetched a bottle of scotch. The lawyer, Gorza-Gongora, told me, "I was always against this meeting with you." Genny brought me the letter. It was dated April 15, 1994.

> Our dear leader, Pastor Elizaphan Ntakirutimana,
>
> How are you! We wish you to be strong in all these problems we are facing. We wish to inform you that we have heard that tomorrow we will be killed with our families. We therefore request you to intervene on our behalf and talk with the Mayor. We believe that, with the help of God who entrusted you the leadership of this flock, which is going to be destroyed, your intervention will be highly appreciated, the same way as the Jews were saved by Esther.
>
> We give honor to you.

The letter was signed by Pastors Ezekiel Semugeshi, Isaka Rucondo, Seth Rwanyabuto, Eliezer Seromba, Seth Sebihe, Jerome Gakwaya, and Ezekias Zigirinshuti.

Dr. Ntaki walked me out to my car. In the driveway, he stopped and said, "If my father committed crimes, even though I am his son, I say he should be prosecuted. But I don't believe any of it."

TWENTY-FOUR HOURS after we met, Pastor Elizaphan Ntakirutimana was in his car, driving south on Interstate 80 toward

Mexico. To the FBI agents who were tailing him, his driving appeared erratic—he would speed up, slow down, change lanes, and again accelerate abruptly. A few miles from the border, they pulled him over and took him into custody. The arrest went almost entirely unnoticed in the American press. A few days later, in the Ivory Coast, the pastor's son Dr. Gerard was also arrested, and he was quickly transferred to the UN tribunal. But the pastor had a United States green card and the rights that came with it, and he retained Ramsey Clark, a former Attorney General, who specialized in defending politically repugnant cases, to fight his extradition. Clark argued, speciously, that it would be unconstitutional for the United States to surrender the pastor—or anybody else— to the tribunal, and Judge Marcel Notzon, who presided over the case in federal district court, agreed. On December 17, 1997, after fourteen months in a Laredo jail, Pastor Ntakirutimana was released unconditionally, and he remained a free man for nine weeks before FBI agents arrested him a second time, pending an appeal of Judge Notzon's decision.

When I heard that Pastor Ntakirutimana had been returned to his family in time for Christmas, I went back through my notes from Mugonero. I had forgotten that after my meetings with survivors, my translator, Arcene, asked me to go with him to the hospital chapel, where there had been a lot of killing; he wanted to pay homage to the dead, who were buried nearby in mass graves. We stood in silence in the empty chapel with its cement pews. On the floor below the altar sat four memorial coffins, draped in white sheets, painted with black crosses. "The people who did this," Arcene said, "didn't understand the idea of a country. What is a country? What is a human being? They had no understanding."

Beware of those who speak of the spiral *of history; they are preparing a boomerang. Keep a steel helmet handy.*

—RALPH ELLISON

Invisible Man

4

IN THE FAMOUS story, the older brother, Cain, was a cultivator, and Abel, the younger, was a herdsman. They made their offerings to God—Cain from his crops, Abel from his herds. Abel's portion won God's regard; Cain's did not. So Cain killed Abel.

Rwanda, in the beginning, was settled by cave-dwelling pygmies whose descendants today are called the Twa people, a marginalized and disenfranchised group that counts for less than one percent of the population. Hutus and Tutsis came later, but their origins and the order of their immigrations are not accurately known. While convention holds that Hutus are a Bantu people who settled Rwanda first, coming from the south and west, and that Tutsis are a Nilotic people who migrated from the north and east, these theories draw more on legend than on documentable fact. With time, Hutus and Tutsis spoke the same language, followed the same religion, intermarried, and lived intermingled, without territorial distinctions, on the same hills, sharing the same social and political culture in small chiefdoms. The chiefs were called Mwamis, and some of them were Hutus, some Tutsis; Hutus and Tutsis fought together in the Mwamis' armies; through marriage and clientage, Hutus could become hereditary Tutsis, and Tutsis could become hereditary Hutus. Because of all this mixing, ethnographers and historians have lately come to agree that Hutus and Tutsis cannot properly be called distinct ethnic groups.

Still, the names Hutu and Tutsi stuck. They had meaning, and though there is no general agreement about what word best describes that meaning—"classes," "castes," and "ranks" are favorites—the source of the distinction is undisputed: Hutus were cultivators and Tutsis were herdsmen. This was the original inequality: cattle are a more valuable asset than produce, and although some Hutus owned cows while some Tutsis tilled the soil, the word Tutsi became synonymous with a political and economic elite. The stratification is believed to have been accelerated after 1860, when the Mwami Kigeri Rwabugiri, a Tutsi, ascended to the Rwandan throne and initiated a series of military and political campaigns that expanded and consolidated his dominion over a territory nearly the size of the present Republic.

But there is no reliable record of the precolonial state. Rwandans had no alphabet; their tradition was oral, therefore malleable; and because their society is fiercely hierarchical the stories they tell of their past tend to be dictated by those who hold power, either through the state or in opposition to it. Of course, at the core of Rwanda's historical debates lie competing ideas about the relationship between Hutus and Tutsis, so it is a frustration that the precolonial roots of that relationship are largely unknowable. As the political thinker Mahmood Mamdani has observed: "That much of what passed as historical fact in academic circles has to be considered as tentative—if not outright fictional—is becoming clear as post-genocidal sobriety compels a growing number of historians to take seriously the political uses to which their writings have been put, and their readers to question the certainty with which many a claim has been advanced."

So Rwandan history is dangerous. Like all of history, it is a record of successive struggles for power, and to a very large extent power consists in the ability to make others inhabit your story of their reality—even, as is so often the case, when that story is written in their blood. Yet some facts, and some understandings, remain unchallenged. For instance, Rwabugiri was the heir to a dynasty that claimed to trace its lineage to the late fourteenth century. Five hundred years is a very long life for any regime, at any time, anywhere. Even if we consider the real possibility that the rememberers of the royal house were exaggerating, or marking time differently than we do, and that Rwabugiri's kingdom was only a few centuries old—that's still a ripe age, and such endurance requires organization.

By the time Rwabugiri came along, the Rwandan state, having expanded gradually from a single hilltop chieftaincy, administered much of what is now southern and central Rwanda through a rigorous, multilayered hierarchy of military, political, and civil chiefs and governors, subchiefs, and deputy governors, subsubchiefs, and deputy deputy governors. Priests, tax collectors, clan leaders, and army recruiters all had their place in the order that bound every hill in the kingdom in fealty to the Mwami. Court intrigues among the Mwami's sprawling entourage were as elaborate and treacherous as any Shakespeare sketched, with the additional complications of official polygamy, and a prize of immense power for the queen mother.

The Mwami himself was revered as a divinity, absolute and infallible. He was regarded as the personal embodiment of Rwanda, and as Rwabugiri extended his domain, he increasingly configured the world of his subjects in his own image. Tutsis were favored for top political and military offices, and through their public identification with the state, they generally enjoyed greater financial power as well. The regime was essentially feudal: Tutsis were aristocrats; Hutus were vassals. Yet status and identity continued to be determined by many other factors as well—clan, region, clientage, military prowess, even individual industry—and the lines between Hutu and Tutsi remained porous. In fact, in some areas of modern-day Rwanda that Mwami Rwabugiri failed to conquer, these categories had no local significance. Apparently,

Hutu and Tutsi identities took definition only in relationship to state power; as they did, the two groups inevitably developed their own distinctive cultures—their own set of ideas about themselves and one another—according to their respective domains. Those ideas were largely framed as opposing negatives: a Hutu was what a Tutsi was not, and vice versa. But in the absence of the sort of hard-and-fast taboos that often mark the boundaries between ethnic or tribal groups, Rwandans who sought to make the most of these distinctions were compelled to amplify minute and imprecise field marks, like the prevalence of milk in one's diet, and, especially, physical traits.

Within the jumble of Rwandan characteristics, the question of appearances is particularly touchy, as it has often come to mean life or death. But nobody can dispute the physical archetypes: for Hutus, stocky and round-faced, dark-skinned, flat-nosed, thick-lipped, and square-jawed; for Tutsis, lanky and long-faced, not so dark-skinned, narrow-nosed, thin-lipped, and narrow-chinned. Nature presents countless exceptions. ("You can't tell us apart," Laurent Nkongoli, the portly vice president of the National Assembly, told me. "*We* can't tell us apart. I was on a bus in the north once and because I was in the north, where they"—Hutus —"were, and because I ate corn, which they eat, they said, 'He's one of us.' But I'm a Tutsi from Butare in the south.") Still, when the Europeans arrived in Rwanda at the end of the nineteenth century, they formed a picture of a stately race of warrior kings, surrounded by herds of long-horned cattle and a subordinate race of short, dark peasants, hoeing tubers and picking bananas. The white men assumed that this was the tradition of the place, and they thought it a natural arrangement.

"Race science" was all the rage in Europe in those days, and for students of central Africa the key doctrine was the so-called Hamitic hypothesis, propounded in 1863 by John Hanning Speke, an Englishman who is most famous for "discovering" the great African lake that he christened Victoria and for identifying it as the source of the Nile River. Speke's basic anthropological theory, which he made up out of whole cloth, was that all culture and civilization in central Africa had been introduced by the taller, sharper-featured people, whom he considered to be a Caucasoid tribe of Ethiopian origin, descended from the biblical King David, and therefore a superior race to the native Negroids.

Much of Speke's *Journal of the Discovery of the Source of the Nile* is devoted to descriptions of the physical and moral ugliness of Africa's "primitive races," in whose condition he found "a strikingly existing proof of the Holy Scriptures." For his text, Speke took the story in Genesis 9, which tells how Noah, when he was just six hundred years old and had safely skippered his ark over the flood to dry land, got drunk and passed out naked in his tent. On emerging from his oblivion, Noah learned that his youngest son, Ham, had seen him naked; that Ham had told his brothers, Shem and Japheth, of the spectacle; and that Shem and Japheth had, with their backs chastely turned, covered the old man with a garment. Noah responded by cursing the progeny of Ham's son, Canaan, saying, "A slave of slaves shall he be to his brothers." Amid the perplexities of Genesis, this is one of the most enigmatic stories, and it has been subjected to many bewildering interpretations—most notably that Ham was the original black man. To the gentry of the American South, the weird tale of Noah's curse justified slavery, and to Speke and his colonial contemporaries it spelled the history of Africa's peoples. On "contemplating these sons of Noah," he marveled that "as they were then, so they appear to be now."

Speke begins a section of his *Journal*, headed "Fauna," with the words: "In treating of this branch of natural history, we will first take man—the true curly-head, flab-nosed, pouch-mouthed negro." The figure of this subspecies confronted Speke with a mystery even greater than the Nile: "How the negro has lived so many ages without advancing seems marvelous, when all the countries surrounding Africa are so forward in comparison; and, judging from the progressive state of the world, one is led to suppose that the African must soon either step out from his darkness, or be superseded by a being superior to himself." Speke believed that a colonial government—"like ours in India"—might save the "negro" from perdition, but otherwise he saw "very little chance" for the breed: "As his father did, so does he. He works his wife, sells his children, enslaves all he can lay hands upon, and unless when fighting for the property of others, contents himself with drinking, singing, and dancing like a baboon, to drive dull care away."

This was all strictly run-of-the-mill Victorian patter, striking only for the fact that a man who had so exerted himself to see the world afresh had returned with such stock observations. (And, really, very little has changed; one need only lightly edit the foregoing passages—the crude caricatures, the question of human inferiority, and the bit about the baboon—to produce the sort of profile of misbegotten Africa that remains standard to this day in the American and European press, and in the appeals for charity donations put out by humanitarian aid organizations.) Yet, living alongside his sorry "negroes," Speke found a "superior race" of "men who were as unlike as they could be from the common order of the natives" by virtue of their "fine oval faces, large eyes, and high noses, denoting the best blood of Abyssinia"—that is, Ethiopia. This "race" comprised many tribes, including the Watusi—Tutsis—all of whom kept cattle and tended to lord it over the Negroid masses. What thrilled Speke most was their "physical appearances," which despite the hair-curling and skin-darkening effects of intermarriage had retained "a high stamp of Asiatic feature, of which a marked characteristic is a bridged instead of a bridgeless nose." Couching his postulations in vaguely scientific terms, and referring to the historical authority of Scripture, Speke pronounced this "semi-Shem-Hamitic" master race to be lost Christians, and suggested that with a little British education they might be nearly as "superior in all things" as an Englishman like himself.

Few living Rwandans have heard of John Hanning Speke, but most know the essence of his wild fantasy—that the Africans who best resembled the tribes of Europe were inherently endowed with mastery—and, whether they accept or reject it, few Rwandans would deny that the Hamitic myth is one of the essential ideas by which they understand who they are in this world. In November of 1992, the Hutu Power ideologue Leon Mugesera delivered a famous speech, calling on Hutus to send the Tutsis back to Ethiopia by way of the Nyabarongo River, a tributary of the Nile that winds through Rwanda. He did not need to elaborate. In April of 1994, the river was choked with dead Tutsis, and tens of thousands of bodies washed up on the shores of Lake Victoria.

ONCE THE AFRICAN interior had been "opened up" to the European imagination by explorers like Speke, empire soon followed. In a frenzy of conquest, Europe's monarchs began staking claims to vast reaches of the continent. In 1885, representatives of the major European powers held a conference in Berlin to sort out the frontiers of their new African real estate. As a rule, the lines they marked on the map, many of which still define African states, bore no relationship to the political or territorial traditions of the places they described. Hundreds of kingdoms and chieftaincies that operated as distinct nations, with their own languages, religions, and complex political and social histories, were either carved up or, more often, lumped together beneath European flags. But the cartographers at Berlin left Rwanda, and its southern neighbor Burundi, intact, and designated the two countries as provinces of German East Africa.*

---

*Because Rwanda and Burundi were administered as a joint colonial territory, Ruanda-Urundi; because their languages are remarkably similar; because both are populated, in equal proportions, by Hutus and Tutsis; and because their ordeals as postcolonial states have been defined by violence between those groups, they are often considered to be the two halves of a single political and historical experience or "problem." In fact, although events in each country invariably influence events in the other, Rwanda and Burundi have existed since precolonial times as entirely distinct, self-contained nations. The differences in their histories are often more telling than the similarities, and comparison tends to lead to confusion unless each country is first considered on its own terms.

No white man had ever been to Rwanda at the time of the Berlin conference. Speke, whose theories on race were taken as gospel by Rwanda's colonizers, had merely peered over the country's eastern frontier from a hilltop in modern-day Tanzania, and when the explorer Henry M. Stanley, intrigued by Rwanda's reputation for "ferocious exclusiveness," attempted to cross that frontier, he was repulsed by a hail of arrows. Even slave traders passed the place by. In 1894, a German count, named von Götzen, became the first white man to enter Rwanda and to visit the royal court. The next year, the death of Mwami Rwabugiri plunged Rwanda into political turmoil, and in 1897, Germany set up its first administrative offices in the country, hoisted the flag of Kaiser Wilhelm's Reich, and instituted a policy of indirect rule. Officially, this meant placing a few German agents over the existing court and administrative system, but the reality was more complicated.

Rwabugiri's death had triggered a violent succession fight among the Tutsi royal clans; the dynasty was in great disarray, and the weakened leaders of the prevailing factions eagerly collaborated with the colonial overlords in exchange for patronage. The political structure that resulted is often described as a "dual colonialism," in which Tutsi elites exploited the protection and license extended by the Germans to pursue their internal feuds and to further their hegemony over the Hutus. By the time that the League of Nations turned Rwanda over to Belgium as a spoil of World War I, the terms Hutu and Tutsi had become clearly defined as opposing "ethnic" identities, and the Belgians made this polarization the cornerstone of their colonial policy.

In his classic history of Rwanda, written in the 1950s, the missionary Monsignor Louis de Lacger remarked, "One of the most surprising phenomena of Rwanda's human geography is surely the contrast between the plurality of races and the sentiment of national unity. The natives of this country genuinely have the feeling of forming but one people." Lacger marveled at the unity created by loyalty to the monarchy—"I would kill for my Mwami"

labeled every Rwandan as either Hutu (eighty-five percent) or Tutsi (fourteen percent) or Twa (one percent). The identity cards made it virtually impossible for Hutus to become Tutsis, and permitted the Belgians to perfect the administration of an apartheid system rooted in the myth of Tutsi superiority.

So the offering of the Tutsi herdsmen found favor in the eyes of the colonial lords, and the offering of the Hutu cultivators did not. The Tutsi upper crust, glad for power, and terrified of being subjected to the abuses it was encouraged to inflict against Hutus, accepted priority as its due. The Catholic schools, which dominated the colonial educational system, practiced open discrimination in favor of Tutsis, and Tutsis enjoyed a monopoly on administrative and political jobs, while Hutus watched their already limited opportunities for advancement shrink. Nothing so vividly defined the divide as the Belgian regime of forced labor, which required armies of Hutus to toil en masse as plantation chattel, on road construction, and in forestry crews, and placed Tutsis over them as taskmasters. Decades later, an elderly Tutsi recalled the Belgian colonial order to a reporter with the words "You whip the Hutu or we will whip you." The brutality did not end with the beatings; exhausted by their communal labor requirements, peasants neglected their fields, and the fecund hills of Rwanda were repeatedly stricken by famine. Beginning in the 1920s, hundreds of thousands of Hutus and impoverished rural Tutsis fled north to Uganda and west to the Congo to seek their fortunes as itinerant agricultural laborers.

Whatever Hutu and Tutsi identity may have stood for in the precolonial state no longer mattered; the Belgians had made "ethnicity" the defining feature of Rwandan existence. Most Hutus and Tutsis still maintained fairly cordial relations; intermarriages went ahead, and the fortunes of *"petits Tutsis"* in the hills remained quite indistinguishable from those of their Hutu neighbors. But, with every schoolchild reared in the doctrine of racial superiority and inferiority, the idea of a collective national identity was steadily laid to waste, and on either side of the Hutu-Tutsi divide there developed mutually exclusionary discourses based on the competing claims of entitlement and injury.

Tribalism begets tribalism. Belgium itself was a nation divided along "ethnic" lines, in which the Francophone Walloon minority had for centuries dominated the Flemish majority. But following a long "social revolution," Belgium had entered an age of greater demographic equality. The Flemish priests who began to turn up in Rwanda after World War II identified with the Hutus and encouraged their aspirations for political change. At the same time, Belgium's colonial administration had been placed under United Nations trusteeship, which meant that it was under pressure to prepare the ground for Rwandan independence. Hutu political activists started calling for majority rule and a "social revolution" of their own. But the political struggle in Rwanda was never really a quest for equality; the issue was only who would dominate the ethnically bipolar state.

In March of 1957, a group of nine Hutu intellectuals published a tract known as the *Hutu Manifesto*, arguing for "democracy"—not by rejecting the Hamitic myth but by embracing it. If Tutsis were foreign invaders, the argument went, then Rwanda was by rights a nation of the Hutu majority. This was what passed for democratic thought in Rwanda: Hutus had the numbers. The *Manifesto* firmly rejected getting rid of ethnic identity cards for fear of "preventing the statistical law from establishing the reality of facts," as if being Hutu or Tutsi automatically signified a person's politics. Plenty of more moderate views could be heard, but who listens to moderates in times of revolution? As new Hutu parties sprang up, rallying the masses to unite in their "Hutuness," the enthusiastic Belgians scheduled elections. But before any Rwandans saw a ballot box, hundreds of them were killed.

ON NOVEMBER 1, 1959, in the central Rwandan province of Gitarama, an administrative subchief named Dominique Mbonyumutwa was beaten up by a group of men. Mbonyumutwa was a Hutu political activist, and his attackers were Tutsi political activists, and almost immediately after they finished with him, Mbonyumutwa was said to have died. He wasn't dead, but the rumor was widely believed; even now, there are Hutus who think that Mbonyumutwa was killed on that night. Looking back, Rwandans will tell you that some such incident was inevitable. But the next time you hear a story like the one that ran on the front page of *The New York Times* in October of 1997, reporting on "the age-old animosity between the Tutsi and Hutu ethnic groups," remember that until Mbonyumutwa's beating lit the spark in 1959 there had never been systematic political violence recorded between Hutus and Tutsis—anywhere.

Within twenty-four hours of the beating in Gitarama, roving bands of Hutus were attacking Tutsi authorities and burning Tutsi homes. The "social revolution" had begun. In less than a week, the violence spread through most of the country, as Hutus organized themselves, usually in groups of ten led by a man blowing a whistle, to conduct a campaign of pillage, arson, and sporadic murder against Tutsis. The popular uprising was known as "the wind of destruction," and one of its biggest fans was a Belgian colonel named Guy Logiest, who arrived in Rwanda from the Congo three days after Mbonyumutwa's beating to supervise the troubles. Rwandans who wondered what Logiest's attitude toward the violence might be had only to observe his Belgian troops standing around idly as Hutus torched Tutsi homes. As Logiest put it twenty-five years later: "The time was crucial for Rwanda. Its people needed support and protection."

Were Tutsis not Rwandan people? Four months before the revolution began, the Mwami who had reigned for nearly thirty years, and was still popular with many Hutus, went to Burundi to see a Belgian doctor for treatment of a venereal disease. The doctor gave him an injection, and the Mwami collapsed and died, apparently from allergic shock. But a deep suspicion that he had

59

been poisoned took hold among Rwanda's Tutsis, further straining their fraying relationship with their erstwhile Belgian sponsors. In early November, when the new Mwami, a politically untested twenty-five-year-old, asked Colonel Logiest for permission to deploy an army against the Hutu revolutionaries, he was turned down. Royalist forces took to the field anyway, but though a few more Hutus than Tutsis were killed in November, the counteroffensive quickly petered out. "We have to take sides," Colonel Logiest declared as Tutsi homes continued to burn in early 1960, and later he would have no regrets about "being so partial against the Tutsis."

Logiest, who was virtually running the revolution, saw himself as a champion of democratization, whose task was to rectify the gross wrong of the colonial order he served. "I ask myself what was it that made me act with such resolution," he would recall. "It was without doubt the will to give the people back their dignity. And it was probably just as much the desire to put down the arrogance and expose the duplicity of a basically oppressive and unjust aristocracy."

That legitimate grievances lie behind a revolution does not, however, ensure that the revolutionary order will be just. In early 1960, Colonel Logiest staged a coup d'état by executive fiat, replacing Tutsi chiefs with Hutu chiefs. Communal elections were held at midyear, and with Hutus presiding over the polling stations, Hutus won at least ninety percent of the top posts. By then, more than twenty thousand Tutsis had been displaced from their homes, and that number kept growing rapidly as new Hutu leaders organized violence against Tutsis or simply arrested them arbitrarily, to assert their authority and to snatch Tutsi property. Among the stream of Tutsi refugees who began fleeing into exile was the Mwami.

"The revolution is over," Colonel Logiest announced in October, at the installation of a provisional government led by Grégoire Kayibanda, one of the original authors of the *Hutu Man-*

ifesto, who gave a speech proclaiming: "Democracy has vanquished feudalism." Logiest also gave a speech, and apparently he was feeling magnanimous in victory, because he issued this prophetic caution: "It will not be a democracy if it is not equally successful in respecting the rights of minorities. . . . A country in which justice loses this fundamental quality prepares the worst disorders and its own collapse." But that was not the spirit of the revolution over which Logiest had presided.

To be sure, nobody in Rwanda in the late 1950s had offered an alternative to a tribal construction of politics. The colonial state and the colonial church had made that almost inconceivable, and although the Belgians switched ethnic sides on the eve of independence, the new order they prepared was merely the old order stood on its head. In January of 1961, the Belgians convened a meeting of Rwanda's new Hutu leaders, at which the monarchy was officially abolished and Rwanda was declared a republic. The transitional government was nominally based on a power-sharing arrangement between Hutu and Tutsi parties, but a few months later a UN commission reported that the Rwandan revolution had, in fact, "brought about the racial dictatorship of one party" and simply replaced "one type of oppressive regime with another." The report also warned of the possibility "that some day we will witness violent reactions on the part of the Tutsis." The Belgians didn't much care. Rwanda was granted full independence in 1962, and Grégoire Kayibanda was inaugurated as President.

So Hutu dictatorship masqueraded as popular democracy, and Rwanda's power struggles became an internal affair of the Hutu elite, very much as the feuds among royal Tutsi clans had been in the past. Rwanda's revolutionaries had become what the writer V. S. Naipaul calls postcolonial "mimic men," who reproduce the abuses against which they rebelled, while ignoring the fact that their past masters were ultimately banished by those they enchained. President Kayibanda had almost certainly read Louis de Lacger's famous history of Rwanda. But instead of Lacger's idea of a Rwandan people unified by "national sentiment," Kayibanda spoke of Rwanda as "two nations in one state."

Genesis identifies the first murder as a fratricide. The motive is political—the elimination of a perceived rival. When God asks what happened, Cain offers his notoriously barbed lie: "I do not know; am I my brother's keeper?" The shock in the story is not the murder, which begins and ends in one sentence, but Cain's shamelessness and the leniency of God's punishment. For killing his brother, Cain is condemned to a life as "a fugitive and a wanderer on the earth." When he protests, "Whoever finds me will slay me," God says, "Not so! If anyone slays Cain, vengeance shall be taken on him sevenfold." Quite literally, Cain gets away with murder; he even receives special protection, but as the legend indicates, the blood-revenge model of justice imposed after his crime was not viable. People soon became so craven that "the earth was filled with violence," and God regretted his creation so much that he erased it with a flood. In the new age that followed, the law would eventually emerge as the principle of social order. But that was many fratricidal struggles later.

5

"MY STORY FROM birth?" Odette Nyiramilimo said. "Do you really have time for that?"

I said I had time.

She said, "I was born in Kinunu, Gisenyi, in 1956. So I was three when this history of the genocide began. I can't remember it exactly, but I did see a group of men on the facing hill descending with machetes, and I can still see houses burning. We ran into the bush with our cows and stayed there for two months. So there was milk, but nothing else. Our house was burned to nothing."

Odette sat straight, perched forward on a white plastic lawn chair with her hands folded on the bare white plastic table between us. Her husband was playing tennis; some of her children were paddling around in the pool. It was Sunday at the Cercle Sportif in Kigali—the smell of chicken on the grill, the sounds of swimmers splashing and the pock of tennis balls, the gaudy brilliance of bougainvilleas spilling down the garden wall. We sat in the shade of a tall tree. Odette wore jeans and a white blouse, and a thin gold chain with a pendant charm at her throat. She spoke quickly and directly for several hours.

"I don't remember when we rebuilt the house," she said, "but in 'sixty-three, when I was in the second year of primary school, I remember seeing my father, well dressed, as if for a festival, in a white cloth wrap. He was out on the road, and I was with the other children, and he said, 'Goodbye, my children, I'm going to die.' We cried out, 'No, no.' He said, 'Didn't you see a jeep go by on the road? It had all your maternal uncles on board, and I won't wait for them to hunt me down. I'll wait here to die with them.' We cried and cried and convinced him not to die then, but the others were all killed."

This is how Rwandan Tutsis count the years of their lives: in a hopscotch fashion—'fifty-nine, 'sixty, 'sixty-one, 'sixty-three, and so on, through 'ninety-four—sometimes skipping several years, when they knew no terror, sometimes slowing down to name the months and the days.

President Kayibanda was, at best, a dull leader, and by his habit of reclusiveness he suggested that he knew it. Stirring up the Hutu masses to kill Tutsis was the only way he seemed able to keep the spirit of the revolution alive. The pretext for this popular violence was found in the fact that from time to time armed bands of monarchist Tutsis who had fled into exile would stage raids on Rwanda. These guerrillas were the first to be called "cockroaches," and they used the word themselves to describe their stealth and their belief that they were uncrushable. Their attacks were fitful and feeble, but Hutu retaliation against civilian Tutsis was invariably swift and extensive. It was a rare season in the early years of the republic when Tutsis were not displaced from their homes by arson and murder.

The most dramatic "cockroach" invasion occurred a few days before Christmas in 1963. A band of several hundred Tutsi guerrillas swept into southern Rwanda from a base in Burundi, and advanced to within twelve miles of Kigali before being wiped out by Rwandan forces under Belgian command. Not content with this victory, the government declared a national state of emergency to combat "counterrevolutionaries," and designated a minister to organize Hutu "self-defense" units, tasked with the "work" of "clearing the bush." That meant murdering Tutsis and destroying their homes. Writing in *Le Monde*, a schoolteacher named Vuillemin, employed by the United Nations in Butare, described the massacres in December of 1963 and January of 1964 as "a veritable genocide," and he accused European aid workers and church leaders in the country of an indifference that amounted to complicity in the state-sponsored slaughter. Between December 24 and 28, 1963, Vuillemin reported, well-organized massacres left as many as fourteen thousand Tutsis dead in the southern province of Gikongoro alone. Although educated Tutsi men were the primary victims, he wrote, "In most cases, women and children were also felled by *masu* blows or spearing. The victims were most often thrown in the river after being stripped of their clothes." Many of the Tutsis who survived followed the earlier swarms of refugees into exile; by mid-1964 as many as a quarter million Tutsis had fled the country. The British philosopher Sir Bertrand Russell described the scene in Rwanda that year as "the most horrible and systematic massacre we have had occasion to witness since the extermination of the Jews by the Nazis."

After Odette's uncles were carted off to their deaths, her father hired a truck to take the family to the Congo. But it was a large family—Odette's father had two wives; she was the seventeenth of his eighteen children; with her grandparents, in-laws, aunts, cousins, nephews, and nieces, the extended family numbered thirty-three people—and the truck was too small. One of her grandmothers just wouldn't fit. So her father said, "Let's stay here and die here," and they stayed.

Odette's family made up pretty much the entire remaining Tutsi population of Kinunu. They lived in poverty in the mountains with their cows, and they feared for their lives. Protection came to them in the form of a village councillor, who approached Odette's father and said, "We like you, and we don't want you to die, so we'll make you a Hutu." Odette didn't recall just how this had worked. "My parents never spoke of it for the rest of their lives," she told me. "It was a bit humiliating. But my father took the identity card, and for two years he was a Hutu. Then he was called in for having a fraudulent identity card."

By 1966 the "cockroaches" in exile disbanded their hapless army, weary of seeing Tutsis slaughtered every time they attacked. Kayibanda, confident of his status as the Hutu Mwami, realized that the old colonial model of official discrimination, thwarting the disempowered tribe's access to education, public employment, and the military, might be a sufficient method of pest control to keep Tutsis in their place. To bolster the proportional power of the majority, census figures were edited so that Tutsis counted for just nine percent of the population, and their opportunities were restricted accordingly. Despite the Hutu monopoly on power, the Hamitic myth remained the basis of the state ideology. So a deep, almost mystical sense of inferiority persisted among Rwanda's new Hutu elite, and to give extra teeth to the quota system a reverse meritocracy was imposed on Tutsis competing for the few positions available: those with the lowest scores were favored over those who performed best. "I had a sister who was always first in our class and I was more like tenth," Odette recalled. "But when they read off the names of those who were accepted to secondary school, my name was read and my sister's wasn't—because I was less brilliant, less of a threat."

"THEN IT WAS 'seventy-three," Odette said. "I had left home, for a teachers college in Cyangugu"—in the southwest—"and one morning, while we were eating before going to mass, they closed the windows and the gates. Then some boys from another school came in the dining hall and circled the tables. I was trembling. I remember I had a piece of bread in my mouth, and I couldn't swallow it. The boys shouted, 'Get up, Tutsis. All the Tutsis stand up.' There was a boy from my hill at home. We went to primary school together, and he said, 'You, Odette, you sit down, we know you've been a Hutu forever.' Then some other boy came and pulled my hair and said, 'With this hair we know you're a Tutsi.' "

Hair was one of the great signifiers for John Hanning Speke. When he identified a king as a member of the Hamitic master race, Speke pronounced him a descendant "from Abyssinia and King David, whose hair was as straight as my own," and the king, flattered, said, yes, there was a story that his ancestors had "once been half white and half black, with hair on the white side straight, and on the black side frizzly." Odette was neither tall nor especially skinny, and on the "nasal index" she was probably about average for a Rwandan. But such was Speke's legacy that a hundred years after he shot himself in a "hunting accident," a schoolboy in Rwanda tormented Odette because she liked to wear her hair combed back in soft waves. "And," she went on, "the director of the school, a Belgian woman, said of me, 'Yes, her, she's a Tutsi of the first category, take her.' So we were expelled. Nobody was killed there. Some girls were spat at in the face, and made to walk on their knees, and some were beaten. Then we left on foot."

All across Rwanda, Tutsi students were being beaten and expelled, and many of them walked home to find their houses burning. The trouble this time had been inspired by events in Burundi, where the political landscape appeared very much like Rwanda's through a bloody looking glass: in Burundi, a Tutsi military regime held power and Hutus feared for their lives. In the spring of 1972 some Burundian Hutus had attempted a rebellion, which was quickly put down. Then, in the name of restoring "peace and order," the army conducted a nationwide campaign of extermination against educated Hutus, in which a lot of unschooled Hutus were murdered as well. The genocidal frenzy in Burundi exceeded anything that had preceded it in Rwanda. At least a hundred thousand Burundian Hutus were killed in the spring of 1972, and at least two hundred thousand fled as refugees—many of them to Rwanda.

The influx of Burundian refugees reminded President Kayibanda of the power of ethnic antagonism to galvanize the civic spirit. Rwanda was stagnating in poverty and isolation, and it needed a boost. So Kayibanda asked his army chief, Major General Juvénal Habyarimana, to organize Committees of Public Safety, and Tutsis were once again reminded what majority rule meant in Rwanda. The death toll this time was relatively low—"only," as Rwandans count these things, in the hundreds—but at least a hundred thousand more Tutsis fled Rwanda as refugees.

When Odette spoke of 1973, she didn't mention Burundi, or Kayibanda's political fortunes, or the mass exodus. These circumstances did not figure in her memory. She stuck to her story, which was enough: One morning, while she had her mouth full of bread, her world had once again collapsed because she was Tutsi. "We were six girls, chased out of my school," she told me. "I had my sack, and we walked." After three days they had covered fifty miles, and arrived in Kibuye. Odette had relatives there—"a sister of my brother-in-law who had married a Hutu"—and she figured she would stay with them.

"This man had a sharpening business," she said. "I found him in front of his house at his grinding stone. At first, he ignored me. I thought, Is he drunk? Doesn't he see who is here? I said, 'It's me, Odette.' He said, 'Why are you here? It's school season.' I said, 'But we've been expelled.' Then he said, 'I don't give shelter to cockroaches.' That's what he said. My sister-in-law came along and she embraced me, and"—Odette clapped her hands together over her head and chopped them down in front of her chest—"he separated us roughly." She looked at her outstretched arms and let them fall. Then she laughed, and said, "In 'eighty-two, when I first became a doctor, my first job was at the Kibuye hospital, and the first patient I had was this same man, this brother-in-law. I couldn't face him. I was trembling, and I had to leave the room. My husband was the director of the hospital and I told him, 'I can't treat this man.' He was very sick and I had taken my oath, but—"

IN RWANDA, THE story of a girl who is sent away as a cockroach and comes back as a medicine woman must be, at least in part, a political story. And that was how Odette told it. In 1973, after her brother-in-law rejected her, she kept walking, home to Kinunu. She found her father's house empty and one of his side houses burned. The family was hiding in the bush, camping among their banana trees, and Odette lived with them there for several months. Then, in July, the man in charge of the pogroms, Major General Habyarimana, ousted Kayibanda, declared himself President of the Second Republic, and called a moratorium on attacks against Tutsis. Rwandans, he said, should live in peace and work together for development. The message was clear: the violence had served its purpose, and Habyarimana was the fulfillment of the revolution.

"We really danced in the streets when Habyarimana took power," Odette told me. "At last, a President who said not to kill Tutsis. And after 'seventy-five, at least, we did live in security. But the exclusions were still there." In fact, Rwanda was more tightly regulated under Habyarimana than ever before. "Development" was his favorite political word and it also happened to be a favorite word of the European and American aid donors whom he milked with great skill. By law, every citizen became a member for life of the President's party, the National Revolutionary Movement for Development (MRND), which served as the all-pervasive instrument of his will. People were literally kept in their place by rules that forbade changing residence without government approval, and for Tutsis, of course, the old nine-percent quota rules remained. Members of the armed forces were forbidden to marry Tutsis, and it went without saying that they were not supposed to be Tutsis themselves. Two Tutsis were eventually given seats in

Habyarimana's rubber-stamp parliament, and a token Tutsi was given a ministerial post. If Tutsis thought they deserved better, they hardly complained; Habyarimana and his MRND promised to let them live unmolested, and that was more than they had been able to count on in the past.

The Belgian director of Odette's old school in Cyangugu would not readmit her, but she found a place in a school that specialized in the sciences, and began preparing for a career in medicine. Once again, the headmistress was a Belgian, but this Belgian took Odette under her wing, keeping her name out of the enrollment books, and hiding her when government inspectors came looking for Tutsis. "It was all trickery," Odette said, "and the other girls resented it. One night, they came to my dormitory and beat me with sticks." Odette didn't dwell on the discomfort. "Those were the good years," she said. "The headmistress looked after me, I had become a good student—first in my class—and then I was admitted, with some more trickery, to the national medical school in Butare."

The only thing Odette said about her life as a medical student was: "In Butare once, a professor of internal medicine came up to me and said, 'What a pretty girl,' and he started patting my bottom and tried to set up a date even though he was married."

The memory just popped out of her like that, with no apparent connection to the thought that preceded it or the thought that followed. Then Odette sped ahead, skipping over the years to her graduation and her marriage. Yet, for a moment, that image of her as a young student in an awkward moment of sexual surprise and discomfort hung between us. It seemed to amuse Odette, and it reminded me of all that she wasn't telling as she recited her life story. She was keeping everything that was not about Hutu and Tutsi to herself. Later, I met Odette several times at parties; she and her husband were gregarious and understandably popular. To-gether they ran a private maternity and pediatrics practice called the Good Samaritan Clinic. They were known as excellent doctors and fun people—warm, vivacious, good-humored. They had a charmingly affectionate ease with each other, and one saw right away that they were in the midst of full and engaging lives. But when we met in the garden of the Cercle Sportif, Odette spoke as a genocide survivor to a foreign correspondent. Her theme was the threat of annihilation, and the moments of reprieve in her story—the fond memories, funny anecdotes, sparks of wit—came, if at all, in quick beats, like punctuation marks.

This made sense to me. We are, each of us, functions of how we imagine ourselves and of how others imagine us, and, looking back, there are these discrete tracks of memory: the times when our lives are most sharply defined in relation to others' ideas of us, and the more private times when we are freer to imagine ourselves. My own parents and grandparents came to the United States as refugees from Nazism. They came with stories similar to Odette's, of being hunted from here to there because they were born as a this and not a that, or because they had chosen to resist the hunters in the service of an opposing political idea. Near the end of their lives, both my paternal grandmother and my maternal grandfather wrote their memoirs, and although their stories and their sensibilities were markedly different, both ended their accounts of their lives right in the middle of those lives, with a full stop at the moment they arrived in America. I don't know why they stopped there. Perhaps nothing that came afterward ever made them feel so vividly, or terribly, aware and alive. But listening to Odette, it occurred to me that if others have so often made your life their business—made your life into a question, really, and made that question their business—then perhaps you will want to guard the memory of those times when you were freer to imagine yourself as the only times that are truly and inviolably your own.

It was the same with nearly all the Tutsi survivors I met in Rwanda. When I pressed for stories of how they had lived during the long periods between bouts of violence—household stories, village stories, funny stories, or stories of annoyance, stories of school, work, church, a wedding, a funeral, a trip, a party, or a feud—the answer was always opaque: in normal times we lived normally. After a while I stopped asking, because the question seemed pointless and possibly cruel. On the other hand, I found that Hutus often volunteered their memories of life's engrossing daily dramas before the genocide, and these stories were, just as the Tutsi survivors had said, normal: variations, in a Rwandan vein, of stories you might hear anywhere.

So remembering has its economy, like experience itself, and when Odette mentioned the hand of the professor of internal medicine on her bottom, and grinned, I saw that she had forgotten that economy and wandered in her memories, and I felt that we were both glad of it. A professor had imagined her susceptible and she had imagined that as a married man and her teacher he should know greater restraint. They had each other wrong. But people have the strangest notions as they navigate each other in this life —and in the "good years," the "normal times," that isn't the end of the world.

ODETTE'S HUSBAND, JEAN-BAPTISTE Gasasira, had a Tutsi father and a Hutu mother, but his father had died when Jean-Baptiste was very young, and his mother had succeeded in arranging for him to have Hutu identity papers. "That hadn't prevented him from being beaten up in 'seventy-three," Odette said, "but it meant the children had Hutu papers." She had two sons and a daughter, and might have had more if she and Jean-Baptiste hadn't been traveling abroad a great deal in the 1980s, to pursue specialized medical studies, "a big opportunity for Tutsis," which was facilitated by their friendship with the Secretary-General of the Ministry of Education.

When Habyarimana took over, Rwanda was significantly poorer than any of its neighbor states, and by the mid-1980s it was economically better off than any of them. Odette and Jean-Baptiste, who had settled into well-paid jobs at the Central Hospital of Kigali, were living very close to the top of the Rwandan ladder, with government housing and cars and a busy social life among the Kigali elite. "Our best friends were Hutus, ministers and those who were in power from our generation," Odette recalled. "This was our crowd. But it was a bit hard. Even though Jean-Baptiste was hired as a Hutu, he was seen to have the face and manner of a Tutsi, and we were known as Tutsis."

The sense of exclusion could be subtle, but with time it became increasingly blunt. In November of 1989, a man came to the maternity ward asking for Dr. Odette. "He was very impatient and insisted we had to talk. He said, 'You're needed at the Presidency, at the office of the Secretary-General of Security.'" Odette was terrified; she assumed that she would be interrogated about her habit, during occasional trips to neighboring countries and to Europe, of visiting family members and Rwandan friends living in exile.

Since 1959, the diaspora of exiled Rwandan Tutsis and their children had grown to include about a million people; it was the largest and oldest unresolved African refugee problem. Nearly half of these refugees lived in Uganda, and in the early 1980s a number of young Rwandans there had joined the rebel leader Yoweri Museveni in his fight against the brutal dictatorship of President Milton Obote. By January of 1986, when Museveni claimed victory and was sworn in as President of Uganda, his army included several thousand Rwandan refugees. Habyarimana felt threatened. For years he had pretended to negotiate with refugee groups who demanded the right to return to Rwanda, but, citing the country's chronic overpopulation, he had always refused to let the exiles come home. Ninety-five percent of Rwanda's land was under cultivation, and the average family consisted of eight people living as subsistence farmers on less than half an acre. Shortly after Museveni's victory in Uganda, Habyarimana had simply declared that Rwanda was full: end of discussion. Thereafter, contact with refugees was outlawed, and Odette knew how thorough Habyarimana's spy network could be. As she drove to the Presidency, she realized that she had no idea what to say if her visits to exiles had been discovered.

"Dr. Odette," Habyarimana's security chief said, "they say you're a good doctor."

Odette said, "I don't know."

"Yes," he went on. "You're said to be very intelligent. You studied at these good schools without the right. But what did you say in the hospital corridor recently, after the death of President Habyarimana's brother?"

Odette didn't know what he was talking about.

The security chief told her: "You said that demons should take the whole Habyarimana family."

Odette, who had been trembling with fear, laughed. "I'm a doctor," she said. "You think I believe in demons?"

The security chief laughed, too. Odette went home, and the next morning, as usual, she went to work. "I started my rounds," she recalled. "Then a colleague came up to me and said, 'You're always going away. Where are you going to go now, to Belgium, or where?' And he took me to see—my name had been struck from the doors to the wards, and everyone was told I didn't work there anymore."

6

TUTSIS WERE NOT alone in their disappointment as the Second Republic calcified into a mature totalitarian order, in which Habyarimana, running unopposed, claimed a comical ninety-nine percent of the vote in the presidential elections. The President's entourage was drawn overwhelmingly from his home base in the northwest, and southern Hutus felt increasingly alienated. Among the peasant masses, Hutus remained very nearly as downtrodden as Tutsis, and they were put to hard use after Habyarimana revived the despised colonial regime of mandatory communal work details. Of course, everyone turned out, as the ubiquitous MRND-party enforcers required, to chant and dance in adulation of the President at mass pageants of political "animation," but such mandatory civic cheer could not mask the growing political discontent in much of Rwandan society. While the country as a whole had grown a bit less poor during Habyarimana's tenure, the great majority of Rwandans remained in circumstances of extreme poverty, and it did not go unnoticed that the omnipotent President and his cronies had grown very rich.

Then again, it had never been otherwise in Rwandan memory, and compared to much of the rest of postcolonial Africa, Rwanda appeared Edenic to foreign-aid donors. Just about everywhere else you turned on the continent, you saw the client dictators of the

Cold War powers ruling by pillage and murder, and from the rebels who opposed them you heard the loud anti-imperial rhetoric that makes white development workers feel bitterly misunderstood. Rwanda was tranquil—or, like the volcanoes in the northwest, dormant; it had nice roads, high church attendance, low crime rates, and steadily improving standards of public health and education. If you were a bureaucrat with a foreign-aid budget to unload, and your professional success was to be measured by your ability not to lie or gloss too much when you filed happy statistical reports at the end of each fiscal year, Rwanda was the ticket. Belgium shoveled money into its old stomping ground; France, ever eager to expand its neocolonial African empire—*la Francophonie*—had begun military assistance to Habyarimana in 1975; Switzerland sent more development aid to Rwanda than to any other country on earth; Washington, Bonn, Ottowa, Tokyo, and the Vatican all counted Kigali as a favorite charity. The hills were thick with young whites working, albeit unwittingly, for the greater glory of Habyarimana.

Then, in 1986, the prices of Rwanda's chief exports, coffee and tea, crashed on the world market. The only easy profits left were to be had from scamming foreign-aid projects, and the competition was intense among the northwesterners, who had risen to prominence on Habyarimana's coattails. In criminal syndicates like the Mafia, a person who has become invested in the logic and practices of the gang is said to be owned by it. This concept is organic to Rwanda's traditional social, political, and economic structures, the tight pyramids of patron-client relationships that are the one thing no change of regime has ever altered. Every hill has its chief, every chief has his deputies and his sub-bosses; the pecking order runs from the smallest social cell to the highest central authority. But if the Mwami—or, now, the President—essentially owned Rwanda, who owned him? Through control of parastatal businesses, of the MRND political apparatus, and of the army, a knot of northwesterners had by the late 1980s turned the

Rwandan state into little more than an instrument of their will—and with time the President himself stood more as a product of regional power than as its source.

From Rwanda's state radio and its generally timid newspapers, one would have been hard pressed to guess that Habyarimana was not entirely the lord and owner of his public face. Yet everyone knew that the President was a man of insignificant lineage, possibly even the grandson of a Zairean or Ugandan immigrant, while his wife, Agathe Kanzinga, was the daughter of big shots. Madame Agathe, a great churchgoer, fond of binge shopping in Paris, was the muscle behind the throne; it was her family and their cronies who had bestowed their aura on Habyarimana, who had spied for him, and who occasionally and with great secrecy had killed for him, and when the national belt began tightening in the late 1980s, it was *le clan de Madame* that prevailed in profiteering from foreign aid.

BUT THERE IS so much you should know here—all at once. Permit me a quick aside.

In the fall of 1980, the naturalist Dian Fossey, who had spent the past thirteen years in the mountains of northwestern Rwanda studying the habits of mountain gorillas, withdrew to Cornell University to finish a book. Her deal with Cornell required her to teach a course, and I was one of her students. One day, before class, I found her in one of her famously dark moods. She had just caught her cleaning lady removing the hair from her—Fossey's—comb. I was impressed: a cleaning lady, much less such a diligent one, struck my undergraduate imagination as highly exotic. But Fossey had had a row with the woman; she may even have given her the sack. She told me that her hair and, for that matter, her fingernail clippings were for her to dispose of. Burning was best, though a flush toilet was OK, too. So the cleaning lady was a scapegoat; it was herself whom Fossey was mad at. Leaving her hair lying about like that was bad form: anybody could get hold of it and work a spell on her. I didn't know at the time that Fossey was popularly known in Rwanda as "the sorceress." I said, "You really believe that hocus-pocus?" Fossey shot back, "Where I live, if I didn't I'd be dead."

Five years passed, and I saw in the newspaper that Dian Fossey had been murdered in Rwanda. Somebody killed her with a machete. Much later, there was a trial in Rwanda, a murky proceeding: a Rwandan defendant was found hanged in his cell before he could testify, and one of Fossey's American research assistants was tried in absentia, found guilty, and sentenced to death. The case was closed, but suspicions remained that it had not been solved. Many Rwandans still speak of a cousin or in-law of Madame Agathe Habyarimana as the true sponsor of the murder; his motive was said to have something to do with gold and drug-smuggling operations—or perhaps gorilla poaching—in the national park around Fossey's research station. It was all very murky.

When Odette told me of her talk with Habyarimana's security chief about the question of demons, I thought of Fossey. Power is terribly complex; if powerful people believe in demons it may be best not to laugh at them. A United Nations press officer in Rwanda gave me a photocopy of a document he had picked up in the wreckage of Habyarimana's home after the genocide. (Among the President's possessions, trophy seekers also found a movie version of Hitler's *Mein Kampf*, with a hagiographic portrait of the Führer on the package.) The document consisted of a prophecy delivered in 1987 by a Catholic visionary, known as Little Pebbles, who claimed direct communication with Our Blessed Mother Virgin Mary, and who foresaw imminent desolation and the end of time. Little Pebbles' scenario for the coming years involved a Communist attempt on the Vatican, civil war in every country on earth, a series of nuclear explosions, including that of a Russian reactor on the North Pole that would cause a shield of ice to form in the stratosphere, blocking out the sun and leading to the death of a quarter of the world's population; thereafter, earthquakes would

make whole nations disappear, and famine and plague would elim-
inate many of the people who had bothered to survive so far.
Finally, after a total nuclear war and three days of darkness, Little
Pebbles promised, "Jesus Christ will return to earth on Easter
Sunday, 1992."

I can't say that Habyarimana ever read this forecast, only that
it found its way into his household, and that it was close in spirit
to views that fascinated his powerful wife. A hill called Kibeho,
which stands near the center of Rwanda, became famous in the
1980s as a place where the Virgin Mary had the habit of appearing
and addressing local visionaries. In Rwanda—the most Christian-
ized country in Africa, where at least sixty-five percent of the population were Catholics and fifteen percent were Protestants—the
Kibeho visionaries quickly attracted a strong following. The Catholic Church got up an official "scientific commission of inquiry"
into the phenomenon, and declared it to be largely authentic. Kibeho was a big deal. Pilgrims came from all over the world, and
Madame Agathe Habyarimana was a frequent visitor. With the
encouragement of the Bishop of Kigali, Monsignor Vincent Nsengiyumva (himself an enthusiastic member of the central committee
of the MRND), Madame Agathe often brought several Kibeho
visionaries along on international trips. These young women had
much to report from their colloquies with the Virgin, but among
the Marian messages that made the strongest popular impression
was the repeated assertion that Rwanda would, before long, be
bathed in blood. "There were messages announcing woe for
Rwanda," Monsignor Augustin Misago, who was a member of the
church commission on Kibeho, told me. "Visions of the crying
Virgin, visions of people killing with machetes, of hills covered
with corpses."

Rwandans often describe themselves as an uncommonly suspicious people, and with some reason. Wherever you go in
Rwanda—to a private home, a bar, a government office, or a refugee camp—drinks are served with the bottle caps on, and opened

only before the eyes of the drinker. It is a custom that honors the fear of poison. An open bottle, even a bottle with a visibly loose cap, is unacceptable. Glasses, too, are suspect. When, as with the potent banana beer consumed by the peasantry, a drink comes unbottled from a common pot, or when a drink is to be shared, the provider must take the first sip, like a food taster in a medieval court, to prove that it is safe.

Tales of alleged poisoning regularly punctuate Rwanda's historical lore. Marc Vincent, a pediatrician from Brussels who served with the colonial administration during the early 1950s, found that the locals regarded poisoning and sorcery as the root causes of all fatal illnesses. In his monograph *L'enfant au Ruanda-Urundi*, Vincent recalled overhearing a very sick ten-year-old boy telling his father, "When I die, you must see who poisoned me." And an eight-year-old told Vincent, "Yes, death exists, but all those who die here, it's not ordinary death, it's sorcery: when you spit on the ground, one takes your saliva, one takes the dust on which you walked. My parents have told me to watch out." Such attitudes, Vincent reported, pervaded all levels of society: "The natives see poisoners everywhere."

Even today, deaths are often explained on *radio trottoir*—sidewalk radio, the ever-warping word of the street—and in the more formal media as the work of invisible poisoners. In the absence of evidence to prove or disprove such rumors, the enduring fear of poison takes on the quality of metaphor. When death is always the work of enemies, and the power of the state considers itself in concert with the occult, distrust and subterfuge become tools of survival, and politics itself becomes a poison.

SO HABYARIMANA WAS shadowed by his wife, and his wife, at least, had forebodings of total destruction. Rwandans seemed to think she should know. On *radio trottoir*, Madame Agathe was called Kanjogera, after the wicked queen mother of Mwami Musinga, the Lady Macbeth of Rwandan legend. *Le clan de Ma-*

dame, Agathe's court within the court, was known as the *akazu*, the little house. The *akazu* was the core of the concentric webs of political, economic, and military muscle and patronage that came to be known as Hutu Power. When the President crossed the *akazu*, he was quickly set straight. For instance, Habyarimana once cultivated a protégé from outside the *akazu*, Colonel Stanislas Mayuya; he liked Mayuya so much that one of the chiefs of the *akazu* had Mayuya shot dead. The gunman was arrested; then he and the prosecutor on the case were also killed.

Mayuya's assassination occurred in April of 1988. A strange year followed. The International Monetary Fund and the World Bank demanded that Rwanda implement a program of "structural adjustment," and the government's budget for 1989 was slashed nearly in half. At the same time, taxes and forced-labor demands increased. Inadequate rains and a mismanagement of resources created pockets of famine. Details of corruption scandals leaked out, and several of Habyarimana's critics suffered so-called automobile accidents, in which they were run over and killed. To prevent Rwanda's sterling image from being tarnished in the eyes of international aid donors, the Kigali police launched vice squads to arrest "prostitutes," a category that included any number of women who had run afoul of the high authorities. The Interior Ministry deputized Catholic militants to vandalize shops that sold condoms. Independent-minded journalists who took note of all this mischief were thrown in jail; they were followed by unemployed idlers whose heads had been shaved in preparation for a "re-education" program.

The more trouble there was, the more new troublemakers emerged. Hutu oppositionists of diverse stripes began finding their voices and lobbying for attention from the Western governments whose aid allocations underwrote about sixty percent of Rwanda's annual budget. The timing was perfect. Following the breach of the Berlin Wall in November of 1989—the same month that Odette was fired—the victorious Cold War powers of Western

Europe and North America began demanding gestures of democratization from their client regimes in Africa. It took a good deal of bullying, but after a meeting with his chief foreign patron, President François Mitterrand of France, Habyarimana suddenly announced, in June of 1990, that it was time to establish a multiparty political system in Rwanda.

Habyarimana's embrace of reform was conspicuously half-hearted, a capitulation to foreign coercion, and instead of simple relief and enthusiasm, the prospect of an open competition for power provoked widespread alarm in Rwanda. It was universally understood that the northwesterners, who depended on his power and on whom his power increasingly depended, would not readily surrender their percentage. While Habyarimana spoke publicly of a political opening, the *akazu* tightened its grip on the machinery of the state. As repression quickened in direct proportion to the threat of change, a number of the leading advocates of reform fled into exile.

And then, in the early afternoon of October 1, 1990, a rebel army, calling itself the Rwandese Patriotic Front, invaded northeastern Rwanda from Uganda, declaring war on the Habyarimana regime, and propounding a political program that called for an end to tyranny, corruption, and the ideology of exclusion "which generates refugees."

EVERY WAR IS unconventional after its own fashion. Hutu Power's unconventionality did not take long to show. The RPF invasion began with fifty men crossing the border, and although hundreds soon followed, the field of combat was clearly demarcated: a patch of national park in the northeast. If it was the RPF you wanted to fight, all you had to do was go up to the front. But on the night of October 4—three days after the invasion—there was a lot of shooting in and around Kigali. In the morning, the government announced that it had successfully put down a rebel attempt on the capital. This was a lie. There had been no battle.

The gunfire was a charade, and its object was simple: to exaggerate Rwanda's danger and to create the impression that rebel accomplices had infiltrated the country to its core.

The RPF invasion offered the Habyarimana oligarchy its best weapon yet against pluralism: the unifying specter of a common enemy. Following the logic of the state ideology—that identity equals politics and politics equals identity—all Tutsis were considered to be RPF "accomplices," and Hutus who failed to subscribe to this view were counted as Tutsi-loving traitors. Habyarimana's crowd didn't want a border war, but they welcomed nationwide turmoil as a pretext for rounding up "internal enemies." Lists had already been prepared: educated Tutsis, prosperous Tutsis, and Tutsis who traveled abroad were among the first to be arrested, and prominent Hutus who were, for one reason or another, considered to be out of step with the regime were picked up as well.

Odette's husband, Jean-Baptiste, received a call from a presidential deputy, who said, "We know you're a Hutu, but you're very close to these Tutsis because of your wife. If you love your family, tell these Tutsis to write a letter to the President, confessing their acts of treason with the RPF." The deputy dictated a sample letter. Jean-Baptiste replied that his friends had nothing to do with the RPF, which was true. Before the RPF struck, almost nobody outside of its ranks had known of its existence. But Habyarimana had repeatedly expressed his fear that the Rwandans in the Ugandan army were plotting against him, and the RPF invasion had, in fact, involved a mass desertion from the Ugandan ranks. As far as Habyarimana and his entourage were concerned, that was proof that anybody they suspected was, by virtue of their suspicion, an enemy agent.

Jean-Baptiste told his interrogator that he had no contacts with exiles. Odette didn't know why he was left alone after that; nearly ten thousand people were arrested in October and November of 1990. But all sorts of mistakes were made. For instance, when men were sent to the hospital to arrest Odette they got the wrong person. "I had been given my job back," she said, "and I had a colleague who had the same name. She was Hutu and she denied that she was me, but she was much taller than I am and they said, 'There's only one Tutsi doctor named Odette.' So she was imprisoned and tortured, and in 1994 she was again mistaken for a Tutsi, and killed."

Throughout the first weeks of the war, the government called on the population to keep calm. But the fake attack on Kigali, and the mass arrests, sent another message. On October 11, just ten days after the RPF invasion, local officials in the village of Kibilira, in Gisenyi, instructed Hutus that their communal work duty for the month would consist of fighting their Tutsi neighbors, with whom they had lived in peace for at least fifteen years. The Hutus went to work with singing and drumming, and the slaughter lasted three days; some three hundred fifty Tutsis were killed, and three thousand fled their homes. For those whose memories do not extend as far back as Odette's, the massacre at Kibilira is remembered as the beginning of the genocide.

7

BACK IN 1987, a newspaper called *Kanguka* began appearing in Rwanda. *Kanguka* means "Wake Up," and the paper, edited by a Hutu from the south and backed by a prominent Tutsi businessman, was critical of the Habyarimana establishment. Its originality lay in presenting an analysis of Rwandan life based on economic rather than ethnic conflict. *Kanguka*'s courageous staff faced constant harassment, but the paper was a hit with the small public who could read it. So in early 1990, Madame Agathe Habyarimana secretly convened several leaders of the *akazu* with the idea of launching a rival publication. They didn't know the first thing about newspapers, but they were experts on human weakness—especially vanity and venality—and as their editor they hired a small-time hustler and big-time self-promoter named Hassan Ngeze, a former bus-fare collector who had established himself as an entrepreneur, selling newspapers and drinks outside a gas station in Gisenyi, and from that vantage point had turned himself into a humorous man-on-the-street correspondent for *Kanguka*.

The paper Ngeze produced, *Kangura*—"Wake It Up"—billed itself as "the voice that seeks to awake and guide the majority people." It began as little more than a lampoon of *Kanguka*, with an identical format that tricked readers into buying it. This ruse was helped along by the fact that just as *Kangura* appeared, the

85

government seized several numbers of *Kanguka*. But the paper's irreverent tone was a bit too much like its opposite's for the tastes of the *akazu*, and it annoyed Ngeze's sponsors that he devoted large portions of the first issues to photo-essays extolling his own virtues. In July of 1990, when Habyarimana's security force arrested the editor of *Kanguka* on charges of high treason, they made a show of balance by simultaneously jailing Hassan Ngeze for disturbing the public order. The ploy worked on several levels. Western human rights groups like Amnesty International issued joint appeals for the release of the two editors, bestowing on Ngeze an aura of antiestablishment martyrdom, when the truth was that he was a propagandist of the regime who had disappointed his patrons. At the same time, prison taught Ngeze that his welfare depended on his being a more diligent flunky, and he was an ambitious man who took the lesson to heart.

In October of 1990, as Rwanda's jails were being packed with alleged RPF accomplices, Ngeze was released to relaunch *Kangura*. (The editor of *Kanguka* remained conveniently locked away.) With the war as his backdrop, Ngeze struck a clever balance between his persona as a prison-accredited gadfly of the regime and his secret status as front man for the *akazu*. Even as he harangued Hutus to unite behind the President in the struggle against the Tutsi menace, he chided the President for failing to lead that struggle with sufficient vigilance. While government officials still felt publicly constrained by international pressure from speaking openly of ethnicity, Ngeze published what he claimed were RPF documents which purportedly "proved" that the rebel movement was part of an ancient Tutsi-supremacist conspiracy to subjugate Hutus in feudal bondage. He ran lists of prominent Tutsis and Hutu accomplices who had "infiltrated" public institutions, accused the government of betraying the revolution, and called for a rigorous campaign of national "self-defense" to protect the "gains" of 1959 and 1973. And he did all of this with his printing costs defrayed by government credit, giving away most of each print run to Rwanda's mayors to distribute free.

A host of new periodicals had appeared in Rwanda in 1990. All but *Kangura* served as voices of relative moderation, and all but *Kangura* are now largely forgotten. More than anybody else, Hassan Ngeze, the Hutu supremacist with the populist touch, plucked from obscurity by the President's wife to play the court jester, was writing the script for the coming Hutu crusade. It would be foolish to dispute his brilliance as a salesman of fear. When another paper ran a cartoon depicting Ngeze on a couch, being psychoanalyzed by "the democratic press"—

Ngeze: I'm sick Doctor!!
Doctor: Your sickness?!
Ngeze: The Tutsis . . . Tutsis . . . Tutsis!!!!!!!

—Ngeze picked it up and ran it in *Kangura*. He was one of those creatures of destruction who turn everything hurled at them into their own weapon. He was funny and bold, and in one of the most repressed societies on earth, he presented the liberating example of a man who seemed to know no taboos. As a race theorist, Ngeze made John Hanning Speke look like what he was: an amateur. He was the original high-profile archetype of the Rwandan Hutu *génocidaire*, and his imitators and disciples were soon legion.

Although he was a practicing member of Rwanda's small Muslim community—the only religious community, according to one Christian leader, that "apparently behaved quite well, and as a group was not active in the genocide, even seeking to save Tutsi Muslims"—Ngeze's true religion was "Hutuness." His most famous article, published in December of 1990, was the credo of this newly crystallized faith: "The Hutu Ten Commandments." In a few swift strokes, Ngeze revived, revised, and reconciled the Hamitic myth and the rhetoric of the Hutu revolution to articulate a doctrine of militant Hutu purity. The first three commandments addressed the stubborn perception, constantly reinforced by the tastes of visiting white men and Hutus with status, that the beauty of Tutsi women surpasses that of Hutu women. According to Ngeze's protocols, all Tutsi women were Tutsi agents; Hutu men who married, befriended, or employed a Tutsi woman "as a secretary or concubine" were to be considered traitors, and Hutu women, for their part, were commanded to guard against the Tutsi-loving impulses of Hutu men. From sex, Ngeze moved on to matters of business, declaring every Tutsi dishonest—"his only aim is the supremacy of his ethnic group"—and any Hutu who had financial dealings with Tutsis an enemy of his people. The same held for political life; Hutus should control "all strategic positions, political, administrative, economic, military, and security." Hutus were further commanded to have "unity and solidarity" against "their common Tutsi enemy," to study and spread "the Hutu ideology" of the revolution of 1959, and to regard as a traitor any Hutu who "persecutes his brother Hutu" for studying or spreading this ideology.

"The Hutu Ten Commandments" were widely circulated and immensely popular. President Habyarimana championed their publication as proof of Rwanda's "freedom of the press." Community leaders across Rwanda regarded them as tantamount to law, and read them aloud at public meetings. The message was hardly unfamiliar, but with its whiff of holy war and its unforgiving warnings to lapsed Hutus, even Rwanda's most unsophisticated peasantry could not fail to grasp that it had hit an altogether new pitch of alarm. The eighth and most often quoted commandment said: "Hutus most stop having mercy on the Tutsis."

IN DECEMBER OF 1990, the same month that Hassan Ngeze published "The Hutu Ten Commandments," *Kangura* also hailed President Mitterrand of France with a full-page portrait, captioned "A friend in need is a friend indeed." The salutation was apt.

Fighting alongside Habyarimana's Forces Armées Rwandaises, hundreds of superbly equipped French paratroopers had kept the RPF from advancing beyond its first foothold in the northeast. Initially, Belgium and Zaire also sent troops to back up the FAR, but the Zaireans were so given to drinking, looting, and raping that Rwanda soon begged them to go home, and the Belgians withdrew of their own accord. The French remained, and their impact was such that after the first month of fighting Habyarimana pronounced the RPF defeated. In fact, the battered rebel forces merely retreated westward from the open grasslands of northeastern Rwanda to establish a new base on the jagged, rain-forested slopes of the Virunga volcanoes. There—cold, wet, and poorly supplied—the RPF suffered greater losses to pneumonia than to fighting, as they trained a steady trickle of new recruits into a fierce, and fiercely disciplined, guerrilla army that might have swiftly forced Habyarimana to the negotiating table, or brought him to outright defeat, had it not been for France.

A military agreement signed in 1975 between France and Rwanda expressly forbade the involvement of French troops in Rwandan combat, combat training, or police operations. But President Mitterrand liked Habyarimana, and Mitterrand's son Jean-Christophe, an arms dealer and sometime commissar of African affairs in the French Foreign Ministry, liked him, too. (As military expenditures drained Rwanda's treasury and the war dragged on, an illegal drug trade developed in Rwanda; army officers set up marijuana plantations, and Jean-Christophe Mitterrand is widely rumored to have profited from the traffic.) France funneled huge shipments of armaments to Rwanda—right through the killings in 1994—and throughout the early 1990s, French officers and troops served as Rwandan auxiliaries, directing everything from air traffic control and the interrogation of RPF prisoners to frontline combat.

In January of 1991, when the RPF took the key northwestern city of Ruhengeri, Habyarimana's home base, government troops backed by French paratroopers drove them out within twenty-four hours. A few months later, when the United States ambassador to Rwanda suggested that the Habyarimana government should abolish ethnic identity cards, the French ambassador quashed the initiative. Paris regarded Francophone Africa as "*chez nous*," a virtual extension of the motherland, and the fact that the RPF had emerged out of Anglophone Uganda inspired the ancient French tribal phobia of an Anglo-Saxon menace. Swaddled in this imperial security blanket, Habyarimana and his ruling clique were free to ignore the RPF for long stretches and to concentrate on their campaign against the unarmed "domestic enemy."

A few days after the RPF's overnight occupation of Ruhengeri, in January of 1991, Habyarimana's FAR faked an attack on one of its own military camps in the northwest. The RPF was blamed and, in retaliation, a local mayor organized massacres of the Bagogwe, a quasi-nomadic Tutsi subgroup that subsisted in extreme poverty; scores were killed, and the mayor had them buried deep in his own yard. More massacres followed; by the end of March hundreds of Tutsis in the northwest had been slaughtered.

"We were really terrorized in that period," Odette recalled. "We thought we were going to be massacred." In 1989, when she was fired from the hospital, Odette had been furious at the speed with which people she had trusted as friends turned away from her. A year later, she looked back on that time as the good old days. Like many Rwandan Tutsis, Odette first reacted to the war with indignation toward the refugee rebels for placing those who had stayed in the country in jeopardy. "We always thought those on the outside were well settled and better off," she told me. "We had come to see our situation here as normal. I used to tell my exiled cousins, 'Why come back? Stay there, you're much better off,' and they said, 'Odette, even you have adopted the discourse of Habyarimana.' The RPF had to make us aware that they suffered, living in exile, and we started to realize that we hadn't thought of these exiles for all this time. Ninety-nine percent of the Tutsis had no idea that the RPF would attack. But we began to discuss it, and realized these were our brothers coming and that the Hutus we'd lived with didn't regard us as equals. They rejected us."

When Odette and her husband, Jean-Baptiste, visited the wives of imprisoned Tutsis, Jean-Baptiste got a call from the Secretary-General of Intelligence, whom he considered a good friend. The intelligence chief's friendly advice was: "If you want to die, keep going to those people."

For those in jail, like Bonaventure Nyibizi, a staffer at the Kigali mission of the United States Agency for International Development, the expectation of death was even greater. "They were killing prisoners every night, and on October 26, I was going to be killed," he told me. "But I had cigarettes. The guy came and said, 'I'm going to kill you,' and I gave him a cigarette, so he said, 'Well, we're killing people for nothing and I'm not going to kill you tonight.' People were dying every day from torture. They were taken out, and when they came back, they were beaten, bayoneted, and they were dying. I slept with dead people several nights. I think the initial plan was to kill everybody in prison, but the Red Cross started registering people, so it became difficult. The regime wanted to keep a good international image."

One of Bonaventure's best friends in prison was a business-man named Froduald Karamira. Bonaventure and Karamira both came from Gitarama, in the south, and both were Tutsi by birth. But early in life, Karamira had acquired Hutu identity papers, and he had benefited accordingly; in 1973, when Bonaventure was expelled from school because he was Tutsi, Karamira, who attended the same seminary, was left unmolested. "But the Habyarimana government didn't like the Hutus from Gitarama, and Karamira was rich, so they arrested him," Bonaventure explained. "He was a very nice person in prison, always trying to help people out, buying cigarettes, a place to sleep, blankets. When he got out of prison before me, my wife was pregnant with our first child, and he went straightaway to visit her. After March of 1991, when the government released all of us from prison, I saw him several times. He used to come to my house, or my office. And then one night"—Bonaventure snapped his fingers—"he changed completely. We couldn't talk anymore because I am Tutsi. This happened with so many people. They changed so quickly that you would say, 'Is this the same person?' "

In the summer of 1991, the much anticipated multiparty order had begun in Rwanda. Such a leap from totalitarianism to a political free market will be tumultuous even when it is undertaken by sincerely well-intentioned leaders, and in Rwanda the political opening was contrived in conspicuously bad faith. Most of the dozen parties that suddenly began scrapping for attention and influence were simply puppets of Habyarimana's MRND, created by the President and the *akazu* to sow confusion and make a mockery of the pluralist enterprise. Only one of the genuine opposition parties had a significant Tutsi membership; the rest were divided between committed reformers and Hutu extremists who swiftly transformed the "democratic debate" into a wedge that further polarized the divided citizenry by presenting Rwandan politics as a simple question of Hutu self-defense. It was us against them— all of us against all of them: anybody who dared to suggest an alternative view was one of them and could prepare for the consequences. And it was Froduald Karamira, the convert to Hutuness, who gave this tidy proposition, and the cacophony of ideological discourse that crackled behind it, the enthusiastic name of Hutu Power.

"I don't know exactly what happened," Bonaventure told me. "People say that Habyarimana paid him tens of millions to change, and he did become the head of ElectroGaz"—the national utility company. "All I know is that he became one of the most important extremists, and that is not the way he was before. So much was changing so suddenly, and still it was hard to see—hard to believe—how much it was changing."

ONE DAY IN January of 1992, soldiers visited Bonaventure's home in Kigali, while he and his wife were out. "They broke the doors," Bonaventure said. "They took everything, they tied up the house staff, and I had a son who was nine months old—they left grenades with him. He was there playing with a grenade in the living room, for three hours. Then somebody passed by and noticed, and fortunately my son was not killed."

So it went—an attack here, a massacre there—as the increasingly well-organized Hutu extremists stockpiled weapons, and Hutu youth militias were recruited and trained for "civil defense." First among these militias was the *interahamwe*—"those who attack together"—which had its genesis in soccer fan clubs sponsored by leaders of the MRND and the *akazu*. The economic collapse of the late 1980s had left tens of thousands of young men without any prospect of a job, wasting in idleness and its attendant resentments, and ripe for recruitment. The *interahamwe*, and the various copycat groups that were eventually subsumed into it, promoted genocide as a carnival romp. Hutu Power youth leaders, jetting around on motorbikes and sporting pop hairstyles, dark glasses, and flamboyantly colored pajama suits and robes, preached ethnic solidarity and civil defense to increasingly packed rallies, where alcohol usually flowed freely, giant banners splashed with hagiographic portraits of Habyarimana flapped in the breeze, and paramilitary drills were conducted like the latest hot dance moves. The President and his wife often turned out to be cheered at these spectacles, while in private the members of the *interahamwe* were organized into small neighborhood bands, drew up lists of Tutsis, and went on retreats to practice burning houses, tossing grenades, and hacking dummies up with machetes.

Play first turned to work for the *interahamwe* in early March of 1992, when the state-owned Radio Rwanda announced the "discovery" of a Tutsi plan to massacre Hutus. This was pure misin-formation, but in preemptive "self-defense" militia members and villagers in the Bugesera region, south of Kigali, slaughtered three hundred Tutsis in three days. Similar killings occurred at the same time in Gisenyi, and in August, shortly after Habyarimana—under intense pressure from international donors—signed a cease-fire with the RPF, Tutsis were massacred in Kibuye. That October, the cease-fire was expanded to embrace plans for a new, transi-tional government that would include the RPF; one week later, Habyarimana delivered a speech dismissing the truce as "nothing but a scrap of paper."

Still, the foreign-aid money poured into Habyarimana's cof-fers, and weapons kept arriving—from France, from Egypt, from apartheid South Africa. Occasionally, when donors expressed concern about the killings of Tutsis, there were arrests, but re-leases followed swiftly; nobody was brought to trial, much less prosecuted for the massacres. To soothe foreign nerves, the gov-ernment portrayed the killings as "spontaneous" and "popular" acts of "anger" or "self-protection." The villagers knew better: massacres were invariably preceded by political "consciousness-raising" meetings at which local leaders, usually with a higher of-ficer of the provincial or national government at their side, described Tutsis as devils—horns, hoofs, tails, and all—and gave the order to kill them, according to the old revolutionary lingo, as a "work" assignment. The local authorities consistently profited from massacres, seizing slain Tutsis' land and possessions, and sometimes enjoying promotions if they showed special enthusiasm, and the civilian killers, too, were usually rewarded with petty spoils.

In retrospect, the massacres of the early 1990s can be seen as dress rehearsals for what proponents of Hutuness themselves called the "final solution" in 1994. Yet there was nothing inevi-table about the horror. With the advent of multipartyism, the President had been compelled by popular pressure to make substantial concessions to reform-minded oppositionists, and it required a dogged uphill effort for Habyarimana's extremist entourage to prevent Rwanda from slipping toward moderation. Violence was the key to that effort. The *interahamwe* was bankrolled and supervised by a consortium of *akazu* leaders, who also ran their own death squads, with names like the Zero Network and the Bullets group. Madame Habyarimana's three brothers, along with a bevy of colonels and leaders of the northwestern business mafia, were founding members of these outfits, which first rolled into action alongside the *interahamwe* during the Bugesera massacre in March of 1992. But the most crucial innovation at Bugesera was the use of the national radio to prepare the ground for slaughter, and the ratcheting up of the suggestive message of us against them to the categorically compelling kill or be killed.

Genocide, after all, is an exercise in community building. A vigorous totalitarian order requires that the people be invested in the leaders' scheme, and while genocide may be the most perverse and ambitious means to this end, it is also the most comprehensive. In 1994, Rwanda was regarded in much of the rest of the world as the exemplary instance of the chaos and anarchy associated with collapsed states. In fact, the genocide was the product of order, authoritarianism, decades of modern political theorizing and indoctrination, and one of the most meticulously administered states in history. And strange as it may sound, the ideology—or what Rwandans call "the logic"—of genocide was promoted as a way not to create suffering but to alleviate it. The specter of an absolute menace that requires absolute eradication binds leader and people in a hermetic utopian embrace, and the individual—always an annoyance to totality—ceases to exist.

The mass of participants in the practice massacres of the early 1990s may have taken little pleasure in obediently murdering their neighbors. Still, few refused, and assertive resistance was extremely rare. Killing Tutsis was a political tradition in postcolonial Rwanda; it brought people together.

IT HAS BECOME a commonplace in the past fifty years to say that the industrialized killing of the Holocaust calls into question the notion of human progress, since art and science can lead straight through the famous gate—stamped with the words "Work Makes You Free"—to Auschwitz. Without all that technology, the argument goes, the Germans couldn't have killed all those Jews. Yet it was the Germans, not the machinery, who did the killing. Rwanda's Hutu Power leaders understood this perfectly. If you could swing the people who would swing the machetes, technological underdevelopment was no obstacle to genocide. The people were the weapon, and that meant everybody: the entire Hutu population had to kill the entire Tutsi population. In addition to ensuring obvious numerical advantages, this arrangement eliminated any questions of accountability which might arise. If everybody is implicated, then implication becomes meaningless. Implication in what? A Hutu who thought there was anything to be implicated in would have to be an accomplice of the enemy.

"We the people are obliged to take responsibility ourselves and wipe out this scum," explained Leon Mugesera, in November of 1992, during the same speech in which he urged Hutus to return the Tutsis to Ethiopia by way of the Nyabarongo River. Mugesera was a doctor, a vice president of the MRND, and a close friend and adviser of Habyarimana. His voice was the voice of power, and most Rwandans can still quote from his famous speech quite accurately; members of the *interahamwe* often recited favorite phrases as they went forth to kill. The law, Mugesera claimed, mandated death to "accomplices" of the "cockroaches," and he asked, "What are we waiting for to execute the sentence?" Members of opposition parties, he said, "have no right to live among us," and as a leader of "the Party" he invoked his duty to spread the alarm and to instruct the people to "defend themselves." As for the "cockroaches" themselves, he wondered, "What are we waiting for to decimate these families?" He called on those who had prospered under Habyarimana to "finance operations to eliminate these people." He spoke of 1959, saying it had been a terrible mistake to allow Tutsis to survive. "Destroy them," he said. "No matter what you do, do not let them get away," and he said, "Remember that the person whose life you save will certainly not save yours." He finished with the words "Drive them out. Long live President Habyarimana."

Mugesera had spoken in the name of the law, but it happened that the Minister of Justice at the time was a man named Stanislas Mbonampeka, who saw things differently. Mbonampeka was a man of parts: he was a well-to-do Hutu from the northwest, the owner of a half share in a toilet paper factory, and he was also an oppositionist, a lawyer and human rights advocate in the top ranks of the Liberal Party, the only opposition party with a sizable Tutsi membership. Mbonampeka studied Mugesera's speech and issued an arrest warrant against him for inciting hatred. Of course, Mugesera didn't go to jail—he went to the army for protection, then emigrated to Canada—and Mbonampeka was soon dismissed as Justice Minister. Mbonampeka saw which way the wind was blowing. By early 1993, all of Rwanda's newborn opposition parties had split into two factions—Power and anti-Power—and Mbonampeka went with Power. Before long, he could be heard on Radio Rwanda, warning the RPF: "Stop fighting this war if you do not want your supporters living inside Rwanda to be exterminated."

In the summer of 1995, I found Mbonampeka living in a drab little room at the Protestant Guest House in Goma, Zaire, about a mile from the Rwandan border. "In a war," he told me, "you can't be neutral. If you're not for your country, are you not for its attackers?" Mbonampeka was a large man with a calm and steady demeanor. He wore gold wire-rimmed spectacles, neatly pressed trousers, and a pink-and-white-striped shirt, and he had the absurd

title of Minister of Justice in the Rwandan government in exile—
a self-appointed body culled largely from officers of the regime
that had presided over the genocide. Mbonampeka was not in that
government in 1994, but he had operated informally as its agent,
pleading the Hutu Power cause both at home and in Europe, and
he regarded this as a normal career development.

"I said Mugesera must be arrested because he sets people
against each other, which is illegal, and I also said that if the RPF
continued to fight we must have civil defense," Mbonampeka told
me. "These positions are consistent. In both cases I was for the
defense of my country." And he added, "Personally, I don't believe in the genocide. This was not a conventional war. The enemies were everywhere. The Tutsis were not killed as Tutsis, only
as sympathizers of the RPF."

I wondered if it had been difficult to distinguish the Tutsis
with RPF sympathies from the rest. Mbonampeka said it wasn't.
"There was no difference between the ethnic and the political,"
he told me. "Ninety-nine percent of Tutsis were pro-RPF."

Even senile grandmothers and infants? Even the fetuses
ripped from the wombs of Tutsis, after radio announcers had reminded listeners to take special care to disembowel pregnant
victims?

"Think about it," Mbonampeka said. "Let's say the Germans
attack France, so France defends itself against Germany. They
understand that all Germans are the enemy. The Germans kill
women and children, so you do, too."

By regarding the genocide, even as he denied its existence, as
an extension of the war between the RPF and the Habyarimana
regime, Mbonampeka seemed to be arguing that the systematic
state-sponsored extermination of an entire people is a provokable
crime—the fault of the victims as well as the perpetrators. But
although the genocide coincided with the war, its organization and
implementation were quite distinct from the war effort. In fact,
the mobilization for the final extermination campaign swung into

full gear only when Hutu Power was confronted by the threat of peace.

ON AUGUST 4, 1993, at a conference center in Arusha, Tanzania, President Habyarimana signed a peace agreement with the RPF, officially bringing the war to an end. The so-called Arusha Accords ensured a right of return for Rwanda's refugee diaspora, promised the integration of the two warring armies into a single national defense force, and established a blueprint for a Broad-Based Transitional Government, composed of representatives of all the national political parties, including the RPF. Habyarimana would remain President, pending elections, but his powers would be basically ceremonial. And, crucially, throughout the peace-implementation period a United Nations peacekeeping force would be deployed in Rwanda.

The RPF had never really expected to win its war on the battlefield; its objective had been to force a political settlement, and at Arusha it appeared to have done that. "You use war when there is no other means, and Arusha opened a means to come and struggle politically," Tito Ruteremara, one of the RPF leaders who negotiated the Accords, told me. "With Arusha we could go inside Rwanda, and if we had good ideas and a very nice organization, we'd make it. If we failed, it meant that our ideas were no good. The struggle wasn't ethnic, it was political, and Habyarimana feared us because we were strong. He had never wanted peace, because he saw that we could be politically successful."

For Habyarimana, it was true that the Arusha Accords amounted to a political suicide note. Hutu Power leaders cried treason, and charged that the President himself had become an "accomplice." Four days after the signing at Arusha, Radio Television Libres des Milles Collines, a new radio station funded by members and friends of the *akazu*, and devoted to genocidal propaganda, began broadcasting from Kigali. RTLM was a *Kangura* of the airwaves; its reach was virtually ubiquitous in radio-saturated

Rwanda, and it became wildly popular with its mixture of rousing oratory and songs by such Hutu Power pop stars as Simon Bikindi, whose most famous number was probably "I Hate These Hutus"—a song of "good neighborliness":

> I hate these Hutus, these arrogant Hutus, braggarts, who
>   scorn other Hutus, dear comrades . . .
> I hate these Hutus, these de-Hutuized Hutus, who have
>   disowned their identity, dear comrades.
> I hate these Hutus, these Hutus who march blindly,
>   like imbeciles,
> this species of naive Hutus who are manipulated, and who
>   tear themselves up, joining in a war whose cause they
>   ignore.
> I detest these Hutus who are brought to kill,
> to kill, I swear to you,
> and who kill the Hutus, dear comrades.
> If I hate them, so much the better . . .

And so on; it is a very long song.

"Anyone who thinks that the war is over as a result of the Arusha Accords is deceiving himself," Hassan Ngeze warned in *Kangura*, in January of 1994. Ngeze had railed against Arusha as a sellout from the start, and with the arrival of the blue-helmeted soldiers of the United Nations Assistance Mission in Rwanda at the end of 1993, he had a new target. UNAMIR, Ngeze proclaimed, was nothing but a tool "to help the RPF take power by force." But, he reminded his readers, the record showed that such peacekeepers were generally cowardly, inclined to "watching as spectators" when violence broke out. He predicted that there would be plenty to watch, and he explicitly warned UNAMIR to stay out of the way. "If the RPF has decided to kill us, then let's kill each other," he urged. "Let whatever is smoldering erupt. . . . At such a time, a lot of blood will be spilled."

8

IN 1991, ODETTE had left her job at the hospital to serve as the doctor for the United States Peace Corps mission in Kigali. Two years later, when Washington suspended the program in Rwanda, Odette put her kids in school in Nairobi, and took a series of short-term Peace Corps postings—in Gabon, Kenya, and Burundi. She liked being in Burundi, because it was easy to get home to see her family, and because Burundi appeared, at last, to have become a country where Hutus and Tutsis were committed to sharing power peacefully. In August of 1993, after nearly thirty years of brutal Tutsi dictatorship, a Hutu was sworn in as Burundi's first popularly elected president. The transfer of power was smoothly accomplished, and Burundi was celebrated at home and abroad as a beacon of hope for Africa. Then, in November, four months after the new President took office, some Tutsi military men assassinated him. The President's death triggered a Hutu uprising and a violent crackdown by the Tutsi army that eventually left at least fifty thousand people dead. The violence in Burundi provided great grist for the mills of Rwanda's Hutu Power purveyors of fear, who trumpeted the news as proof of Tutsi treachery, but it left Odette without a job.

She didn't want to go back to Kigali. With Habyarimana resisting the implementation of the Arusha Accords, attacks on Tutsis and Hutu oppositionists were becoming ever more frequent, and Odette had only to tune her radio to RTLM to feel that her days there would be numbered. But the Peace Corps wanted to resume operations in Rwanda, and Odette was offered twenty-five dollars an hour—in a country where the average income was less than twenty-five dollars a month—to help prepare the program. She was tired of moving her kids around and being apart from Jean-Baptiste. What's more, following the Arusha Accords, a contingent of six hundred RPF soldiers had arrived in Kigali. And there was UNAMIR.

"Really," Odette said, "it was UNAMIR that tricked us into staying. We saw all these blue helmets, and we talked with Dallaire"—Major General Roméo Dallaire, the Canadian in command of the UN force. "We thought even if Hutus start to attack us the three thousand men of UNAMIR should be enough. Dallaire gave us his phone number and his radio number, and said, 'If anything happens you call me immediately.' So we trusted them."

One night in January of 1994, just after she returned to Kigali from Burundi, Odette was driving two visiting cousins back to their hotel when her car was suddenly surrounded by a swarm of shouting *interahamwe*. She hit the accelerator, and the *interahamwe* threw two grenades. The explosion blew out all the windows, showering Odette and her passengers with glass, and it took them a few minutes to realize that they were unhurt. "I called Dallaire," she said, "but nobody came from UNAMIR. I realized then that these people would never protect us."

DISTRUST OF UNAMIR was the one thing which Hutu Power and those it wanted dead shared as deeply as their distrust of one another. And with good reason. In the months following the signing of the Arusha Accords, Rwandans had watched UN peacekeeping missions in Bosnia and Somalia being humiliated by impotence and defeat. On October 3, 1993, five weeks before

UNAMIR arrived in Kigali, eighteen American Rangers serving alongside the UN force in Somalia were killed, and television images of their bodies being dragged through the streets of Mogadishu were beamed around the world. UNAMIR had a much more limited mandate than the Somalian mission: it was prohibited from using force except in self-defense, and even for that it was poorly equipped.

On January 11, 1994, when the issue of *Kangura* warning UNAMIR to "consider its danger" was fresh off the press, Major General Dallaire sent an urgent fax to the Department of Peace-keeping Operations at UN headquarters in New York. The fax, headed "Request for Protection for Informant," explained that Dallaire had developed a remarkable intelligence source from within the highest echelons of the *interahamwe* and that he needed help in guaranteeing the man's security. The informant, Dallaire wrote, was a former member of the President's security staff, who was getting paid nearly a thousand dollars a month by the army chief of staff and the president of the MRND to serve as a "top level" *interahamwe* trainer. A few days earlier, Dallaire's informant had been in charge of coordinating forty-eight plainclothes commandos, an MRND minister, and several local government officials in a plot to kill opposition leaders and Belgian soldiers during a ceremony at the parliament. "They hoped to provoke the RPF . . . and provoke a civil war," the fax said. "Deputies were to be assassinated upon entry or exit from parliament. Belgian troops" —the mainstay of the UNAMIR force—"were to be provoked and if Belgian soldiers resorted to force a number of them were to be killed and thus guarantee Belgian withdrawal from Rwanda." That plan had been aborted—for the moment—but Dallaire's informant told him that more than forty *interahamwe* cells of forty men each were "scattered" around Kigali, after being trained by the Rwandan army in "discipline, weapons, explosives, close combat, and tactics." The fax continued:

- Since UNAMIR mandate [the informant] has been ordered to register all Tutsi in Kigali. He suspects it is for their extermination. Example he gave is that in twenty minutes his personnel could kill up to a thousand Tutsis.

- Informant states he disagrees with anti-Tutsi extermination. He supports opposition to RPF but cannot support killing of innocent persons. He also stated that he believes the President does not have full control over all elements of his old Party/Faction.

- Informant is prepared to provide location of major weapons cache with at least a hundred thirty-five weapons. . . . He was ready to go to the arms cache tonight—if we gave him the following guarantee. He requests that he and his family (his wife and four children) be placed under our protection.

This was not the first time, nor would it be the last, that General Dallaire would learn that Kigali—designated a "weapons-free zone" in the Arusha Accords—was a Hutu Power arms bazaar. It was hardly a secret: grenades and Kalashnikov assault rifles were openly displayed and affordably priced in the central city market; planes carrying French, or French-sponsored, arms shipments kept arriving; the government was importing machetes from China in numbers that far exceeded the demand for agricultural use; and many of these weapons were being handed around free to people with no known military function—idle young men in zany *interahamwe* getups, housewives, office workers—at a time when Rwanda was officially at peace for the first time in three years. But Dallaire's fax offered a far more precise blueprint of what was to come than any other document that has emerged from the time known as "Before." Everything his informant told him came true three months later, and it was clearly Dallaire's judgment at the time that his source should be taken very seriously. He announced his intention to raid an arms cache within thirty-six hours, and wrote, "It is recommended the informant be granted protection and evacuated out of Rwanda."

Dallaire labeled his fax "most immediate," and signed off in French: *"Peux ce que veux. Allons'y"* ("Where there's a will, there's a way. Let's go"). The response from New York was: Let's not. The chief of UN peacekeeping at the time was Kofi Annan, the Ghanaian who would become Secretary-General. Annan's deputy, Iqbal Riza, replied to Dallaire the same day, rejecting the "operation contemplated" in his fax—and the extension of protection to the informant—as "beyond the mandate entrusted to UNAMIR." Instead, Dallaire was instructed to share his information with President Habyarimana, and tell him that the activities of the *interahamwe* "represent a clear threat to the peace process" and a "clear violation" of the "Kigali weapons-secure area." Never mind that Dallaire's informant had explicitly described the plans to exterminate Tutsis and assassinate Belgians as emanating from Habyarimana's court: the mandate said that peace-treaty violations should be reported to the President, and New York advised Dallaire, "You should assume that he"—Habyarimana—"is not aware of these activities, but insist that he must immediately look into the situation."

Dallaire was also told to share his information with the ambassadors to Rwanda from Belgium, France, and the United States, but no effort was made at peacekeeping headquarters to alert the United Nations Secretariat or the Security Council of the startling news that an "extermination" was reportedly being planned in Rwanda. Still, in May of 1994, when the extermination of Tutsis was at its peak in Rwanda, Kofi Annan told a Senate hearing in Washington, D.C., that UN peacekeepers "have the right to defend themselves, and we define self-defense in a manner that includes preemptive military action to remove those armed elements who are preventing you from doing your work. And yet our commanders in the field, whether in Somalia or Bosnia, have been very reticent about using force." In the light of Dallaire's fax, Annan's failure to mention Rwanda was striking.

"I was responsible," Iqbal Riza, who wrote the response to Dallaire, later told me, adding, "This is not to say that Mr. Annan was oblivious of what was going on." The correspondence, he said, was on Annan's desk within forty-eight hours, and copies would also have been passed on to the office of Boutros Boutros-Ghali, who was then the Secretary-General. But, according to one of Boutros-Ghali's closest aides, the Secretariat was unaware of it at the time. "It's astonishing—an amazing document," the aide said, when I read him Dallaire's fax over the phone. "This is all at a level of drama that I don't remember experiencing except once or twice in the last five years at the UN. It's just incredible that a fax like that could come in and not be noticed." In fact, Boutros-Ghali did eventually become aware of the fax, but he made light of it, after the genocide, remarking, "Such situations and alarming reports from the field, though considered with the utmost seriousness by United Nations officials, are not uncommon within the context of peacekeeping operations."

Riza took a similar view. In hindsight, he told me, "you can see all this very clearly—when you are sitting with your papers before you, with your music on, or whatever, and you can say, 'Ah, look, there's this.' When it's happening in the heat of the moment, it's something else." He described Dallaire's fax as just one piece of an ongoing daily communication with UNAMIR. "We get hyperbole in many reports," he said, and then he invoked hindsight himself, saying, "If we had gone to the Security Council three months after Somalia, I can assure you no government would have said, 'Yes, here are our boys for an offensive action in Rwanda.'"

So General Dallaire, following his orders from New York, advised Habyarimana that he had a leak in his security apparatus, and there—but for the genocide—the matter might have ended. Not surprisingly, Dallaire's informant stopped informing, and years later, when the Belgian Senate established a commission to sort out the circumstances under which some of its soldiers had wound up slaughtered while on duty for UNAMIR, Kofi Annan refused to testify or to allow General Dallaire to testify. The UN Charter, Annan explained in a letter to the Belgian government, granted UN officials "immunity from legal process in respect of their official acts," and he did not see how waiving that immunity "was in the interest of the Organization."

TOWARD THE END of March of 1994, Odette had a dream: "We were fleeing, people shooting left and right, airplanes strafing, everything burning." She described these images to a friend of hers named Jean, and a few days later Jean called her and said, "I've been traumatized since you described that dream. I want you to go with my wife to Nairobi because I feel we're all going to die this week."

Odette welcomed the idea of leaving Kigali. She promised Jean she'd be ready to go on April 15, the day her contract with the Peace Corps ended. She remembers telling him, "I, too, am tired of this."

Similar exchanges were taking place throughout Kigali. Just about every Rwandan I spoke with described the last weeks of March as a time of eerie premonition, but nobody could say exactly what had changed. There were the usual killings of Tutsis and Hutu opposition leaders and the usual frustration with Habyarimana's failure to implement the peace agreement—the "political deadlock," which the Belgian Foreign Minister, Willy Klaes, warned the UN Secretary-General in mid-March "could result in an irrepressible explosion of violence." But Rwandans remember something more, something inchoate.

"We were sensing something bad, the whole country," Paul Rusesabagina, director of the Hôtel des Diplomates in Kigali, told me. "Everybody could see there was something wrong somewhere. But we couldn't see exactly what it was." Paul was a Hutu, an independent-minded critic of the Habyarimana regime who described himself as "always in the opposition." In January of 1994, after he was attacked in his car, he had moved into the hotel for a while, and then he had gone to Europe on vacation with his wife and one-year-old son. When he told me that they had returned to Kigali on March 30, he laughed and his face took on a look of astonishment. "I had to come back for work," he said. "But you could feel it was wrong."

Bonaventure Nyibizi told me that he often wondered why he hadn't left Rwanda in those days. "Probably the main reason was my mother," he said. "She was getting old and I probably felt it would be difficult to move her without knowing where to go. And we were hoping that things would get better. Also, since I was born, since I was four or five years old, I have seen houses destroyed, I have seen people being killed, every few years, 'sixty-four, 'sixty-six, 'sixty-seven, 'seventy-three. So probably I told myself it's not going to be serious. Yah—but obviously I knew it was going to be serious."

On April 2, about a week after Odette's dream of destruction, Bonaventure drove down to Gitarama to visit his mother. On his way home he stopped at a roadside bar, co-owned by Froduald Karamira, his prison friend turned Hutu Power leader. Bonaventure had a beer and spoke for a long time with Karamira's barman about how Karamira had changed and where the country was going. The barman told Bonaventure that Karamira was saying everyone should follow Hutu Power and Habyarimana, and that later they would get rid of Habyarimana. "I asked him how," Bonaventure recalled. "I said, 'You're giving a lot of power to Habyarimana, how are you hoping to get rid of him?' " Bonaventure laughed and said, "He didn't want to tell me."

Hassan Ngeze was telling anybody who would buy his newspaper. In the March issue of *Kangura*, he ran the banner headline "HABYARIMANA WILL DIE IN MARCH." An accompanying cartoon depicted the President as a Tutsi-loving RPF accomplice, and the article explained that he would "not be killed by a Tutsi" but by a "Hutu bought by the cockroaches." *Kangura* proposed a scenario strikingly similar to the schemes described by the informant in Dallaire's fax—the President assassinated "during a mass celebration" or "during a meeting with his leaders." The article opened with the words "Nothing happens that we did not predict," and ended, "Nobody likes Habyarimana's life better than he does. The important thing is to tell him how he will be killed."

9

ON THE EVENING of April 6, 1994, Thomas Kamilindi was in high spirits. His wife, Jacqueline, had baked a cake for a festive dinner at their home in Kigali. It was Thomas's thirty-third birthday, and that afternoon he had completed his last day of work as a reporter for Radio Rwanda. After ten years at the state-owned station, Thomas, who was a Hutu, had resigned in protest against the lack of political balance in news programming. He was taking a shower when Jacqueline began pounding on the bathroom door. "Hurry up!" she shouted. "The President has been attacked!" Thomas locked the doors of his house and sat by the radio, listening to RTLM. He disliked the Hutu Power station's violent propaganda, but the way things were going in Rwanda that propaganda often served as a highly accurate political weather forecast. On April 3, RTLM had announced that during the next three days "there will be a little something here in Kigali, and also on April 7 and 8 you will hear the sound of bullets or grenades exploding." Now the station was saying that President Habyarimana's plane, returning from Dar es Salaam, Tanzania, had been shot down over Kigali and had crashed into the grounds of his own palace. The new Hutu President of Burundi and several of Habyarimana's top advisers had also been on board. There were no survivors.

Thomas, who had well-placed friends, had heard that large-scale massacres of Tutsis were being prepared nationwide by the President's extremist entourage, and that lists of Hutu oppositionists had been drawn up for the first wave of killings. But he had never imagined that Habyarimana himself might be targeted. If Hutu Power had sacrificed him, who was safe?

The radio normally went off the air at 10 p.m., but that night it stayed on. When the bulletins ceased, music began to play, and to Thomas the music, which continued through his sleepless night, confirmed that the worst had been let loose in Rwanda. Early the next morning, RTLM began blaming Habyarimana's assassination on the Rwandese Patriotic Front and members of UNAMIR. But if Thomas had believed that, he would have been at the microphone, not at the receiver.

Odette and Jean-Baptiste were also listening to RTLM. They'd been drinking whiskey with a visitor, when a friend called to tell them to tune in. It was 8:14 p.m., Odette recalled, and the radio announced that Habyarimana's plane had been seen falling in flames over Kigali. Jean-Baptiste's immediate reaction was "We're leaving. Everyone get in the jeep, or we'll all be massacred." His idea was to head south, to Butare, the only province with a Tutsi governor and a stronghold of anti-Power sentiment. When Jean-Baptiste showed such adamance, their visitor said, "OK, me too. I'm getting out of here. Keep your whiskey." Odette smiled when she told me this. She said, "This man liked his whiskey. He was handicapped, and he'd come over to show off his new television and video player, because my husband is very generous and he had given this guy money to buy it. Being a handicapped man, he used to say, 'I'm going to die if I don't have a TV to watch.' Unfortunately he never got to watch his TV. He was killed that night."

Odette wiped at her eyes, and said, "That's a story I've always kept inside—about this handicapped guy—because he was so happy with his TV." She smiled again. "So," she said. "So. So.

So." It was the only time she wept in telling me her story. She covered her face with one hand, and the fingers of the other tapped a fast pulse against the table. Then she said, "I'm going to get us some sodas." She came back five minutes later. "Better now," she said. "I'm sorry. It was this handicapped guy—Dusabi was his name—that upset me. It's difficult to call this up, but I think of it every day. Every day."

Then she told me about the rest of that "first" night in April. Jean-Baptiste was impatient to get going. Odette said they had to take her sister, Vénantie, who was one of the few Tutsi deputies in the parliament. But Vénantie kept them waiting. "She was phoning around, phoning everyone," Odette said. "Finally Jean-Baptiste told her, 'We're going to have to leave you.' Vénantie said, 'You can't. How will you feel forever afterward if I'm killed?' I said, 'Why won't you come?' She said, 'If Habyarimana's dead, who'll kill us? He was the one.'" Then RTLM announced that everybody had to stay in their homes, which was precisely what Jean-Baptiste had feared. He put on his pajamas, and said, "Whoever survives will regret that we stayed for the rest of his life."

The next day, the family heard shooting in the streets and began to receive news of massacres. "Children called to say, 'Mother and Father are dead.' A cousin called with news like that," Odette said. "We tried to find out how to get to Gitarama, where it was still calm. People always think I'm crazy when I recount this, but I called the governor. He said, 'Why do you want to come?'" Odette told him her cousin had died in Gitarama and they had to attend the funeral. The governor said, "If they're dead they won't be suffering, and if you try to come you might die on the way."

"ON APRIL 6," Paul Rusesabagina, the hotel manager, told me, "I was here at the Diplomates, having a drink on the terrace, when Habyarimana was killed. But my wife and four children were at home—we used to live near the airport—and my wife heard the missile which hit the airplane. She rang and told me, 'I've just heard something I never heard before. Try to get home immediately.' "

A military man who was staying at the hotel saw Paul leaving and advised him to avoid his usual route, because there was already a roadblock set up. Paul still didn't know what had happened. Driving home, he found the streets deserted, and as soon as he entered his house, the phone rang. It was the Dutchman who managed the Hôtel des Milles Collines, which was owned by Sabena, the same Belgian company that ran the Diplomates. "Come back to town immediately," he told Paul. "Your President's dead." Paul rang people he knew at UNAMIR to ask for an escort. "They said, 'No way. There are roadblocks all over Kigali, and people are being killed on the roads,' " Paul told me. "This was one hour after the President was killed—just one hour."

Nobody, at that moment, was entirely sure who was in charge of the decapitated government, but the roadblocks, the confident tone of the RTLM announcers, and the reports of killing in the streets left little doubt that Hutu Power was conducting a coup d'état. And it was. Although Habyarimana's assassins have never been positively identified, suspicion has focused on the extremists in his own entourage—notably the semiretired Colonel Théoneste Bagasora, an intimate of Madame Habyarimana, and a charter member of the *akazu* and its death squads, who had said in January of 1993 that he was preparing the apocalypse. But regardless of who killed Habyarimana, the fact remains that the organizers of the genocide were primed to exploit his death instantaneously. (While Rwanda's Hutu Power elite spent the night cranking up the genocidal engines, in Burundi, whose President had also been killed, the army and the United Nations broadcast calls for calm, and this time Burundi did not explode.)

In the early evening of April 6, Colonel Bagasora had taken dinner as the guest of the Bangladeshi battalion of UNAMIR. An hour after the President's death, he was presiding over a meeting of a self-anointed "crisis committee," a mostly military gathering at which Hutu Power ratified its own coup and, because General Dallaire and the special representative of the UN Secretary-General were in attendance, paid lip service to continuing the Arusha process. The meeting broke up around midnight. By then the capital was already crawling with soldiers, *interahamwe*, and members of the elite Presidential Guard, equipped with lists of people to kill. The assassins' first priority was to eliminate Hutu opposition leaders, including the Hutu Prime Minister, Agathe Uwilingiyimana, whose house was one of many that were surrounded at daybreak on April 7. A contingent of ten Belgian UNAMIR soldiers arrived on the scene, but the Prime Minister fled over her garden wall and was killed nearby. Before the Belgians could leave, a Rwandan officer drove up and ordered them to surrender their arms and to come with him. The Belgians, outnumbered, were taken to Camp Kigali, the military base in the center of town, where they were held for several hours, then tortured, murdered, and mutilated.

After that, the wholesale extermination of Tutsis got underway, and the UN troops offered little resistance to the killers. Foreign governments rushed to shut down their embassies and evacuate their nationals. Rwandans who pleaded for rescue were abandoned, except for a few special cases like Madame Agathe Habyarimana, who was spirited to Paris on a French military transport. The RPF, which had remained prepared for combat throughout the stalled peace-implementation period, resumed its war less than twenty-four hours after Habyarimana's death, simultaneously moving its troops out of their Kigali barracks to secure an area of high ground around the parliament, and launching a major offensive from the "demilitarized zone" in the northeast. The government army fought back fiercely, allowing the people to get on with their murderous work. "You cockroaches must know you are made of flesh," a broadcaster gloated over RTLM. "We won't let you kill. We will kill you."

With the encouragement of such messages and of leaders at every level of society, the slaughter of Tutsis and the assassination of Hutu oppositionists spread from region to region. Following the militias' example, Hutus young and old rose to the task. Neighbors hacked neighbors to death in their homes, and colleagues hacked colleagues to death in their workplaces. Doctors killed their patients, and schoolteachers killed their pupils. Within days, the Tutsi populations of many villages were all but eliminated, and in Kigali prisoners were released in work gangs to collect the corpses that lined the roadsides. Throughout Rwanda, mass rape and looting accompanied the slaughter. Drunken militia bands, fortified with assorted drugs from ransacked pharmacies, were bused from massacre to massacre. Radio announcers reminded listeners not to take pity on women and children. As an added incentive to the killers, Tutsis' belongings were parceled out in advance—the radio, the couch, the goat, the opportunity to rape a young girl. A councilwoman in one Kigali neighborhood was reported to have offered fifty Rwandan francs apiece (about thirty cents at the time) for severed Tutsi heads, a practice known as "selling cabbages."

On the morning of April 9, Paul Rusesabagina, who had been trapped in his house by the twenty-four-hour-a-day curfew, saw someone climbing over the wall into his garden. If these people have come for me, he thought, let me die alone before my children and my wife and all the people here are killed. He went out into his yard, and learned that Colonel Bagasora's "crisis committee" had just appointed a new "interim government," composed entirely of loyal Hutu Power puppets. This government wanted to make the Hôtel des Diplomates its headquarters, but all the rooms at the hotel were locked and the keys were in a safe in Paul's office. Twenty soldiers had been sent for him. Paul gathered his family, and the friends and neighbors who had taken refuge at his house, about thirty people in all, and they drove off with their escort. They found themselves in a stricken city—"horrible," Paul said, "our neighbors were all dead"—and they hadn't gone a mile when their escort suddenly pulled over and stopped.

"Mister," one of the soldiers said, "do you know that all the managers of businesses have been killed? We've killed them all. But you're lucky. We're not killing you today, because they sent us to look for you and get you for the government." Remembering this speech, Paul laughed, a few hard breathy gasps. "I'm telling you," he said. "I was sweating. I started negotiating, telling them, 'Listen, killing won't gain you anything. There's no profit from that. If I give you some money, you profit, you go and get what you need. But if you kill someone—this old man, for instance, he's now sixty years old, he has finished his life in this world—what are you gaining from that?' " Parked on the roadside, Paul negotiated in this vein for at least an hour, and before he was allowed to proceed he had given up more than five hundred dollars.

In 1993, when Sabena had named Paul director-general of the Diplomates, he was the first Rwandan ever to have risen so high in the corporate ranks of the Belgian company. But on April 12, 1994—three days after he moved into the hotel with the new, genocidal government—when the Dutchman who managed the Hôtel des Milles Collines called Paul to say that, as a European, he had arranged to be evacuated, it was understood that, as a Rwandan, Paul would be left behind. The Dutchman asked Paul, who had worked at the Milles Collines from 1984 to 1993, to take care of the hotel in his absence. At the same time, the Hutu Power government at the Hôtel des Diplomates suddenly decided to flee Kigali, where combat with the RPF was intensifying, and install itself at Gitarama. A heavily armored convoy was being prepared for the journey. Paul loaded his family and friends into a hotel van, and when the government convoy began to move, he pulled out behind it, following as if he was a part of it until it rolled past the Milles Collines, where he swung into the driveway of his new home.

It was a strange scene at the Milles Collines, Kigali's premier hotel, an icon of international business-class prestige, where the staff dressed in livery and a night's lodging cost a hundred twenty-five dollars—about half the average Rwandan annual income. The guests included a few officers of the Forces Armées Rwandaises and of UNAMIR, and hundreds of local sanctuary seekers—mostly well-off or well-connected Tutsis and Hutu oppositionists and their families, who were officially slated for death but who had, through connections, bribery, or sheer luck, made it to the hotel alive, hoping that the UN presence would protect them.

A few foreign journalists were still at the hotel when Paul arrived, but they were evacuated two days later. Josh Hammer, a *Newsweek* correspondent who spent twenty-four hours in Kigali on April 13 and 14, recalled standing at a window of the Milles Collines with some of the hotel's Tutsi refugees, watching a gang of *interahamwe* running down the street outside: "You could literally see the blood dripping off their clubs and machetes." When Hammer went out with colleagues to explore the city, they couldn't go more than two or three blocks before being turned around by *interahamwe*. At military roadblocks, he said, "They'd let you through, and wave to you, then you'd hear two or three shots and you'd come back and there'd be fresh bodies." On the day of Hammer's visit, a Red Cross truck, loaded with injured Tutsis bound for a hospital, was stopped at an *interahamwe* roadblock, and all the Tutsis were taken out and slaughtered "on the spot." The distant pounding of RPF artillery shook the air, and when Hammer went to the Milles Collines' rooftop restaurant, government soldiers blocked the doors. "It looked like the whole military command was in there, plotting strategy and genocide," he said.

So the journalists left for the airport with a UNAMIR convoy, and Paul remained to take care of a hotel filled with the condemned. Except for the mostly symbolic protection provided by a resident handful of UN soldiers, the Milles Collines was physically undefended. Hutu Power leaders and officers of the FAR came and went freely, *interahamwe* bands ringed the hotel grounds, the six outside telephone lines of the hotel switchboard were cut off, and as the number of refugees packed into the rooms and corridors came close to a thousand, it was periodically announced that they would all be massacred. "Sometimes," Paul told me, "I felt myself dead."

"Dead?" I said. "Already dead?"

Paul considered for a moment. Then he said, "Yeah."

ON THE MORNING before Paul moved into the Milles Collines, Odette and Jean-Baptiste attempted to leave Kigali. They had been paying three hundred dollars a day in protection money to a trio of neighborhood policemen, and they were nearly out of cash. Odette had signed over several thousand dollars of traveler's checks, but the cops were suspicious of this form of payment. Odette feared that they might discover her sister, Vénantie, when the money ran out. Vénantie had hidden for three days in a chicken coop that belonged to some nuns who lived next door, then she'd come out, saying she'd rather die. Odette had already learned that at least one of her sisters had been killed in the north, and she understood, too, that most of the Tutsis in Kigali had been massacred. Her friend Jean, who had asked her to take his wife to Nairobi, had gone there by himself to find a house for his family, and his wife had been killed along with their four children. Garbage trucks were plying the streets, picking up corpses.

But the killing hadn't yet reached the south. Odette and Jean-Baptiste thought that if they could get there they might be safe, only the Nyabarongo River stood in the way, and there was no hope of getting over the bridge just south of Kigali. They decided to try their luck in the papyrus marshes that lined the riverbank —to cross by boat and continue on foot through the bush. In exchange for an escort to the river, they signed over their jeep, their television, their stereo, and other household goods to their police protectors. The police even went and found Odette's nephew and his wife and baby, who were hiding somewhere in Kigali, and put them in a school for safety. But the nephew was killed the next day, along with all the other men in the school.

The night before leaving Kigali, Odette went to her neighbors, the nuns, and told the Sister Superior of her plan. The nun drew Odette aside and gave her more than three hundred dollars. "A lot of money," Odette told me. "And she was a Hutu." Odette gave some of the money to each of her children, who were fourteen, thirteen, and seven years old, and she tucked slips of paper into the children's shoes with the addresses and phone numbers of family and friends, and with her and Jean-Baptiste's bank account numbers—in case, Odette had to tell them, they got separated or killed.

The family rose at four in the morning. The police never showed up. They had taken the last of Odette's traveler's checks and vanished. So Jean-Baptiste drove. At that early hour, the roadblocks were mostly abandoned. Vénantie, who was well known as a parliamentarian, disguised herself in the car as a Muslim with scarves wrapped around her face. At a small village near the river, where the mayor was a friend of Jean-Baptiste's, they arranged for a local police escort—two men in front, one behind, for about thirty dollars a man—and set out on foot, carrying a little water and biscuits and a kilo of sugar through papyrus that grew higher than their heads. At the water's edge they saw a boat on the far bank and called to the boatman, but the boatman said, "No, you're Tutsis."

The marshes were teeming with Tutsis, hiding or trying to cross the river, and lurking among the papyrus, there were also many *interahamwe*. When Odette heard her daughter crying out, "No, don't kill us, we have money, I have money, don't kill me," she realized the children had been caught.

"We ran over," Odette told me. "Jean-Baptiste said, 'See, I'm just a Hutu fleeing the RPF,' and we threw all our money and everything we had at them. As they divided it up, we ran away, back toward the village where we'd left the jeep. Then another group of *interahamwe* came and spotted my sister. While we were running, they were calling from hill to hill, 'There's a deputy with them, you've got to get her.' My sister was older than me and heavier, and we were very tired. We drank from a bottle of fruit syrup, and it gave us strength, but my sister was panting. She had a little pistol with her and Jean-Baptiste was running fast with the kids, and I said, 'Wait, Jean-Baptiste, if we're going to die we should die together.' Then a group of *interahamwe* pounced on us, and they put grenades to our necks. That was when I heard the shots. I never could look. I never saw my sister's corpse. They shot her with her own pistol."

Odette was speaking quickly and she kept right on going: "Oh, I forgot to say that during the crisis before April, Jean-Baptiste had bought two Chinese grenades very cheaply here in the market. I didn't like it. I was always afraid they'd blow up." But the grenades had come in handy. When the *interahamwe* had caught the children, and again when they caught the whole family and Vénantie was shot, Jean-Baptiste brandished the grenades, telling the killers they would die along with his family. "So they didn't kill us," Odette said. "Instead, they took us to the village for interrogation, and the mayor, whom we knew, brought some rice and made it look like we were prisoners to protect us."

By then it was late in the afternoon, and it began to rain— the sort of blinding, deafening, open-spigot rain that dumps over Rwanda on April afternoons—and Jean-Baptiste led the family through it in a crouching run to their jeep. *Interahamwe* mobbed the car. Jean-Baptiste drove through them and headed for Kigali. He drove fast, stopping for nothing, and twelve hours after leaving their house the family returned to it. That night, they listened to Radio Muhabura, the RPF station, where the names of Tutsis who had been reported killed were read each day on the air. Partway through the roll call of the dead, they heard their own names.

THOMAS KAMILINDI HAD remained locked in his house for a week. He worked his phone, collecting news from around the country and filing reports for a French radio service. Then, on April 12, he got a call from Radio Rwanda saying that Eliezer Niyitigeka wanted to see him. Niyitigeka, a former radio colleague, had just been appointed Minister of Information in the Hutu Power government, replacing an oppositionist who had been killed. Thomas walked to the station, which was near his house, and Niyitigeka told him that he had to come back to work. Thomas reminded him that he'd quit as a matter of conscience, and the minister said, "OK, Thomas, let the soldiers decide." Thomas hedged: he wouldn't take a job under threat but would wait for an official letter of employment. Niyitigeka agreed, and Thomas returned home to learn from his wife, Jacqueline, that, while he was gone, two soldiers from the Presidential Guard had appeared, carrying a list with his name on it.

Thomas wasn't surprised to learn that he was on an assassins' list. At Radio Rwanda, he had refused to speak the language of Hutu Power and had led two strikes; he was a member of the Social Democratic Party, which had ties to the RPF, and he was from the south, from Butare. Considering these factors, Thomas was determined to seek a safer refuge than his home. The next morning, three soldiers came to his door. He invited them to have a seat, but the leader of the contingent said, "We don't sit when we're working." The soldier said, "Come with us." Thomas said he wasn't budging until he knew where he was going. "You come with us or your family will have trouble," the soldier said.

Thomas left with the soldiers and walked up the hill, past the deserted American Embassy and along the Boulevard de la Révolution. At the corner, in front of the Soras Insurance Building, across from the Ministry of Defense, a knot of soldiers stood around a newly erected bunker. The soldiers scolded Thomas for describing their activities in his reports to the international media. He was ordered to sit on the street. When he refused, the soldiers beat him. They beat him hard and slapped him repeatedly, shouting insults and questions. Then someone kicked him in the stomach, and he sat down. "OK, Thomas," one of the men said. "Write a letter to your wife and say what you like, because you're going to die."

A jeep drove up, and the soldiers in it got out and kicked Thomas some more. Then he was given pen and paper, and he wrote, "Listen, Jacqueline, they're going to kill me. I don't know why. They say I'm an accomplice of the RPF. That's why I'm going to die, and here's my testament." Thomas wrote his will, and handed it over.

One of the soldiers said, "OK, let's finish this," and stood back, readying his rifle.

"I didn't look," Thomas recalled, when he told me of his ordeal. "I really believed they would shoot me. Then another vehicle came up, and suddenly I saw a major with a foot up on the armored car, and he said, 'Thomas?' When he called me I came out of a sort of dream. I said, 'They're doing me in.' He told them to stop, and he told a sergeant to take me home."

Thomas is spry, compact, and bright-eyed. His face and hands are as expressive as his speech. He is a radio man, a raconteur, and however bleak his tale, the telling gave him pleasure. After all, he and his family were still alive. His was what passed for a happy story in Rwanda. Still, I had the impression, with him more than with others, that as he told it he was seeing the events he described afresh; that as he stared into the past the outcome was not yet obvious, and that when he looked at me, with his clear eyes a touch hazy, he was still seeing the scenes he described, perhaps even hoping to understand them. For the story made no sense: the major who had spared his life may have recognized

Thomas, but to Thomas the major was a stranger. Later, he learned his name: Major Turkunkiko. What was Thomas to Major Turkunkiko that he should have been allowed to live? It wasn't unusual for one or two people to survive large massacres. When you "clear the bush," a few weeds always escape the blade—a man told me that his niece was macheted, then stoned, then dumped in a latrine, only to get up each time and stagger away—but Thomas had been deliberately reprieved, and he could not say why. He shot me a look of comic astonishment—eyebrows high, forehead furrowed, a quirky smile working his mouth—to say that his survival was far more mysterious than his peril had been.

Thomas told me that he had been trained as a Boy Scout "to look at danger, and study it, but not to be afraid," and I was struck that each of his encounters with Hutu Power had followed a pattern: when the minister ordered him back to work, when the soldiers came for him, and when they told him to sit on the street, Thomas always refused before complying. The killers were accustomed to encountering fear, and Thomas had always acted as if there must be some misunderstanding for anyone to feel the need to threaten him.

Such subtleties should have been irrelevant. An accomplice was an accomplice; there could be no exceptions, and efficiency was essential. During the genocide, the work of the killers was not regarded as a crime in Rwanda; it was effectively the law of the land, and every citizen was responsible for its administration. That way, if a person who should be killed was let go by one party he could expect to be caught and killed by somebody else.

I met with Thomas on a soft summer evening in Kigali—the hour of sudden equatorial dusk when flocks of crows and lone buzzards reel, screaming, between the trees and the rooftops. Walking back to my hotel, I passed the corner where Thomas had expected to be killed. The Soras Insurance Building's plate-glass portico was a tattered web of bullet holes.

"If I don't kill that rat he'll die," says Clov in Samuel Beckett's *Endgame*. But those who commit genocide have chosen to make nature their enemy, not their ally.

ON THE MORNING of April 12, at the same time that the Presidential Guard first came for Thomas at his house, Bonaventure Nyibizi learned that his family was to be killed that afternoon. They had been hiding in and around his house, spending some nights crouched in ditches. Many of their neighbors had been killed, and he told me, "I remember that already on April 10 there was a communiqué on the radio from the provincial administration calling all the drivers with big trucks, because only four days after the genocide started there were such a lot of dead people here that it was necessary to bring the trucks."

Bonaventure did not doubt that his family's luck had run out at home. "So we decided that instead of being killed by a machete, we'd choose to be killed by a grenade or by being shot," he said. "We took my car and drove outside my compound. We were able to make it up to the church of Sainte Famille. It was at most half a mile, and it was very difficult to drive because there were a lot of roadblocks. But we drove there, and on April 15 they came for us. They killed about a hundred fifty people in Sainte Famille that day, and they were looking for me all the time."

The Catholic cathedral of Sainte Famille, an immensity of brick, stands right off one of Kigali's main arteries, a few hundred yards downhill from the Hôtel des Milles Collines. Because of its prominence, and its consequent visibility to the few international observers who were still circulating in Kigali, Sainte Famille was one of half a dozen places in the city—and fewer than a dozen in all of Rwanda—where Tutsis who sought refuge in 1994 were never exterminated en masse. Instead, the killing in such places was incremental, and for those who were spared the terror was constant. Sainte Famille was initially protected by policemen, but, as usual, their resistance to the neighborhood *interahamwe* and to the soldiers who came hunting for Tutsis quickly collapsed. In the beginning, the killers who staked out the church contented themselves with attacking new refugees as they arrived. The massacre on April 15 was the first massive incursion into Sainte Famille, and it was quite carefully organized by the *interahamwe* and the Presidential Guard.

Only males were killed on that day, picked out individually from the throng of several thousand in the church and its outbuildings. The killers had lists, and many of them were neighbors of the victims and could recognize them on sight. A young man who had worked for Bonaventure as a domestic was killed. "But I was lucky," Bonaventure said. "I went inside a small room with my family, and just as I went in and closed the door, Sainte Famille filled with military and militia and police. They started asking for me, but fortunately they did not break down the door where I was. I stayed there with the kids and my wife. There were about twenty people altogether in that small, small place." Bonaventure had a three-month-old daughter with him, and he said, "Keeping her quiet was the hardest."

I asked him what the priests had done when the killing began. "Nothing," he said. "One of them was good, but he was threatened himself, so he went into hiding on April 13, and the other one in charge was very comfortable with the militia. This is the famous Father Wenceslas Munyeshyaka. He was very close to the military and the militia, and he was going around with them. He was not actually denouncing anybody at first, but he would do nothing for the people."

After the massacre, a junior priest, named Paulin, did help to install Bonaventure in a safer hiding place—the back office of a church garage—where he stayed, alone with a friend, from April 15 until June 20. "He was a Hutu, this priest, but he was kind," Bonaventure said. "Sometimes he would open the door so that our wives could bring us water or food. Rumors went around that I had been killed, so all I had to do was stay hidden."

WALKING HOME FROM his aborted execution, Thomas Kamilindi was told by the sergeant who escorted him that he was still condemned to die. "They're going to kill you today if you don't leave," the sergeant said. Thomas had no idea where to go. He wrote a new will, and gave it to his wife, saying, "I'm leaving, I don't know where, maybe someday this paper can help you."

When he stepped outside again, it was raining. He began walking, and wound up at the radio station. "I was afraid," he said, "because the radio was practically a military camp." But nobody seemed to mind him there. "I watched television until the evening. I called my wife, and told her I was at the radio, and I spent the night under a table on a mat. I had nothing to eat, but I slept well." Thomas could not imagine how he would have survived if he were a Tutsi. In the morning, he told the editor-in-chief of the radio that he had nearly been killed. "Do the morning news, and perhaps they'll think you're with us," the editor said.

"So I did the six-thirty a.m. broadcast," Thomas told me, "but I couldn't go on like that." He called around to various embassies, and found that they had all been evacuated. Then he tried the Hôtel des Milles Collines: "The guy at the reception recognized my voice, and said, 'Thomas! You're still alive. That's incredible. We thought you were dead.' He said, 'If you can get here, you might be OK.'" It was forbidden to go around in a vehicle without escort or papers, so Thomas persuaded a soldier to drive him. He arrived at the hotel without money, but he was given a room. "If people came, we said we'd worry about money later," a hotel staffer told me. That night as Thomas settled in, his phone rang. It was an army major, Augustin Cyiza, who was also staying in the hotel. Cyiza was sympathetic to the refugees—he eventually deserted the FAR to join the RPF—but Thomas didn't know that at the time. He went to Cyiza's room assuming that he would be killed, or at least arrested. Instead the two men drank beer and talked late into the night, and the next day Cyiza went out and returned with Thomas's wife and daughter.

Beer saved many lives at the Hôtel des Milles Collines. Recognizing that the price of drinks could only go up in the embattled city, the caretaker manager Paul Rusesabagina worked through diverse middlemen to keep the hotel cellars well stocked. This trade, by which he also arranged for enough sweet potatoes and rice to keep his guests from starvation, required extensive dealings with the military command, and Paul took advantage of the contacts. "I was using drinks to corrupt people," he told me, and laughed, because the people he was corrupting were Hutu Power leaders, and what he meant by corrupting them was feeding them liquor so they wouldn't kill the refugees under his roof. "I gave drinks and sometimes I even gave money," he said. Major General Augustin Bizimungu, the commander of the FAR, was one of many regular, unsavory visitors to the hotel whom Paul kept well lubricated. "Everybody came," Paul said. "I had what they wanted. That was not my problem. My problem was that nobody should be taken out of my hotel."

Paul is a mild-mannered man, sturdily built and rather ordinary-looking—a bourgeois hotel manager, after all—and that is how he seemed to regard himself as well, as an ordinary person who did nothing extraordinary in refusing to cave in to the insanity that swirled around him. "People became fools. I don't know why," he said to me. "I kept telling them, 'I don't agree with what you're doing,' just as openly as I'm telling you now. I'm a man who's used to saying no when I have to. That's all I did—what I felt like doing. Because I never agree with killers. I didn't agree with them. I refused, and I told them so." Many Rwandans didn't agree with the genocide, of course, but many overcame their disagreements and killed, while many more simply saved their own skins. Paul sought to save everybody he could, and if that meant negotiating with everybody who wanted to kill them—so be it.

Shortly before dawn one morning, Lieutenant Apollinaire Hakizimana from military intelligence walked up to the reception desk, rang Paul in his room, and said, "I want you to get everybody out of this hotel within thirty minutes." Paul had been asleep, and he woke up negotiating. "I said, 'Mister, do you know that these people are refugees? What security do you guarantee? Where are they going? How are they going? Who's taking them?' " Lieutenant Hakizimana said, "Did you hear what I said? We want everybody out, and within half an hour." Paul said, "I'm still in bed. Give me thirty minutes. I'll take my shower, and then get everybody out." Paul quickly sent for several of the refugees he trusted most, who were well connected with the regime—including François Xavier Nsanzuwera, the former Attorney General of Rwanda, a Hutu who had once investigated Hakizimana as a leader of Hutu Power death squads. Together, Paul and his friends began working the phone, calling General Bizimungu, various colonels, and anyone else they could think of who might pull rank on the lieutenant. Before the half hour was out, an army jeep arrived at the hotel with orders for Hakizimana to leave.

"They got that boy out," Paul said. Then he paused for a moment in his memories, and his perspective zoomed out, so that I pictured him peering through his window at the Milles Collines as he said, "And what was around us—around the hotel compound? Soldiers, *interahamwe*—armed with guns, machetes, everything." Paul seemed determined to register his own proper size. He hadn't said, "*I* got that boy out"—he'd said *they* did— and by showing me the ranks of killers massed at the hotel gate, he was underscoring the point.

In discussions of us-against-them scenarios of popular violence, the fashion these days is to speak of mass hatred. But while hatred can be animating, it appeals to weakness. The "authors" of the genocide, as Rwandans call them, understood that in order to move a huge number of weak people to do wrong, it is necessary to appeal to their desire for strength—and the gray force that

128

really drives people is power. Hatred and power are both, in their different ways, passions. The difference is that hatred is purely negative, while power is essentially positive: you surrender to hatred, but you aspire to power. In Rwanda, the orgy of misbegotten power that led to genocide was carried out in the name of Hutuness, and when Paul, a Hutu, set out to defy the killers, he did so by appealing to their passion for power: *"they"* were the ones who had chosen to take life away and he grasped that that meant they could also choose to extend the gift of retaining it.

AFTER HEARING THE announcement of their own deaths on the radio, Odette and her family stayed in their house. "We never turned on the light and never answered the phone except with a prearranged signal for people who knew us—ring once, hang up, call again." Two weeks went by like that. Then Paul called from the Milles Collines. He was an old friend, and he was just checking around—to see who was alive, whom he might save. "He said he'd send Froduald Karamira to pick us up," Odette recalled. "I said, 'No, I don't want to see him. If he comes he will kill us.' But that was Paul. He maintained contact with people like that right to the end." Paul made no apologies. "Of course I talked to Karamira," he told me. "I talked to him because everybody was coming to the Milles Collines. I had many contacts and I had my stock of drinks, and I was sending them to get people and bring them to the Milles Collines. It wasn't only Odette and Jean-Baptiste and their children who were saved in that way. There were so many others."

On April 27, a lieutenant showed up at Odette's house to shuttle the family to the hotel in his jeep. Even an army officer could be stopped and have his passengers taken from him by the *interahamwe*, so it was decided to make three separate trips. Odette went first. "In the streets," she said, "there were barriers, machetes, corpses. But I wouldn't look. I didn't see a corpse in that whole time, except in the river. When we were there in the marshes, my son said, 'What's that, Mother?' and I said it was statues that had fallen into the river and were floating past. I don't know where that came from. My son said, 'No, it's corpses.' "

When the lieutenant and Odette reached the hotel and found the gate surrounded—not to protect those inside, of course, but to prevent new refugees from entering—she held out a handful of malaria pills and aspirin, and said she was a doctor coming to treat the manager's children. "Normally," she told me, "I don't drink, but when I walked into the hotel, I said, 'Give me a beer.' I had a little beer, and got completely drunk from it."

The lieutenant went to fetch Odette's children, and as he drove with them toward the hotel, they were stopped. The militia at the roadblock asked the children, "If your parents aren't dead, or Tutsi, why aren't you with them?" Odette's son didn't hesitate. He said, "My father's manning a roadblock, and my mother's at the hospital." But the killers weren't convinced. Two hours passed in edgy discussion. Then a car pulled up carrying Georges Rutaganda, the first vice president of the *interahamwe* and a member of the MRND central committee. Rutaganda recognized the children from earlier times—when he and people like Odette and Jean-Baptiste had moved in the same social universe—and for a moment, apparently, his atrophied soul stirred him to magnanimity. According to Odette: "He told the *interahamwe* who were hassling those kids, 'Don't you listen to the radio? The French said if we don't stop killing children they'll stop arming and helping us.' Then he said, 'You kids, get in that car and go.' "

So Rutaganda had violated the eighth "Hutu commandment" and showed mercy to Odette's children, but she felt no warmth for the man. Many people who participated in the killing—as public officials, as soldiers or militia members, or as ordinary citizen butchers—also protected some Tutsis, whether out of personal sympathy or for financial or sexual profit. It was not uncommon for a man or a woman who regularly went forth to kill to keep a few favorite Tutsis hidden in his or her home. Later, such people sometimes pleaded that they took some lives in order not to attract attention to their efforts to save others. To their minds, it seemed, their acts of decency exonerated the guilt of their crimes. But to survivors, the fact that a killer sometimes spared lives only proved that he could not possibly be judged innocent, since it demonstrated plainly that he knew murder was wrong.

"That the person who cut off my sister's head should have his sentence reduced? No!" Odette said to me. "Even this Mr. Rutaganda, who saved my children, should be hanged in a public place, and I will go there." The children were in tears when they reached the hotel. The lieutenant himself was crying. It took a good deal of persuading, on Odette's part, before he made the final trip and brought Jean-Baptiste and their adopted mulatto child to the hotel. "Mulattoes," Odette explained, "were seen as the children of Tutsis and Belgians."

10

PAUL RUSESABAGINA REMEMBERED that in 1987 the Hôtel des Milles Collines had acquired its first fax machine, and an auxiliary telephone line had been installed to support it. In mid-April of 1994, when the government cut outside service to and from the hotel's main switchboard, Paul discovered that—"miraculously," as he said—the old fax line still had a dial tone. Paul regarded this line as the greatest weapon in his campaign for the protection of his guests. "We could ring the King of Belgium," Paul told me. "I could get through to the Ministry of Foreign Affairs of France immediately. We sent many faxes to Bill Clinton himself at the White House." As a rule, he said, he would stay up until four in the morning—"sending faxes, calling, ringing the whole world."

The Hutu Power leaders in Kigali knew Paul had a phone, but, he said, "they never had my number, so they didn't know how to cut it off, and they had other problems to think about." Paul guarded his phone carefully, but not absolutely; refugees with useful foreign contacts were given access to it. Odette sent regular faxes to her former employers at Peace Corps headquarters in Washington, and on April 29, Thomas Kamilindi used the hotel phone to give an interview to a French radio station. "I described how we lived, with no water—drinking the swimming pool—and how it was with the killing, and how the RPF was advancing,"

Thomas told me. The interview was broadcast, and the next morning, Major Cyiza told Thomas, "You fucked up. They've decided to kill you. Get out of here if you can."

Thomas had nowhere to go. He moved into a friend's room, and that afternoon he got word that a soldier had arrived at the hotel to assassinate him. Using the house phone, Thomas asked his wife to find out the soldier's name. It was Jean-Baptiste Iradukunda. "He had been a friend since childhood," Thomas told me, "so I called him and said, 'OK, I'm coming,' and I went. He explained that the military command wanted me dead. I asked who decided this, their names, and who had sent him. He hesitated. Then he said, in effect, 'I don't know who's going to kill you. I can't do it. But I'm leaving the hotel and they'll send someone for sure to kill you.'"

"Nobody else came for me," he said. "The situation normalized. I went out in the corridor again after a while, and we stayed put."

When I asked Paul about Thomas's trouble, he laughed. "That interview wasn't good for the refugees," he said, and he added, "*They* wanted to take him out, but I refused."

I asked Paul how that had worked, why his refusal was heeded.

He said, "I don't know," and again he laughed. "I don't know how it was, but I refused so many things."

MEANWHILE, ALL ACROSS Rwanda: murder, murder, murder, murder, murder, murder, murder, murder, murder . . .

Take the best estimate: eight hundred thousand killed in a hundred days. That's three hundred and thirty-three and a third murders an hour—or five and a half lives terminated every minute. Consider also that most of these killings actually occurred in the first three or four weeks, and add to the death toll the uncounted legions who were maimed but did not die of their wounds, and the systematic and serial rape of Tutsi women—and then you can grasp what it meant that the Hôtel des Milles Collines was the only place in Rwanda where as many as a thousand people who were supposed to be killed gathered in concentration and, as Paul said very quietly, "Nobody was killed. Nobody was taken away. Nobody was beaten."

Down the hill from the hotel, in his hideaway at the church of Sainte Famille, Bonaventure had a radio, and listening to RTLM, he heard how well the killing was going. He heard the radio announcers' gentle encouragements to leave no grave half full, and the more urgent calls for people to go here or go there because more hands were needed to complete this or that job. He heard the speeches of potentates from the Hutu Power government, as they traveled around the country, calling on the people to redouble their efforts. And he wondered how long it would be before the slow but steady massacre of refugees in the church where he was hiding caught up with him. On April 29, RTLM proclaimed that May 5 was "cleanup" day for the final elimination of all Tutsis in Kigali.

James Orbinski, a Canadian physician who was one of about fifteen international relief workers still stationed in Kigali, described the city as "literally a no-man's-land." He said, "The only thing alive was the wind, except at the roadblocks, and the road-blocks were everywhere. The *interahamwe* were terrifying, blood-thirsty, drunk—they did a lot of dancing at roadblocks. People were carrying family to hospitals and orphanages. It would take them days to go two or three miles." And getting to a hospital was no guarantee of safety. When Orbinski visited the hospital where Odette and Jean-Baptiste had worked, he found it littered with bodies. He went to an orphanage, hoping to evacuate the children, and met a Rwandan officer who said, "These people are POWs, and as far as I'm concerned they're insects, and they'll be crushed like insects."

By the end of April, the city was divided across its main valley: to the east, where Orbinski was based, the RPF had control, and to the west, the city belonged to the government. UNAMIR and the few emergency workers like Orbinski spent hours each day in negotiation, trying to arrange exchanges of prisoners, refugees, and the wounded across the front lines. Their effectiveness was extremely limited. "I went to Sainte Famille every day, bringing medical supplies, making lists," Orbinski told me. "I'd go back the next day—twenty people killed, forty people killed."

When Paul recalled how he had used his telephone at the Milles Collines to focus international attention on the plight of his guests, he said, "But, you know, Sainte Famille also had a working phone line, and that priest, Father Wenceslas, never used it. My goodness."

It was true that the phone worked at the church. Even Bonaventure Nyibizi, in his hiding place, had been aware of it, and one day in mid-May he had been able to sneak out and get access to it. "I called Washington—the USAID mission," he told me. "They said, 'You know what the situation is. Whenever you have a chance to leave, contact the nearest mission.'" Hardly a message of hope; but for Bonaventure, to make contact, and to know that others knew he was alive and where, was a comfort.

Why didn't Father Wenceslas make similar calls? Why hadn't more people acted as Paul had? "That's a mystery," Paul said. "Everybody could have done it. But, for instance, Wenceslas himself wore a pistol, yet he was a priest. I can't say that he killed anyone. I never saw him killing. But I saw him with a pistol. One day he came to my room. He was talking about what was happening in the country, how people were shooting from Sainte Famille—from his church!—soldiers with armored cars. He said he gave them drinks *because* they've killed people. I said, 'Mister, I don't agree with that.' And my wife said, 'Priest, instead of carrying your Bible, why do you carry a pistol? Why don't you put this pistol down and take up your Bible? A priest should not be seen in blue jeans and a T-shirt with a pistol.'"

Later, Odette told me the same story, and she said that Father

Wenceslas had replied, "Everything has its time. This is the time for a pistol, not a Bible."

Paul remembered the exchange differently. By his account, Father Wenceslas had said, "They've already killed fifty-nine priests. I don't want to be the sixtieth." Paul's response was: "If someone comes and shoots you now, do you think that with a pistol you won't die?"

After the genocide, Wenceslas fled with the help of French missionaries to a village in southern France, where he was assigned to active pastoral duty. In July of 1995, he was arrested and charged under French law with crimes of genocide in Kigali, but his case quickly snagged on legal technicalities. After two weeks in a French jail, he was released to resume his ministry. In January of 1998, France's Supreme Court ruled that he could be prosecuted after all. He stood charged, among other things, with providing killers with lists of Tutsi refugees at his church, flushing refugees out of hiding to be killed, attending massacres without interfering, sabotaging UNAMIR's efforts to evacuate refugees from the church, and coercing refugee girls to have sex with him. In 1995, he was asked by two interviewers—a Rwandan whose mother and sisters had been refugees at Sainte Famille and a French journalist—whether he regretted his actions during the genocide. "I didn't have a choice," Wenceslas replied. "It was necessary to appear pro-militia. If I had had a different attitude, we would have all disappeared."

THE LAST RECORDED apparition of the Virgin Mary at the hilltop shrine of Kibeho occurred on May 15, 1994, at a time when the few surviving Tutsis in the parish were still being hunted. In the preceding month, thousands of Tutsis had been killed in Kibeho. The largest massacre there had occurred in the cathedral, and it lasted several days, until the killers got tired of working by hand and set the building ablaze, immolating the living and the dead. During the days before the fire, Father Pierre Ngoga, a local priest, had sought to defend the refugees and paid for it with his life, while another local priest, Father Thadée Rusingizandekwe, was described by survivors as one of the leaders of several *interahamwe* attacks. Clad, like the militia members, in a drapery of banana leaves, Father Thadée reportedly carried a rifle and shot into the crowd.

With the church leadership so divided, the May 15 apparition offered a theological resolution to the question of genocide. The exact words attributed to the Holy Mother by the visionary Valentine Nyiramukiza have been lost. But the message was broadcast on Radio Rwanda at the time, and a number of Rwandan priests and journalists—including Thomas Kamilindi, who heard it at the Hôtel des Milles Collines—told me that the Virgin was reported to have said that President Habyarimana was with her in heaven, and that her words were widely interpreted as an expression of divine support for the genocide.

The Bishop of Gikongoro, Monsignor Augustin Misago, who wrote a book about the Kibeho apparitions, told me that Valentine's suggestion that "the killing of Tutsis was approved in heaven" struck him as "impossible—a message prepared by the politicians." But then, the messages sent by church leaders frequently carried a political edge during the killings. In fact, Bishop Misago was often described as a Hutu Power sympathizer; he had been publicly accused of barring Tutsis from places of refuge, criticizing fellow members of the clergy who helped "cockroaches," and asking a Vatican emissary who visited Rwanda in June 1994 to tell the Pope "to find a place for Tutsi priests because the Rwandan people do not want them anymore." What's more, on May 4 of that year, shortly before the last Marian apparition at Kibeho, the bishop appeared there himself with a team of policemen, and told a group of ninety Tutsi schoolchildren, who were being held in preparation for slaughter, not to worry, because the police would protect them. Three days later, the police helped to massacre eighty-two of the children.

Bishop Misago was a large, imposing man. A portrait of him
—dressed, as I found him, in a long, purple-buttoned white
robe—hung near a much smaller portrait of the Pope on the wall
of the room where he received me at the bishopric. Minutes after
I arrived, a major thunderstorm broke. The room grew darker, the
bishop's robe appeared to grow brighter, and his voice rose to a
shout against the din of rain on the corrugated-metal roofing. He
seemed glad to shout. He was not at all happy about my visit—I
had come without an appointment, carrying a notebook—and his
conversation was accompanied by a lot of wild gesticulations, in
between which he leafed constantly through a tiny pocket calendar
without looking at it. He also had the unfortunate habit of laughing a loud, nervous, "Ha-ha-ha!" whenever he mentioned an awkward situation like a massacre.

"What could I do?" he said, when I asked him about the
eighty-two dead Tutsi schoolchildren at Kibeho. He told me that
he had gone to Kibeho with the commander of the Gikongoro
police and an intelligence officer "to see how to restore order and
unity." He said he had no choice but to work with such authorities. "I don't have an army. What could I do by myself? Nothing.
That's elementary logic." He had found that the Tutsi students at
Kibeho were inadequately protected, and he said, "The conclusion
was that the number of police should be augmented. Before, there
had been five. Now, they sent about twenty."

The bishop laughed, and went on: "We returned to Gikongoro, confident that the situation would be better. The unfortunate
thing was that among those policemen there were some accomplices of the *interahamwe*. I couldn't have known that. These decisions were made in the army. So the director of the school came
to Gikongoro to explain the situation and to ask that the police
team be changed, and when he got home he discovered that the
massacre had happened. You see? Ha-ha-ha! First we were badly
informed, and then we were powerless to fix the situation. So, you

are also an adult and able to judge that one does not imagine that a person will kill children."

In fact, it seemed to me that in the fourth week of the genocide no adult in Rwanda could have imagined that the police were reliable protectors of Tutsis. The bishop insisted that he had been helpless. "You—you Westerners—left and abandoned us all," he said. "Even the Papal Nuncio left on April 10. It's not just the poor Bishop of Gikongoro."

"But you were still a man of influence," I said.

"No, no, no," the bishop said. "That's an illusion." He laughed his nervous laugh. "When men become like devils, and you don't have an army, what can you do? All paths were dangerous. So how could I influence? Even the Church—we are not like extraterrestrials who can foresee things. We could have been victims of a lack of information. When one is poorly informed, one hesitates to take a position. And there was powerful official misinformation. As a journalist, when you are not sure, you don't publish it—you go verify it. The global accusations against the Church are not scientific. That's ideological propaganda."

The bishop wasn't really denying that he'd committed a major blunder at Kibeho. But he didn't seem to think it was a crime, and although he said he was "embarrassed" to have been taken in by official propaganda, he gave no sign of remorse. He wanted to be thought of as a victim of the same deception that had resulted in eighty-two children being slaughtered. If I understood him correctly, he was saying that he had been a profoundly ignorant man who was duped by demons. Perhaps. But it was curious that he treated my questions about his traffic with those demons as an attack on the institution of the Roman Catholic Church, and when I did ask him about the Church, his response hardly seemed to qualify as a defense.

"To my knowledge," he said, "no official of the Church publicly declared anything that was happening to be unacceptable.

Monsignor Vincent Nsengiyumva, the old Archbishop of Kigali, is the best example. He made no secret of his friendship with President Habyarimana. Of course, the other bishops and the other clergy disapproved. But, you know, profane society in the West likes very much to make exposés with journalism, film, and TV, while we are in the habit of doing things in secret and quietly without beating the drum or sounding the trumpet. If you spoke out, one could have said that you'd become a heretic."

It was true that for many Rwandans to go against Hutu Power would have felt like heresy. But Bishop Misago seemed to have second thoughts about his outburst. A few minutes later, he said, "I was tired when you arrived. I was going to lie down. I was a bit tired and a bit agitated, so that may have colored my answers. And then, you ask such questions."

Clearly, Bishop Misago hadn't behaved as wickedly as Father Wenceslas. Still, it surprised me that a man with his reputation had stayed in Rwanda after the genocide. A number of priests had been arrested for their conduct in 1994, and an official at the Ministry of Justice in Kigali told me that a strong case could be made for arresting Misago. But, he added, "the Vatican is too strong, and too unapologetic for us to go taking on bishops. Haven't you heard of infallibility?"

DURING ONE OF his visits to the Hôtel des Milles Collines, Father Wenceslas had invited Paul Rusesabagina to join him for a drink at the Sainte Famille church. But Paul never left the hotel, and for that, even Wenceslas should have been grateful, since he had delivered his own mother to Paul for safekeeping at the hotel. In fact, a number of men affiliated with the Hutu Power regime had installed their Tutsi wives at the Milles Collines, and while their presence there surely contributed to the hotel's overall safety, Paul felt that it reflected shamefully on the men. "Wenceslas knew himself that he wasn't even able to protect his mother,"

Paul said. "And he was so arrogant that when he brought her, he told me, 'Paul, I bring you my cockroach.' Do you understand? He was talking about his mother. She was a Tutsi."

Wenceslas, Paul told me, was "just a —how do you call it? —a bastard. He didn't know his father." But what does that explain? Lots of people who behaved as badly or worse than Wenceslas had fathers, and would never have called their mothers cockroaches, while many people who were ill at ease with their origins didn't run criminally amok. I wasn't interested in what made Wenceslas weak; I wanted to know what had made Paul strong—and he couldn't tell me. "I wasn't really strong," he said. "I wasn't. But maybe I used different means that other people didn't want to use." Only later—"when people were talking about that time"—did it occur to him that he had been exceptional. "During the genocide, I didn't know," he told me. "I thought so many people did as I did, because I know that if they'd wanted they could have done so."

Paul believed in free will. He understood his actions during the genocide in the same way that he understood those of others, as choices. He didn't seem to think that he could be called righteous, except when measured against the criminality of others, and he rejected that scale. Paul had devoted all his diverse energies to avoiding death—his own and others'—but what he feared even more than a violent end was living or dying as what he called a "fool." Regarded in this light, the option of kill or be killed translated into the questions: kill for what? be killed as a what?—and posed no great challenge.

The riddle to Paul was that so many of his countrymen had chosen to embrace inhumanity. "It was more than a surprise," he told me. "It was a disappointment. I was disappointed by most of my friends, who immediately changed with that genocide. I used to see them just as gentlemen, and when I saw them with the killers I was disappointed. I still have some friends that I trust. But the genocide changed so many things—within myself, my own behavior. I used to go out, feel free. I could go and have a drink with anyone. I could trust. But now I tend not to do so."

So Paul had a rare conscience, and knew the loneliness that came with it, but there was nothing false about his modesty regarding his efforts on behalf of the refugees at the Milles Collines. He hadn't saved them, and he couldn't have saved them—not ultimately. Armed with nothing but a liquor cabinet, a phone line, an internationally famous address, and his spirit of resistance, he had merely been able to work for their protection until the time came when they were saved by someone else.

THE FIRST MAJOR evacuation from the hotel was attemped by UNAMIR on May 3. Trucks arrived to take sixty-two refugees, who had been offered asylum in Belgium, including Thomas, Odette and Jean-Baptiste, and their families, to the airport. But as the refugees boarded the trucks, government spies milled through the parking lot, making lists of the evacuees, and the call went out on RTLM to stop the convoy. About a mile from the hotel, a rapidly growing mob of *interahamwe* and soldiers halted the trucks at a roadblock. The refugees were forced to climb down; some were beaten and kicked. *Interahamwe* with radios tuned to RTLM listened as the names of well-known evacuees were read, then sought those people out for special abuse. The former Attorney General, François Xavier Nsanzuwera, got the worst of it. With UNAMIR officers looking on, he was knocked to the pavement with a rifle butt. As he lay there, bleeding from the head, several shots were fired at him. The shots missed. But the mob grew more excited and began demanding the right to massacre the evacuees. Rwandan military officers held them off, at the same time refusing to allow the convoy to budge. I've heard many accounts of the hours the evacuees spent at the roadblock and not one clear explanation of why, in the end, the convoy was allowed to retreat

142

back to the hotel, but it was, and Odette spent the evening with a sewing kit, stitching wounds.

Twelve days later, an officer from military intelligence turned up at the hotel and informed Paul that everybody in it would be killed that night. There was no question of relying on UNAMIR for help. Once again, Paul rallied all of his connections, in the government and abroad, and called on every refugee with plausible contacts to do the same. Paul remembers speaking with the director-general of the Ministry of Foreign Affairs in Paris, and telling him "Mister, if you want these people to be saved, they will be saved. But if you want them to die, they will die today, and you French people will pay in one way or another for the people who are killed in this hotel today." Almost immediately after this conversation, General Bizimungu of the FAR high command and General Dallaire of UNAMIR came to Paul to assure him that the hotel would not be touched.

Paul made the effort, but the life-and-death decision lay, as always, with the killers and, tellingly in this case, with their French patrons. That night a single bullet crashed through a window of the Milles Collines, as if to say that the hand of death was only temporarily stayed. But by then, the battle for Kigali was raging, and the hotel and several other high-profile houses of "refuge," such as the church of Sainte Famille, had become bargaining chips. The RPF was holding thousands of government prisoners in a stadium across town, and the RPF command proposed the kind of deal that Hutu Power understood: you kill those, and we'll kill these. An exchange was negotiated across the front lines. UNAMIR helped to mediate the arrangement, and provided transportation, and it was widely reported at the time that the UN had saved the refugees. But the truth lies elsewhere: they were saved by the RPF's threat to kill others.

The evacuation proceeded slowly, truckload by truckload, day by day. There were many days when no trucks moved, and even as some refugees were being trucked to safety, massacres continued at Sainte Famille and elsewhere in Kigali. On June 17, when only a handful of refugees remained at the Milles Collines, Paul went to the Hôtel des Diplomates, in search of liquor for General Bizimungu. When he returned to the Milles Collines, he found that a mob of *interahamwe* had broken into the suite where he was staying with his family. His wife and children hid in the bathroom, while the militia tore up the living room. Paul ran into some of the invaders in the corridor. "They asked me, 'Where's the manager?' I was in a T-shirt and jeans and they think a manager is always in a tie. I said, 'The manager? You haven't met him?' They said, 'No, where is he?' I said, 'He's gone that way,' and I went the other way. I met some more of them on the stairs, and they asked, 'Where's the manager?' " Paul laughed. Once again, he sent them off in the other direction. Then he went looking for General Bizimungu, who was waiting for his liquor handout. The general instructed one of his sergeants to chase the militia out. As Paul remembered it, Bizimungu said, "Go up there and tell those militia that if they kill someone, I'll kill them. Even if they beat someone, I'll kill them. And if they stay in this hotel for the next five minutes, I'll shoot."

The next day, Paul and his family joined a UNAMIR convoy to the RPF zone. He had done what he could. But had the RPF not been pounding Hutu Power from across the valley, there would have been no convoy—and probably no survivors.

. . . and it might well happen to most of us dainty people that we were in the thick of the battle of Armageddon without being aware of anything more than the annoyance of a little explosive smoke and struggle on the ground immediately about us.

—GEORGE ELIOT
Daniel Deronda

11

THE NIGHTS WERE eerily quiet in Rwanda. After the birds fell silent, there were hardly even any animal sounds. I couldn't understand it. Then I noticed the absence of dogs. What kind of country has no dogs? I started to keep watch in the markets, in the streets, in the countryside, in churchyards, schoolyards, farmyards, graveyards, junkyards, and the flowering yards of fine villas. Once, far out in the hills, I thought I spotted a boy leading a dog on a tether down a dirt lane. But it was a goat at the end of the rope. Village life without dogs? Children without dogs? Poverty without dogs? There were plenty of cats—the first pets to disappear in a famine, but famine was not Rwanda's problem—and I began to wonder whether, in Rwanda, cats had won their eternal war with dog-kind.

During my first three months in the country, between May and August of 1995, I kept a list of the dogs I saw: A Belgian lady at the Hôtel des Milles Collines had a pair of toy poodles that trotted beside her on her morning strolls through the garden around the swimming pool; the French landlady of a Dutch aid worker I knew had a fat golden retriever; a team of American and Belgian sappers had some German shepherds who assisted them in land-mine removal; and once I saw a scrawny bitch gnawing a fish skeleton behind a restaurant in the northwestern town of Gi-senyi, but that dog might have just slipped over the border from Zaire a few hundred yards away, and after a moment a cook spotted her and chased her away with loud cries and a whack of a long wooden spoon. Studying this list, you might conclude that dog ownership corresponded to skin color: white people had dogs and Africans did not. But Africans are generally as fond of dogs as the rest of humanity, so the impressive doglessness of Rwanda perplexed me.

I made inquiries, and I learned that right through the genocide dogs had been plentiful in Rwanda. The words people used to describe the dog population back then were "many" and "normal." But as the RPF fighters had advanced through the country, moving down from the northeast, they had shot all the dogs.

What did the RPF have against dogs? Everyone I asked gave the same answer: the dogs were eating the dead. "It's on film," someone told me, and I have since seen more Rwandan dogs on video monitors than I ever saw in Rwanda—crouched in the distinctive red dirt of the country, over the distinctive body piles of that time, in the distinctive feeding position of their kind.

I was told about an Englishwoman from a medical relief organization who got very upset when she saw RPF men shooting the dogs that were feeding off a hallful of corpses at the great cathedral center and bishopric of Kabgayi, which had served as a death camp in central Rwanda. "You can't shoot dogs," the Englishwoman told the soldiers. She was wrong. Even the blue-helmeted soldiers of UNAMIR were shooting dogs on sight in the late summer of 1994. After months, during which Rwandans had been left to wonder whether the UN troops knew how to shoot, because they never used their excellent weapons to stop the extermination of civilians, it turned out that the peacekeepers were very good shots.

The genocide had been tolerated by the so-called international community, but I was told that the UN regarded the corpse-eating dogs as a health problem.

ON DECEMBER 11, 1946, the General Assembly of the United Nations declared genocide a crime under international law. On December 9, 1948, the General Assembly went further, adopting Resolution 260A(III), the Convention on the Prevention and Punishment of the Crime of Genocide, which obliged "Contracting Parties" to "undertake to prevent and to punish . . . acts committed with intent to destroy, in whole or in part, a national, ethnical, racial or religious group."

Just as a state's police swear to prevent and punish murder, so the signers of the Genocide Convention swore to police a brave new world order. The rhetoric of moral utopia is a peculiar response to genocide. But those were heady days, just after the trials at Nuremberg, when the full scale of the Nazi extermination of Jews all over Europe had been recognized as a fact of which nobody could any longer claim ignorance. The authors and signers of the Genocide Convention knew perfectly well that they had not fought World War II to stop the Holocaust but rather—and often, as in the case of the United States, reluctantly—to contain fascist aggression. What made those victorious powers, which dominated the UN then even more than they do now, imagine that they would act differently in the future?

Rwanda is landlocked and dirt-poor, a bit larger than Vermont and a bit less populous than Chicago, a place so dwarfed by neighboring Congo, Uganda, and Tanzania that for the sake of legibility its name has to be printed on most maps outside the lines of its frontiers. As far as the political, military, and economic interests of the world's powers go, it might as well be Mars. In fact, Mars is probably of greater strategic concern. But Rwanda, unlike Mars, is populated by human beings, and when Rwanda had a genocide, the world's powers left Rwanda to it.

On April 14, 1994, one week after the murder of the ten Belgian blue-helmets, Belgium withdrew from UNAMIR—precisely as Hutu Power had intended it to do. Belgian soldiers, aggrieved by the cowardice and waste of their mission, shredded their UN berets on the tarmac at Kigali airport. A week later, on April 21, 1994, the UNAMIR commander, Major General Dallaire, declared that with just five thousand well-equipped soldiers and a free hand to fight Hutu Power, he could bring the genocide to a rapid halt. No military analyst whom I've heard of has ever questioned his judgment, and a great many have confirmed it. The radio transmitter of RTLM would have been an obvious, and easy, first target. Yet, on the same day, the UN Security Council passed a resolution that slashed the UNAMIR force by ninety percent, ordering the retreat of all but two hundred seventy troops and leaving them with a mandate that allowed them to do little more than hunker down behind their sandbags and watch.

The desertion of Rwanda by the UN force was Hutu Power's greatest diplomatic victory to date, and it can be credited almost single-handedly to the United States. With the memory of the Somalia debacle still very fresh, the White House had just finished drafting a document called Presidential Decision Directive 25, which amounted to a checklist of reasons to avoid American involvement in UN peacekeeping missions. It hardly mattered that Dallaire's call for an expanded force and mandate would not have required American troops, or that the mission was not properly peacekeeping, but genocide prevention. PDD 25 also contained what Washington policymakers call "language" urging that the United States should persuade others not to undertake the missions that it wished to avoid. In fact, the Clinton administration's ambassador to the UN, Madeleine Albright, opposed leaving even the skeleton crew of two hundred seventy in Rwanda. Albright went on to become Secretary of State, largely because of her reputation as a "daughter of Munich," a Czech refugee from Nazism with no tolerance for appeasement and with a taste for projecting

U.S. force abroad to bring rogue dictators and criminal states to heel. Her name is rarely associated with Rwanda, but ducking and pressuring others to duck, as the death toll leapt from thousands to tens of thousands to hundreds of thousands, was the absolute low point in her career as a stateswoman.

A week after UNAMIR was slashed, when the ambassadors of Czechoslovakia, New Zealand, and Spain, sickened by the barrage of irrefutable evidence of genocide in Rwanda, began pushing for the return of UN troops, the United States demanded control of the mission. But there was no mission to control. The Security Council, where Rwanda conveniently occupied a temporary seat in 1994, could not even bring itself to pass a resolution that contained the word "genocide." In this proud fashion, April gave way to May. As Rwanda's genocidal leaders stepped up efforts for a full national mobilization to extirpate the last surviving Tutsis, the Security Council prepared, on May 13, to vote once again on restoring UNAMIR's strength. Ambassador Albright got the vote postponed by four days. The Security Council then agreed to dispatch five thousand five hundred troops for UNAMIR, only—at American insistence—very slowly.

So May became June. By then, a consortium of eight fed-up African nations had proclaimed their readiness to send an intervention force to Rwanda, provided that Washington would send fifty armored personnel carriers. The Clinton administration agreed, but instead of lending the armor to the courageous Africans, it decided to lease it to the UN—where Washington was billions of dollars in arrears on membership dues—for a price of fifteen million dollars, transportation and spare parts included.

IN MAY OF 1994, I happened to be in Washington to visit the United States Holocaust Memorial Museum, an immensely popular tourist attraction adjacent to the National Mall. The ticket line formed two hours before opening time. Waiting amid the crowd, I tried to read a local newspaper. But I couldn't get past a photograph on the front page: bodies swirling in water, dead bodies, bloated and colorless, bodies so numerous that they jammed against each other and clogged the stream. The caption explained that these were the corpses of genocide victims in Rwanda. Looking up from the paper, I saw a group of museum staffers arriving for work. On their maroon blazers, several wore the lapel buttons that sold for a dollar each in the museum shop, inscribed with the slogans "Remember" and "Never Again." The museum was just a year old; at its inaugural ceremony, President Clinton had described it as "an investment in a secure future against whatever insanity lurks ahead." Apparently, all he meant was that the victims of future exterminations could now die knowing that a shrine already existed in Washington where their suffering might be commemorated, but at the time, his meaning seemed to carry a bolder promise.

By early June, the Secretary-General of the UN—and even, in an odd moment, the French Foreign Minister—had taken to describing the slaughter in Rwanda as "genocide." But the UN High Commissioner for Human Rights still favored the phrase "possible genocide," while the Clinton administration actually forbade unqualified use of the g-word. The official formulation approved by the White House was: "acts of genocide may have occurred." When Christine Shelley, a State Department spokeswoman, tried to defend this semantic squirm at a press briefing on June 10, she was asked how many acts of genocide it takes to make a genocide. She said she wasn't in "a position to answer," adding dimly, "There are formulations that we are using that we are trying to be consistent in our use of." Pressed to define an act of genocide, Shelley recited the definition of the crime from the Genocide Convention of 1948, which the United States only got around to signing in 1989, fourteen years after Rwanda itself had done so. A

State Department transcript of the briefing records the ensuing exchange:

> Q: So you say genocide happens when certain acts happen, and you say that those acts have happened in Rwanda. So why can't you say that genocide has happened?

> MS. SHELLEY: Because, Alan, there is a reason for the selection of words that we have made, and I have—perhaps I have—I'm not a lawyer. I don't approach this from the international legal and scholarly point of view. We try, best as we can, to accurately reflect a description in particularly addressing that issue. It's—the issue is out there. People have obviously been looking at it.

Shelley was a bit more to the point when she rejected the denomination of genocide, because, she said, "there are obligations which arise in connection with the use of the term." She meant that if it was a genocide, the Convention of 1948 required the contracting parties to act. Washington didn't want to act. So Washington pretended that it wasn't a genocide. Still, assuming that the above exchange took about two minutes, an average of eleven Tutsis were exterminated in Rwanda while it transpired.

The press and many members of Congress were sufficiently revolted by the administration's shameless evasions on Rwanda that even as Shelley was spinning in Washington, Secretary of State Warren Christopher told reporters in Istanbul: "If there's any particular magic in calling it a genocide, I have no hesitancy in saying that." Clinton's brain trust then produced an inventive new reading of the Genocide Convention. Instead of obliging signatory states to prevent genocide, the White House determined, the Convention merely "enables" such preventive action. This was rubbish, of course, but by neutering the word "genocide" the new spin allowed American officials to use it without anxiety. Meanwhile, the armored personnel carriers for the all-African intervention force sat on a runway in Germany while the UN pleaded for a five-million-dollar reduction of the rental charge. When the White House finally agreed to the discount, transport planes were not available. Desperate to have something to show for the constant American protestations of concern about Rwanda, administration officials took to telling reporters that Washington was contributing to a public-health initiative in Uganda to clean up more than ten thousand Rwandan corpses from the shores of Lake Victoria.

THE HARDER WASHINGTON tried to keep its hands clean of Rwanda, the dirtier they got. At the same time, France was chafing for an opportunity to rescue its investment of military and political prestige in Rwanda. That meant salvaging Habyarimana's Hutu Power heirs from the increasingly likely prospect of a total defeat at the hands of the dreaded Anglophone RPF. Communications between Paris and Kigali remained constant, cordial, and often downright conspiratorial. Hawkish French diplomats and Africa hands generally adopted the official position of Rwanda's genocidal government: that far from being a matter of policy the massacres of Tutsis were the result of mass popular outrage following Habyarimana's assassination; that the "population" had "risen as a single man" to defend itself; that the government and army wanted only to restore order; that the killing was an extension of the war with the RPF; that the RPF started it and was the greater offender—in short, that Rwandans were simply killing each other as they were wont to do, for primordial tribal reasons, since time immemorial.

Such mystification aside, the genocide remained a fact, and although France had rarely hesitated in the past to conduct unilateral, partisan military invasions to prop up its African clients,

154

the genocide made such a move awkward. The French press was crowding the French political and military establishment with exposés of its blatant complicity in the preparation and implementation of the butchery. Then, in mid-June, the French government hit on the idea of billing a military expedition into Rwanda as a "humanitarian" mission and carrying it out under the UN flag, with some rented Senegalese troops along for the ride to create an aura of multilateralism. When asked what he thought of such a scheme, UNAMIR's indignant General Dallaire told the *Independent* of London, "I flat out refuse to answer that question—no way." Many African leaders outside the Francophone bloc, like South Africa's President Nelson Mandela and Archbishop Desmond Tutu, openly questioned French motives, and the RPF pronounced Paris's plan unacceptable. On the nights of June 16 and 18, arms shipments for the Hutu Power regime were landed, with French connivance, in the eastern Zairean city of Goma and shuttled over the border to Rwanda. But on June 22, the Security Council—eager to be relieved of its shame, and apparently blind to the extra shame it was bringing upon itself—endorsed the "impartial" French deployment, giving it a two-month mandate with the permission to use aggressive force that had systematically been denied to UNAMIR.

The next day, the first French troops of *Opération Turquoise* rolled from Goma into northwestern Rwanda, where they were welcomed by enthralled bands of *interahamwe*—singing, waving French tricolor flags, and carrying signs with slogans like "Welcome French Hutus"—while a disc jockey at RTLM advised Hutu women to gussy themselves up for the white men, taunting, "Now that the Tutsi girls are all dead, it's your chance."

The timing of *Opération Turquoise* was striking. By late May, the massacre of Tutsis had slowed down because most of them had already been massacred. The hunt continued, of course, especially in the western provinces of Kibuye and Cyangugu, but Gérard Prunier, a political scientist who was part of the task force that worked out France's intervention scheme, has written that the great worry in Paris as plans for the mobilization got underway in mid-June was whether its troops would find any large concentrations of Tutsis to rescue before the television cameras. In much of Rwanda, Hutu Power's message to the masses had been changed from an order to kill to an order to flee before the RPF advance. On April 28—long ago, in the compressed time frame of the Rwandan apocalypse—a quarter of a million Hutus, bolting before the RPF advance, had streamed over a bridge into Tanzania from the eastern province of Kibungo. This was the largest and speediest mass flight across an international border in modern history, and although it included whole formations of *interahamwe*, military units, town councils, and the civilian throngs who had strewn the church at Nyarubuye and the rest of Kibungo with corpses, those who fled were indiscriminately received with open arms by UN and humanitarian agencies and accommodated as refugees in giant camps.

Before France even began talking of a "humanitarian" military expedition, the RPF controlled eastern Rwanda, and its forces were moving steadily westward in a broad pincer movement to the north and south of Kigali. As they progressed, the full extent of the extermination of Tutsis in the areas they conquered was broadcast to the world. While Rwandan government leaders and RTLM claimed that the RPF was killing every Hutu it found alive, and French military spokesmen promoted the idea of a "two-way genocide" and called the RPF the *Khmer Noir*, the dominant impression in the international press was of an astonishingly disciplined and correct rebel army, determined to restore order. And for Tutsis and most Hutus of good conscience the best hope for salvation was to reach, or be reached by, the RPF zone.

The RPF, which consisted at that time of about twenty thousand fighters, was forcing a national army more than twice its size, backed by militias and a great mass of civilians mobilized for "self-defense," to retreat. For anybody concerned about the welfare of Hutu Power, as so many in France were, the obvious question would seem to have been: What went wrong? The simplest answer was that Rwanda's Hutu Power regime was sapping its frontline military effort in favor of completing the genocide, just as the Germans had done in the final months of World War II. But a subtler dynamic was at work in Rwanda as well. From the start of the war with the RPF in 1990, Hutu extremists had promoted their genocidal aspirations with the world-upside-down rhetoric of Hutu victimization. Now Hutu Power had presided over one of the most outrageous crimes in a century of seemingly relentless mass political murder, and the only way to get away with it was to continue to play the victim. In yielding Rwanda to the RPF and leading vast flocks into exile, the Hutu Power leaders could retain control of their subjects, establish a rump "refugee" state in UN-sponsored camps, and pretend that their worst fears had been justified.

France promised the Security Council that its objective in Rwanda "naturally excludes any interference in the development of the balance of military forces between the parties involved in the conflict." But within a week of their arrival, French troops occupied nearly a quarter of the country, sweeping across southwestern Rwanda to stand face to face with the RPF. At that point, France suddenly reinterpreted its "humanitarian" venture and declared its intention to turn the entire territory it had conquered into a "safe zone." The RPF was not alone in asking: safe for whom? France's own ex-President, Valéry Giscard d'Estaing, accused the French command of "protecting some of those who had carried out the massacres."

The RPF didn't waste much time in argument. It launched an all-out offensive to limit the *Zone Turquoise*. On July 2 it captured Butare, and on July 4 it took Kigali, scuttling Hutu Power's earlier plans to mark that day with a funeral for President Habyarimana and a celebration of the total eradication of Tutsis from the capital.

OPÉRATION TURQUOISE WAS eventually credited with rescuing at least ten thousand Tutsis in western Rwanda, but thousands more continued to be killed in the French-occupied zone. Hutu Power brigades draped their vehicles with French flags to lure Tutsis from hiding to their deaths; and even when real French troops found survivors, they often told them to wait for transport, then went away and returned to find that those they had "saved" were corpses. From the moment they arrived, and wherever they went, the French forces supported and preserved the same local political leaders who had presided over the genocide. While the United States still had not managed to deliver the armored personnel carriers promised to UNAMIR's African volunteers, the French had arrived in Zaire decked for battle, with an awesome array of artillery and armor, and a fleet of twenty military aircraft that was instantly the most imposing flying power in central Africa. And just as they embraced the Hutu Power military regime and its militias as the legitimate authorities of a state under rebel siege, they openly regarded the RPF as the enemy—at least until the fall of Butare. Then the French softened their tone. They didn't exactly back down, but the sneering animosity with which Turquoise spokesmen referred to the rebels suddenly gave way to something like grudging respect, and rumors began to circulate that the RPF had scored a direct military victory against France. Several years later, I asked Major General Paul Kagame, who had led the RPF to victory, whether there was any truth to this theory.

"Something like that," Kagame told me. "It occurred during our approach to Butare. I received from General Dallaire of UNAMIR a message from the French general in Goma telling me that we should not enter Butare. They were trying to tell me there would be a fight." Kagame told Dallaire that he "could not tolerate such a provocation and such arrogance on the part of the French." Then, he recalled, "I told the troops to change course, to move to Butare now. They arrived in the evening. I told them just to surround the town and stay put. I didn't want them to get involved in a firefight at night. So they took positions and waited until morning. When our troops entered, they found that the French had secretly moved out to Gikongoro"—to the west. "But then, through Dallaire, they asked permission to return for some Catholic sisters and some orphans they wanted to take away. I cleared it. The French came back, but they didn't know that we had already secured the route from Gikongoro to Butare. We had set a long ambush, nearly two companies along the road."

The French convoy consisted of about twenty-five vehicles, and as it left Butare, Kagame's forces sprang their trap and ordered the French to submit each vehicle to inspection. "Our interest was to make sure none of these people they were taking were FAR or militias. The French refused. Their jeeps were mounted with machine guns, so they turned them on our troops as a sign of hostility. When the soldiers in the ambush realized there was going to be a confrontation, they came out, and a few fellows who had rocket-propelled grenade launchers targeted the jeeps. When the French soldiers saw that, they were all instructed to point their guns upward. And they did. They allowed our soldiers to carry out the inspection." In one of the last vehicles, Kagame said, two government soldiers were found. One ran away, and was shot dead, and Kagame added, "Maybe they killed the other one, too." At the sound of shooting, the French vehicles that had been cleared to go ahead turned on the road and began firing from afar, but the exchange lasted less than a minute.

Kagame recalled another incident when his men had French troops in custody and tense negotiations had to be carried out through General Dallaire. On that occasion, Kagame said, "They threatened to come in with helicopters and bomb our troops and positions. I told them that I thought the matter was going to be discussed and resolved peacefully, but that if they wanted to fight, I had no problem with that." In the end, he said, the French pleaded for their men back, and he let them go. Kagame, who grew up in Uganda as a Rwandan refugee and spoke English, told me that he couldn't comprehend France's support for the *géno-cidaires*—as even English-speaking Rwandans call the adherents of Hutu Power—and he scoffed at French fears of an Anglophone conquest of Rwanda. "If they wanted people here to speak French, they shouldn't have helped to kill people here who spoke French."

Kagame's feelings about UNAMIR were more nuanced. He said that he appreciated General Dallaire as a man, but not "the helmet he wore," and that he had told Dallaire so directly. "UNAMIR was here, armed—they had armored personnel carriers, tanks, all sorts of weapons—and people got killed while they were watching. I said I would never allow that. I told him, 'In such a situation, I would take sides. Even if I were serving the UN, I would take the side of protecting people.' I actually remember telling him that it is a bit of a disgrace for a general to be in a situation where people are being killed, defenseless, and he is equipped—he has soldiers, he has arms—and he cannot protect them."

Dallaire himself seemed to agree. Two and a half years after the genocide, he said, "The day I take my uniform off will be the day that I will also respond to my soul, and to the traumas . . . particularly of millions of Rwandans." Even among the French troops who served in *Opération Turquoise*, some souls became troubled. "We have been deceived," Sergeant Major Thierry Prungnaud told a reporter at a collection site for emaciated and machete-scarred Tutsi survivors in early July of 1994. "This is not what we were led to believe. We were told that Tutsis were killing Hutus. We thought the Hutus were the good guys and the victims." But individual discomfort aside, the signal achievement of the *Opération Turquoise* was to permit the slaughter of Tutsis to continue for an extra month, and to secure safe passage for the genocidal command to cross, with a lot of its weaponry, into Zaire.

AS THE RPF entered Butare and Kigali in early July, more than a million Hutus took to their heels, following their leaders to the west. What moved them was the fear that the RPF would treat them as Hutu Power had treated its "enemies." That fear has often been described as fear of reprisal, but for those in the crowd who had indeed helped exterminate Tutsis, the fear should properly be called fear of justice or at least of punishment. Of course, to fear justice one must first believe that one has done wrong. To the *génocidaires*, the prospect of an imminent RPF victory proved that they were the victims, and Hutu Power's propaganda engines tried to make the most of that feeling.

"The fifty thousand bodies that can be found in Lake Victoria, which threaten Lake Victoria with pollution—they come from massacres which only the RPF could have committed," declared the RTLM announcer Georges Ruggiu, in a typical broadcast on June 30. Ruggiu, a white, Italian-born Belgian citizen, who had found his calling in life as a Hutu Power misinformation propagandist, went on to suggest, absurdly, that only five thousand people could still be found alive in the RPF zone. The next morning, July 1, was Rwanda's independence day, and Ruggiu wished his listeners "a good national holiday, even if it is probably a holiday where they must still work and fight." Instead, hundreds of thousands of Ruggiu's listeners were fleeing. RTLM itself was forced to shut down for a few days while it moved its studio northwest from Kigali. Broadcasts like Ruggiu's had done a good job of convincing even those without blood on their hands that staying behind was not an option. But flight was often blind—a function of family ties, or mass panic, rather than of reason or individual choice. In many cases, whole communities were herded onto the road and marched along by force of arms, with their mayors and deputy mayors at the front of the pack, and soldiers and *intera-hamwe* at the rear, hustling them onward.

Those who fled south entered the *Zone Turquoise*, while to the north a million and a half people flooded toward Gisenyi and the border with Goma, Zaire. As they went, they grabbed every bit of portable property they could lay hands on and every wheeled vehicle that still rolled to carry themselves and their cargo. What they could not take with them, the Hutu Power mobs systematically looted and laid to waste: government offices, factories, schools, electrical pylons, homes, shops, tea and coffee plantations. They tore away roofing and ripped out windows, slashed water lines and ate or carted off all they could that was edible.

Thousands of children were abandoned along the route of flight, lost in the shuffle, and often deliberately left behind, and who will claim to know why—out of some fantasy that it was safer for the children? or because the parents could move more swiftly unburdened? out of shame or out of shamelessness? Priests led whole congregations into the unknown. Army battalions rolled through the crowd, and businessmen and bureaucrats drove their cars heaped with their household wares, their wives and cousins, their children and grandmothers—and their radios, of course, tuned to RTLM. When tension gripped the crowd, stampedes occurred, and people were crushed to death by the dozens.

The frontline troops of the RPF followed the mob into the Hutu Power heartland of the northwest, securing control of the country from the routed government forces. On July 12, the head of the International Committee of the Red Cross pronounced that a million people had been killed in the genocide. On July 13, the rebels captured Ruhengeri, Habyarimana's old home base, and during the two days that followed an estimated half million Hutus crossed the border into Goma. On July 15, the United States withdrew diplomatic recognition from Rwanda's Hutu Power government and shut down its Washington embassy. On July 16, the Hutu Power President and most of his cabinet fled into the *Zone*

Turquoise. France had promised to arrest them, but on July 17 they moved on with the entourage of Colonel Bagasora to Zaire, where the influx of Rwandans was now said to be a million strong. At the same time, in Kigali, the RPF declared that it would form a new national government, guided by the power-sharing principles of the Arusha Accords and without regard for ethnicity. On July 18, following an intensive artillery battle, the RPF captured Gisenyi and began securing the northwestern border with Zaire. On July 19, the new government—a coalition between the RPF and surviving members of the anti-Hutu Power opposition parties—was sworn in at Kigali, and in New York the UN ambassador of the ousted genocidal regime was forced to give up his seat on the Security Council. Thereafter, Rwanda's national army would be known as the Rwandese Patriotic Army, the exiled Forces Armées Rwandaises would be known as the ex-FAR, and the RPF would be the name only of the former rebel movement's political structure, which formed the backbone of the new regime. On July 20, the ex-FAR and *interahamwe* began raiding emergency shipments of relief food and supplies that were being airlifted into Zaire for the refugees. That same day, in Goma, the first cases of cholera were reported in the teeming new camps. And with that the genocide began to be old news.

THE WORLD THAT had "stood around with its hands in its pockets," as General Kagame put it, during the extermination of Tutsis, responded to the mass flight of Hutus into Zaire with passionate intensity. Goma in the late summer of 1994 presented one of the most bewildering human spectacles of the century, and the suffering on display there made for what cameramen unabashedly call "great TV."

Goma sits on the northern shore of Lake Kivu at the base of a range of towering volcanoes, and north and west of town a vast and inhospitable plain of hardened black lava covered by rough and scraggly bush stretches for miles. The rock is jagged and sharp, lacerating even to the toughened soles of habitually barefoot Rwandan peasants, and yet it is a crumbly rock, and everything that comes near it is quickly coated in a coal-like dust. It was on this bed of brimstone that the Rwandan hordes settled down in six camps more populous than any city in the region—a hundred twenty thousand here, a hundred fifty thousand there, two hundred thousand down the road—and all at once they began dying like flies. More than thirty thousand died in the three or four weeks before the cholera epidemic was contained. A man would be staggering along the road, and then he'd sit, and while the cameras rolled, he would crumple up, tip over, and be gone. And not just men but women and little children—simply because they'd had a sip of water in which somebody had pissed, or shat, or dumped a body. The dead were rolled up in straw mats and deposited along the roadside for collection: mile after mile of neatly bundled bodies. Bulldozers had to be brought in to dig mass graves and plow the bodies under. Picture it: a million people, shifting through the smoke of cooking fires on a vast black field, and behind them—it so happened—the huge dark cone of the Nyaragongo volcano had come to life, burbling with flame that made the night sky red and smoke that further clouded the day.

This scene was broadcast to the world around the clock, and it came across in one of two ways. In the sloppy version, you heard, or read, that there had been a genocide, and then you heard and saw, or read, that a million refugees had wound up in this nearly perfect scene of hell on earth, and you thought genocide plus refugees equals refugees from genocide, and your heart was wrenched. Or else you got the story straight—these were people who had killed or who had been terrified into following the killers into exile—and you heard, or read, or could not but infer, that this nearly perfect scene of hell on earth was some sort of divine retribution, that the cholera was like a biblical plague, that the horror had been equalized, and it was all much more than you could stomach, never mind comprehend, and your heart was wrenched. By this process of compression and imagination, the imponderable sprawl of febrile humanity at Goma blotted out the memory of the graveyard at its back, and an epidemic that came out of bad water and killed tens of thousands eclipsed a genocide that had come out of a hundred years of insane identity politics and resulted in nearly a million murders.

"If it bleeds, it leads," the old newsroom saw has it, and in Rwanda the blood was beginning to dry. The story was in Goma, and it was no longer just a sad, confusing, ugly African story. It was our story, too—the whole world was there to save the Africans from their sad, confusing, ugly story. Planes churned in and out of the Goma airfield twenty-four hours a day, bringing plastic sheeting to build refugee tents, bringing food by the ton, bringing well-digging equipment, medical supplies, fleets of white four-wheel-drive Land Cruisers, office equipment, lime to bury the dead, and nurses, doctors, logisticians, social workers, security officers, and press officers—in the largest, most rapid, and most expensive deployment by the international humanitarian-aid industry in the twentieth century. The United Nations High Commissioner for Refugees led the charge, and behind it came an array of more than a hundred relief agencies frantic to get in on the astonishingly dramatic—and yes, lucrative—action. Almost overnight, Goma became the capital of a new, semiautonomous archipelago of refugee camps, organized with ever-increasing efficiency under the pale blue flag of the UNHCR. Beneath that flag, however, the UN had little control.

Zairean troops had claimed to be disarming Rwandans as they came over the border, and great piles of machetes and guns did accumulate beside the immigration shacks, but sitting in a car, amid the torrent of humanity sweeping through Goma, an American military officer telephoned Washington and dictated a list of the astonishing array of artillery, armor, and light weaponry that was being carried past him by the ex-FAR. Presided over by this largely intact army, and by the *interahamwe*, the camps were rap-

165

idly organized into perfect replicas of the Hutu Power state—same community groupings, same leaders, same rigid hierarchy, same propaganda, same violence. In this regime, the humanitarians were treated rather like the service staff at a seedy mafia-occupied hotel: they were there to provide—food, medicine, housewares, an aura of respectability; if at times they were pandered to, it was only because they were being set up to be cheated; if they needed to be browbeaten, a mob quickly surrounded them; and if they were essentially the dupes of their criminal guests, they were not unwitting about it and, with time, their service effectively made them accessories to the Hutu Power syndicate.

None of this was especially subtle or secretive. By late August, when the French finally withdrew from the *Zone Turquoise*, another half million Hutus—including many Hutu Power loyalists —had moved on to Burundi or, through Bukavu, Zaire, to a network of camps that stretched along the south end of Lake Kivu. Although Goma still had the roughest camps, the ex-FAR and *interahamwe* quickly established a presence wherever the UN set up a refuge. International humanitarian law forbids the establishment of refugee camps within fifty miles of the inhabitants' home country, but all of the camps for Rwandans were closer to home than that, and most lay just a few miles from the Rwandan border in Tanzania, Burundi, and Zaire. Nearly a third of Rwanda's Hutu population was in these camps. Of course, that meant that two-thirds—more than four million people—had chosen to stay in Rwanda, and the cholera and general horror of Goma inspired a number of refugees to reflect that they might have been better off if they, too, had stayed behind. But those who spoke of returning were often denounced as RPF accomplices, and some were killed by the camp militias. After all, if all the innocent refugees left, only the guilty would remain, and Hutu Power's monopoly on international pity might be shaken.

A reporter who was sent into Goma directly from Bosnia told me that he knew what Hutu Power was and that he looked up at the volcano and prayed, "God, if that thing erupts right now, and buries the killers, I will believe that you are just and I will go to church again every day of my life." Many humanitarian-aid workers told me they had similarly anguished thoughts, but that didn't stop most of them from settling in. It bothered them that the camp leaders might be war criminals, not refugees in any conventional sense of the word, but fugitives. It was unpleasant to hear those leaders say that the refugees would never return except as they had come, en masse, and that when they went back they would finish the job they had started with the Tutsis. And it was really disturbing that within weeks of their arrival, even before the cholera had been brought entirely under control, armed bands from the camps began waging a guerrilla war of bloody cross-border raids on Rwanda. Some humanitarian agencies found the extreme politicization and militarization of the camps so distasteful that in November 1994 they pulled out of Goma. But others eagerly filled the empty places.

In the first months after the genocide, there was much discussion at the UN of assembling an international force to disarm the militants in the camps and to separate out the political and criminal elements from the subject masses. For months on end, one high-level international diplomat after another issued alarming statements about violence among the refugees in Zaire, warning that Hutu Power planned a massive invasion of Rwanda and calling for a force to bring order to the camps. But although all the major powers were paying heavily to keep the camps running, when the Secretary-General asked for volunteers for such a force, not a single country was willing to provide troops.

The border camps turned the Rwandan crisis into a regional crisis. It remained, as it had always been, a political crisis, but the so-called international community preferred to treat it as a humanitarian crisis, as if the woe had appeared without any human rhyme or reason, like a flood or an earthquake. In fact, the Rwandan catastrophe *was* widely understood as a kind of natural disaster—Hutus and Tutsis simply doing what their natures dictated, and killing each other. If so many people had fled in such horrible circumstances, the thinking went, they must have been fleeing something even more horrible. So the *génocidaires* scored another extraordinary public-relations victory through the deft manipulation of mass anguish, and—of all things—an appeal to the world's conscience.

IN SEPTEMBER OF 1997, shortly before Secretary-General Kofi Annan muzzled him against testifying before the Belgian Senate, General Dallaire, formerly of UNAMIR, went on Canadian television and said of his tour in Rwanda: "I'm fully responsible for the decisions of the ten Belgian soldiers dying, of others dying, of several of my soldiers being injured and falling sick because we ran out of medical supplies, of fifty-six Red Cross people being killed, of two million people becoming displaced and refugees, and about a million Rwandans being killed—because the mission failed, and I consider myself intimately involved with that responsibility."

Dallaire refused to "pass the buck" to the UN system. Instead he passed it on to the member states of the Security Council and of the General Assembly. If, in the face of genocide, governments fear placing their soldiers at risk, he said, "then don't send soldiers, send Boy Scouts"—which is basically what the world did in the refugee camps. Dallaire was in uniform as he faced the camera; his graying hair was closely cropped; he held his square jaw firmly outthrust; his chest was dappled with decorations. But he spoke with some agitation, and his carefully measured phrases did nothing to mask his sense of injury or his fury.

He said: "I haven't even started my real mourning of the apathy and the absolute detachment of the international community, and particularly of the Western world, from the plight of Rwandans. Because, fundamentally, to be very candid and soldierly, who the hell cared about Rwanda? I mean, face it. Essentially, how many people really still remember the genocide in Rwanda? We know the genocide of the Second World War because the whole outfit was involved. But who really is involved in the Rwandan genocide? Who comprehends that more people were killed, injured, and displaced in three and a half months in Rwanda than in the whole of the Yugoslavian campaign in which we poured sixty thousand troops and the whole of the Western world was there, and we're pouring billions in there, still trying to solve the problem. How much is really being done to solve the Rwandan problem? Who is grieving for Rwanda and really living it and living with the consequences? I mean, there are hundreds of Rwandans whom I knew personally whom I found slaughtered with their families complete—and bodies up to here—villages totally wiped out . . . and we made all that information available daily and the international community kept watching."

The utopian premise of the Genocide Convention had been that a moral imperative to prevent efforts to exterminate whole peoples should be the overriding interest animating the action of an international community of autonomous states. This is a radical notion, fundamentally at odds, as so much of the internationalist experiment has proven to be, with the principle of sovereignty. States have never acted for purely disinterested humanitarian reasons; the novel idea was that the protection of humanity was in every state's interest, and it was well understood in the aftermath of World War II that action against genocide would require a willingness to use force and to risk the lives of one's own. The belief was that the price to the world of such a risk would not be as great as the price of inaction. But whose world were the drafters of the Genocide Convention—and the refugee conventions, which soon followed—thinking of?

I first traveled to Rwanda via Brussels on May 8, 1995. The European papers were full of commemorative articles marking the fiftieth anniversary of V-E Day. The *Herald Tribune* had reprinted its entire front page from May 8, 1945, and the articles impressed me with their fighting spirit: smash the Germans, conquer, then bring justice, then reconstruct. The European *Wall Street Journal* carried news of a poll which found that, fifty years after the fact, sixty-five percent of Germans believed that it was a good thing their country had been defeated. And I wondered: Can we imagine such an outcome for any of the wars of today?

Rwanda had presented the world with the most unambiguous case of genocide since Hitler's war against the Jews, and the world sent blankets, beans, and bandages to camps controlled by the killers, apparently hoping that everybody would behave nicely in the future.

The West's post-Holocaust pledge that genocide would never again be tolerated proved to be hollow, and for all the fine sentiments inspired by the memory of Auschwitz, the problem remains that denouncing evil is a far cry from doing good.

ON TELEVISION, MAJOR General Dallaire was politic. He blamed no governments by name. He said, "The real question is: What does the international community really want the UN to do?" He said, "The UN simply wasn't given the tools." And he said, "We did not want to take on the Rwandan armed forces and the *interahamwe*."

Listening to him, I was reminded of a conversation I had with an American military intelligence officer who was having a supper of Jack Daniel's and Coca-Cola at a Kigali bar.

"I hear you're interested in genocide," the American said. "Do you know what genocide is?"

I asked him to tell me.

"A cheese sandwich," he said. "Write it down. Genocide is a cheese sandwich."

I asked him how he figured that.

"What does anyone care about a cheese sandwich?" he said. "Genocide, genocide, genocide. Cheese sandwich, cheese sandwich, cheese sandwich. Who gives a shit? Crimes against humanity. Where's humanity? Who's humanity? You? Me? Did you see a crime committed against you? Hey, just a million Rwandans. Did you ever hear about the Genocide Convention?"

I said I had.

"That convention," the American at the bar said, "makes a nice wrapping for a cheese sandwich."

Part Two

. . . so here the Archangel paused
Betwixt the world destroyed and world restored . . .

—JOHN MILTON

Paradise Lost

12

IN JULY OF 1995, a year after the installation of Rwanda's new government, Archbishop Desmond Tutu of South Africa visited Kigali and delivered a sermon at a football stadium, begging the assembled multitude: "Please, please, please, our sisters and brothers, please, please, keep quiet. Please, please, stop crying!"

It was an astonishing message to a people whose country had run with blood, particularly from a man who had won a Nobel Peace Prize for refusing to keep quiet. But as he went on to invoke the recent history of blacks wresting power from whites in South Africa, it became clear that Archbishop Tutu had come as much to scold as to console Rwanda for its woes. In South Africa, he said, "They had different languages, they had different races, they had different cultures. . . . You are all black. You speak one language. And I'm trying to discover what have we got in our heads here?" The crowd laughed, but the laughter ceased when the archbishop went on: "Hey? Hey? Hey? Hey? Do you want to tell me that blacks are stupid? Eh? Are you stupid?"

A rather soft "No" rose from the crowd.

"I can't hear you. Are you stupid?" Tutu asked again.

"No."

And a third time, Tutu asked: "Are you stupid?"

The crowd's response, like the archbishop's call, had increased in volume each time around, but even the last and loudest "No!" seemed tempered by a sense that, however ironically the question was meant, it remained an insult of a kind to which Rwandans are unaccustomed.

What did being black have to do with anything in Rwanda? That might be an issue in South Africa, but except for a handful of foreign residents, everyone in Rwanda—stupid and smart, foul and fair, majority and minority—is black, and the archbishop's fixation on the category suggested an alien view of the country's ordeal that lumped violators and violated together as equal partners in the country's affliction.

"I come as an African," Tutu later explained to an assembly of government leaders and diplomats. "I come as one who, willy-nilly, shares in the shame, in the disgrace, in the failures of Africa because I am an African. And what happens here, what happens in Nigeria, wherever—that becomes part of my experience."

A member of parliament seated beside me rolled her eyes. Tutu's insistence on race was meant as an expression of solidarity, but Rwanda wasn't South Africa, or Nigeria, and Africans had done no more to stop the genocide than anyone else. So it was strange to be told that a crime perpetrated by Rwandans against Rwandans was a crime against African pride and progress, and that the shame of it was a private African affair rather than a shame to all humanity. Stranger still to be told to shut up and stop acting like stupid blacks.

WHEN I GOT depressed in Rwanda, which was often, I liked to go driving. On the road, the country resolved itself in rugged glory, and you could imagine, as the scenes rushed past and the car filled with smells of earth and eucalyptus and charcoal, that the people and their landscape—the people in their landscape—were as they had always been, undisturbed. In the fields people tilled, in the markets they marketed, in schoolyards the girls in bright blue dresses and boys in khaki shorts and safari shirts played and squabbled like children anywhere. Across sweeping valleys, and through high mountain passes, the roadside presented the familiar African parade: brightly clad women with babies bound to their backs and enormous loads on their heads; strapping young men in jeans and Chicago Bulls T-shirts ambling along empty-handed —save, perhaps, for a small radio; elderly gents in suits weaving down red-dirt lanes on ancient bicycles; a girl chasing a chicken, a boy struggling to balance the bloody head of a goat on his shoulder; tiny tots in ragged smocks whacking cows out of your way with long sticks.

Life.

You knew, by the statistics, that most of the people you saw were Hutu, but you had no idea who was who; whether that girl, who stared blankly at your oncoming car and at the last minute winked and broke into a wide grin, was a massacre survivor, or whether she was a killer, or both, or what. If you stopped to buy a cold drink and a brochette of grilled goat, or to ask directions, a small crowd gathered to stare and offer commentary, reminding you of your exoticism. If you drove around in the northwest, and pulled over to admire the volcanoes, peasants came out of their fields to express approval that you had no greater purpose, in that moment, than to regard their place with pleasure. If you traveled southwest through the Nyungwe rain forest preserve and got out to watch the colobus monkeys, people in passing minibuses waved and cheered.

Most of Rwanda was once a forest like Nyungwe, a dark knot of vegetation trailed by low thin clouds. But centuries of use had stripped the forest away, and by the time I came along even the steepest slopes were tilled, grazed, and toiled over, shaded only at their summit by a vestigial crown of tall trees. The intensity with which every patch of available land was worked offered visual evidence of Rwanda's population density and the attendant competition for resources, and it has been argued that the genocide was driven, in large measure, by basic economic motives: "to the victor go the spoils" and "there isn't room for both of us"—that sort of thing, as if the killing had been a kind of Darwinian population control mechanism.

No doubt, the promise of material gain and living space did move some killers. But why hasn't Bangladesh, or any other terribly poor and terribly crowded place of the many one might name, had a genocide? Overpopulation doesn't explain why hundreds of thousands of people agreed to murder nearly a million of their neighbors in the course of a few weeks. Nothing really explains that. Consider all the factors: the precolonial inequalities; the fanatically thorough and hierarchical centralized administration; the Hamitic myth and the radical polarization under Belgian rule; the killings and expulsions that began with the Hutu revolution of 1959; the economic collapse of the late 1980s; Habyarimana's refusal to let the Tutsi refugees return; the multiparty confusion; the RPF attack; the war; the extremism of Hutu Power; the propaganda; the practice massacres; the massive importation of arms; the threat to the Habyarimana oligarchy posed by peace through power sharing and integration; the extreme poverty, ignorance, superstition, and fear of a cowed, compliant, cramped—and largely alcoholic—peasantry; the indifference of the outside world. Combine these ingredients and you have such an excellent recipe for a culture of genocide that it's easy to say that it was just waiting to happen. But the decimation had been utterly gratuitous.

And afterward the world was a different place for anyone who chose to think about it. Rwandans had no choice. This was what interested me most about them: not the dead—what can you really say about a million murdered people whom you didn't know?—but how those who had to live in their absence would do so. Rwanda had the memories and the habits of a long past, yet the rupture in that past had been so absolute that the country I was driving through was actually a place that had never existed before. Scenes of rural life that appeared eternal to me, and that impressed Joseph, the driver, as empty, were neither of those things. The

Rwanda I visited in the years after the genocide was a world in limbo.

I SAID EARLIER that power largely consists in the ability to make others inhabit your story of their reality, even if you have to kill a lot of them to make that happen. In this raw sense, power has always been very much the same everywhere; what varies is primarily the quality of the reality it seeks to create: is it based more in truth than in falsehood, which is to say, is it more or less abusive of its subjects? The answer is often a function of how broadly or narrowly the power is based: is it centered in one person, or is it spread out among many different centers that exercise checks on one another? And are its subjects merely subjects or are they also citizens? In principle, narrowly based power is easier to abuse, while more broadly based power requires a truer story at its core and is more likely to protect more of its subjects from abuse. This rule was famously articulated by the British historian Lord Acton in his formula "Power corrupts and absolute power corrupts absolutely."

But like most truisms, Acton's adage is not quite true: to take an example from American history, President Lincoln's power was more absolute than President Nixon's, yet Nixon was surely the more fundamentally corrupt of the two. So, when we judge political power, we need to ask not only what its base is but also how the power is exercised, under what circumstances, toward what ends, at what price, and with what success. These are tough judgments to make, generally open to dispute, and for those of us who live in the astonishing overall security provided by the great Western democracies of the late twentieth century, they are the very stuff of public life. Yet we seem to have a hard time taking seriously the notion that places where mass violence and suffering is so widespread that it is casually called "meaningless" might also be places where people engage in meaningful politics.

When I first went to Rwanda, I was reading a book called

Civil War, which had been receiving great critical acclaim. Writing from an immediate post-Cold War perspective, the author, Hans Magnus Enzensberger, a German, observed, "The most obvious sign of the end of the bipolar world order are the thirty or forty civil wars being waged openly around the globe," and he set out to inquire what they were all about. This seemed promising until I realized that Enzensberger wasn't interested in the details of those wars. He treated them all as a single phenomenon and, after a few pages, announced: "What gives today's civil wars a new and terrifying slant is the fact that they are waged without stakes on either side, that they are wars *about nothing at all*."

In the old days, according to Enzensberger—in Spain in the 1930s or the United States in the 1860s—people used to kill and die for ideas, but now "violence has separated itself from ideology," and people who wage civil wars just kill and die in an anarchic scramble for power. In these wars, he asserted, there is no notion of the future; nihilism rules; "all political thought, from Aristotle and Machiavelli to Marx and Weber, is turned upside down," and "all that remains is the Hobbesian ur-myth of the war of everyone against everyone else." That such a view of distant civil wars offers a convenient reason to ignore them may explain its enormous popularity in our times. It would be nice, we may say, if the natives out there settled down, but if they're just fighting for the hell of it, it's not my problem.

But it *is* our problem. By denying the particularity of the peoples who are making history, and the possibility that they might have politics, Enzensberger mistakes his failure to recognize what is at stake in events for the nature of those events. So he sees chaos—what is given off, not what's giving it off—and his analysis begs the question: when, in fact, there are ideological differences between two warring parties, how are we to judge them? In the case of Rwanda, to embrace the idea that the civil war was a free-for-all—in which everyone is at once equally legitimate and equally

182

illegitimate—is to ally oneself with Hutu Power's ideology of genocide as self-defense.

Politics, after all, mostly operates in the in-between realm of bad—or, if you're an optimist, better—versus worse. On any given day in postgenocide Rwanda, you could collect stories of fresh ugliness, and you could also collect stories of remarkable social and political improvement. The more stories I collected, the more I began to realize that life during the genocide, by virtue of its absoluteness, had evoked a simpler range of responses than the challenge of living with its memory. For those who had endured, stories and questions tended to operate in a kind of call-and-response fashion—stories calling up questions, calling up more stories, calling up more questions—and nobody of any depth seemed to expect precise answers. At best they hoped for understandings, ways of thinking about the defiant human condition at the end of this century of unforeseen extremity. Quite often, I felt that these stories were offered to me the way that shipwrecked people, neither drowned nor saved, send messages in bottles: in the hope that, even if the legends they carry can do the teller no good, they may at some other time be of use to somebody, somewhere else.

Even now, as I write, in the early months of 1998, Rwanda's war against the genocide continues. Perhaps by the time you read this the outcome will be clearer. Rwanda may again have endured incalculable nationwide bloodshed, and Hutu Power may again have prevailed over much, if not all, of the country. There's also a chance that Rwanda will be a place of steady, grinding struggle, with periods and regions of great terror, and periods and regions of edgy stability, which is more or less how it has been since the genocide. Of course, if you're some kind of archaeologist who digs this book up in the distant future, five or fifty or five hundred years from now, there's a chance that Rwanda will be a peaceful land of life, liberty, and the pursuit of happiness; you may be planning your next holiday there, and the stories you find in these pages will offer but a memorial backdrop, the way we now read stories of the genocide of American Indians or of slavery days, or accounts of all the horrible crimes against humanity that marked Europe's progress, and think, as Conrad's Marlow said of England, "We live in the flicker—may it last as long as the old earth keeps rolling! But darkness was here yesterday."

13

IN THE NINE months I spent in Rwanda in the course of six trips, the only freshly killed person I saw was a young man who had died in a car wreck. Three minutes earlier he had been riding along through his life, then his driver swerved to avoid hitting an old woman crossing the road, and now he lay on his side in high grass, locked in a fetal curl, with his head open. If I had a picture of him and reproduced it here with the caption "Tutsi genocide victim," or "Hutu victim of the RPF," you would have no way to perceive the deception. In either case, the appeal to your sympathies and your sense of outrage would be the same.

That is how the story of Rwanda has generally been reported, as the war between the *génocidaires* and the RPF-installed government drags on. In a typical dispatch, headed "Searching in Vain for Rwanda's Moral High Ground," my local paper, *The New York Times*, described a Hutu refugee maimed in an attack by Tutsi soldiers, and a Tutsi refugee maimed by Hutu Power militias, as "victims in an epic struggle between two rival ethnic groups" in which "no one's hands are clean." The impression created by such reports is that because victims on either side of the conflict suffer equally, both sides are equally insupportable. To drive the point home, the *Times* got a sound bite from Filip Reyntjens, a Belgian who is considered one of Europe's leading authorities on

Rwanda. "It's not a story of good guys and bad guys," Reyntjens told the newspaper. "It's a story of bad guys. Period."

It was after reading similar newspaper stories that I first decided to go to Rwanda. A year after the genocide, the Rwandese Patriotic Army had been deployed to close a camp for "internally displaced persons" at Kibeho, the hill famous for apparitions of the Virgin Mary. More than eighty thousand Hutus who had fled their homes after the genocide were living at the Kibeho camp, which the French had originally set up during *Opération Turquoise*. The RPA operation to close the camp had gone awry, and at least two thousand Hutus were reported killed. Once again, a UN battalion had been on hand and had done nothing. I remember a news photograph of a UN soldier holding two dead babies, one in each hand, during the cleanup after the killings.

First the genocide, and now this, I thought: Hutus kill Tutsis, then Tutsis kill Hutus—if that's really all there is to it, then no wonder we can't be bothered with it. Was it really so mindless and simple?

The piled-up dead of political violence are a generic staple of our information diet these days, and according to the generic report all massacres are created equal: the dead are innocent, the killers monstrous, the surrounding politics insane or nonexistent. Except for the names and the landscape, it reads like the same story from anywhere in the world: a tribe in power slaughters a disempowered tribe, another cycle in those ancient hatreds, the more things change the more they stay the same. As in accounts of earthquakes or volcanic eruptions, we are told that experts knew the fault line was there, the pressure was building, and we are urged to be excited—by fear, distress, compassion, outrage, even simple morbid fascination—and perhaps to send a handout for the survivors. The generic massacre story speaks of "endemic" or "epidemic" violence and of places where people kill "each other," and the ubiquity of the blight seems to cancel out any appeal to think about the single instance. These stories flash up from the void and, just as abruptly, return there. The anonymous dead and their anonymous killers become their own context. The horror becomes absurd.

I wanted to know more. The killings at the Kibeho camp offered a preview of one way that the UN border camps—particularly the heavily militarized Hutu Power enclaves in Zaire—might eventually be disbanded. Those camps were themselves havens for war criminals and champions of atrocity, and their very existence placed everyone in and around them in mortal danger. Nobody had any idea how to close them peacefully; in fact, nobody really seemed to believe that was possible. The story of Rwanda had been bothering my mind, and I wanted to explore how the killings at the Kibeho camp related and compared to the genocide that preceded them. According to the human rights orthodoxy of our age, such comparisons are taboo. In the words of Amnesty International: "Whatever the scale of atrocities committed by one side, they can never justify similar atrocities by the other." But what does the word "similar" mean in the context of a genocide? An atrocity is an atrocity and is by definition unjustifiable, isn't it? The more useful question is whether atrocity is the whole story.

Consider General Sherman's march through Georgia at the head of the Union Army near the end of the American Civil War, a scorched-earth campaign of murder, rape, arson, and pillage that stands as a textbook case of gross human rights abuses. Historians don't seem to believe that the atrocities of Sherman's march fulfilled any otherwise unfulfillable strategic imperative. Yet it's generally agreed that the preservation of the Union and the consequent abolition of slavery served the national good, so historians regard Sherman's march as an episode of criminal excess by agents of the state rather than as evidence of the fundamental criminality of the state.

Similarly, in France, during the months immediately following World War II, between ten and fifteen thousand people were killed as fascist collaborators in a nationwide spasm of vigilante justice. Although nobody looks back on those purges as a moment of pride, no national leader has ever publicly regretted them. France, which considers itself the birthplace of human rights, had a venerable legal system, with plenty of policemen, lawyers, and judges. But France had been through a hellish ordeal, and the swift killing of collaborators was widely held to be purifying to the national soul.

The fact that most states are born of violent upheaval does not, of course, mean that disorder leads to order. In writing the history of events that are still unfolding in a state that is still unformed, it is impossible to know which tendencies will prevail and at what price. The safest position is the human rights position, which measures regimes on a strictly negative scale as the sum of their crimes and their abuses: if you damn all offenders and some later mend their ways, you can always take credit for your good influence. Unfortunately, the safest position may not necessarily be the wisest, and I wondered whether there is room—even a need —for exercising political judgment in such matters.

THE CAMP AT Kibeho had been one of dozens of camps for "internally displaced persons"—IDPs—established in the *Zone Turquoise*. When the French withdrew in late August of 1994, the camps held at least four hundred thousand people, and they were placed under the supervision of the refurbished UNAMIR and an assortment of UN and private international humanitarian agencies. The new government had wanted the camps closed immediately. Rwanda, the government claimed, was safe enough for everyone to go home, and significant concentrations of Hutu Power military and militia members among the IDPs made the camps themselves a major threat to the national security. The relief agencies agreed in principle, but insisted that departure from the camps should be entirely voluntary.

The IDPs, however, were not eager to leave the camps, where they were well fed, and provided with good medical care by the relief agencies, and where rumors that the RPF was exterminating Hutus en masse were being circulated by the *génocidaires*, who maintained a powerful influence over the population. As in the border camps, *interahamwe* agents didn't hesitate to threaten and attack those who wished to leave Kibeho, fearing that a mass desertion of the civilian population would leave them isolated and exposed. The *génocidaires* also made frequent sorties out of the camps to terrorize and steal from the surrounding communities, attacking Tutsi genocide survivors and Hutus whom they suspected might bear witness against them. Kibeho was the epicenter of such activity. According to Mark Frohardt, who worked with the UN's Rwanda Emergency Office and later served as deputy chief of the UN's Human Rights mission in Rwanda, UNAMIR "determined that a disproportionately high percentage of the murders that were taking place in Rwanda, in late November and early December of 1994, had occurred within a twenty-kilometer radius of Kibeho."

That December, UNAMIR and the RPA ran their only joint operation ever, a one-day sweep of Kibeho in which about fifty "hard-core elements"—that is, *génocidaires*—were arrested and some weapons were confiscated. Shortly afterward, the RPA began closing the smaller camps. The preferred strategy was one of nonviolent coercion: people were evicted from their shanties, then the shanties were torched. The IDPs got the message, and relief agencies, too, went along with the program, helping to move more than a hundred thousand people home. Follow-up studies by international relief workers, and UN human rights monitors, found that at least ninety-five percent of these IDPs resettled peacefully in their homes. At the same time, many *génocidaires* fled to other camps, especially to Kibeho, while some IDPs who returned to their villages were arrested on accusations of genocide, and some were alleged to have been killed in acts of revenge or banditry.

By early 1995, a quarter of a million IDPs remained in the camps, of which Kibeho was the largest and home to the largest collection of hard-core *génocidaires*. The UN and relief agencies, fearing the consequences of coercive closings, offered to come up with an alternative course of action. The government waited. Months went by; but the humanitarians could not agree on a coherent closing plan. In late March, the government announced that time was running out, and in mid-April the RPA was redeployed to do the job: camp by camp, the army sent at least two hundred thousand Hutus home in an orderly fashion.

Kibeho was left for last. Before dawn on April 18, the RPA ringed the camp, which still held at least eighty thousand men, women, and children. Alarmed by the soldiers, and worked into a panic by the resident Hutu Power operatives, the IDPs rushed pell-mell up the hill and gathered in a tight knot around the heavily sandbagged and razor wire-fortified headquarters of Zambatt—UNAMIR's Zambian contingent. In this stampede, at least eleven children were crushed to death, and hundreds of people were severely burned by overturned cooking pots or badly cut up as they were forced against the UN razor wire.

The RPA tightened its cordon around the throng, and over the next two days, several gates were established around the perimeter. Relief agencies set up registration tables, and about five thousand people from the camp were searched and transported to their homes. But the gates were too few, the registration process was slow, there weren't enough trucks to speed it up, the *génocidaires* among the IDPs were putting pressure on the rest not to cooperate, and some foreign relief workers were also advising camp residents to resist evacuation. Little food or water remained in the camp. Most people could barely move; they stood in their own urine and feces. On April 19, some IDPs hurled rocks at the RPA, and some reportedly attempted to grab RPA weapons. Soldiers opened fire, killing several dozen people. In the course of the day members of the Australian medical battalion of UNAMIR, Ausmed, began arriving at the camp to reinforce the Zambians.

Toward evening on April 20, a hard rain began to fall. That

night, in the packed camp, some people began hacking at those around them with machetes. There was also sporadic shooting by RPA soldiers and by armed elements within the camp. By morning, at least twenty-one people had been killed, primarily by gunfire, and many more were wounded, primarily by machetes. Children kept getting trampled to death. The RPA kept tightening its cordon. Throughout the next day, people continued to file through the registration points and to leave the camp, mostly on foot, because the rain had made the roads largely impassable. The RPA restricted IDPs' access to medical and water supplies and periodically fired into the air to drive the crowd toward the registration points. Acts of violence continued within the camp. "At the Zambian company," an Ausmed officer later recalled, "a group kept running for shelter and hiding in the compound. We helped the Zambians push them back past the wire."

Late in the morning of April 22, the wet and tormented mass of IDPs at Kibeho once again surged and stampeded against the RPA lines, breaching the cordon at the downhill end of the camp. A stream of IDPs ran through the opening, heading across the valley to the facing hills. RPA troops opened fire, shooting nonstop and indiscriminately into the crowd, and scores of soldiers set out in pursuit of those who had fled, shooting and lobbing grenades at them. The RPA barrage continued for hours; in addition to machine guns, rocket-propelled grenades and at least one mortar were fired into the camp.

Barred by their mandate from using force except in self-defense, the UNAMIR peacekeepers in the Zambatt compound took up weapons only to fend off invasion by the crush of IDPs. Many later recalled weeping in distress and confusion as death and mutilation surrounded them. In typical testimony, a member of Ausmed described seeing "through a window a man attacking a woman with a machete," then IDPs "throwing bricks, etc., at us," then RPA soldiers firing rifles and tossing grenades at IDPs, then an IDP shooting at the peacekeepers, then "four RPA chase a

191

young girl behind the Casualty Collection Point and shoot her eighteen times," then a "vehicle-mounted machine gun . . . mowing down a large crowd of IDPs in long bursts," then "RPA kill two old women . . . kick them downhill."

Another Ausmed man recalled watching RPA soldiers murdering women and children, and said, "They seemed to be enjoying it." And yet another Ausmed testimony described a couple of RPA soldiers firing into the crowd: "They were jumping around laughing and carrying on. It was like they were in a frenzy." The same man also said, "It was pretty horrific to see at least four RPA stand around one IDP and empty a magazine each into him. Some of the IDPs stopped, so the RPA threw rocks at them to make them run again so they could shoot at them again. These IDPs were unarmed and frightened."

By four o'clock that afternoon, when Mark Cuthbert-Brown, a British major who was serving as provost marshal of UNAMIR, arrived at Kibeho by helicopter, the shooting had tapered off to a sporadic background popping and small bursts of automatic fire. From the air, Cuthbert-Brown had seen long files of thousands of IDPs being searched and registered at RPA checkpoints and heading down the road, away from Kibeho. The Australians, the Zambians, and relief workers had been able to go out and begin collecting the dead and wounded, although their access was often blocked by RPA men. Then, after an hour in the camp, Major Cuthbert-Brown heard "a sudden rise in the tempo of firing." Once again, the IDPs had broken through the RPA cordon and spilled down the hill, and the earler scenes of atrocity repeated themselves for several hours. Crouched behind sandbags with binoculars, Cuthbert-Brown watched RPA soldiers hunt the IDPs down the valley and across the far hills, while other RPA soldiers continued to process thousands of IDPs for departure.

Shortly after nightfall, the second wave of intensive shooting abated. Cuthbert-Brown took notes:

20:10 HRS. Become aware of a background wailing from the area of the compound to the west (but this may have built up gradually over a period of time).

21:00 HRS. Wailing continues but there is a letup in firing and grenade explosions.

21:20 HRS. A few grenade explosions heard near the Zambatt HQ.

21:30 HRS. Sporadic single shots in the same area.

21:33 HRS. Six rounds fired by the camp wall.

21:55 HRS. Hysterical screaming rises above the background wailing; Zambian officers speculate that it is related to a machete fight in the compound. Shortly gives way to normal level of wailing; it remains throughout the night.

An Ausmed man said, "We finished up that day disgusted with the RPA and why the UN didn't send more people in than just a company of Zambians and approximately twenty-five Australians."

In the night the RPA stopped shooting. "Soon after first light," Major Cuthbert-Brown wrote in his log, "look over wall . . . and see bodies strewn around the area." In the course of the day, tens of thousands of IDPs were marched and trucked out of the devastated camp, as UN teams and relief workers tended to the wounded and counted the dead. By early afternoon, reporters arrived in the camp and Cuthbert-Brown wrote "Media jamboree settles around the graves." The first death toll to hit the wires was eight thousand, but that was quickly revised down to between two and four thousand—the largest number of them crushed to death in the stampedes, many killed by the RPA, and quite a few hacked, bludgeoned, and even speared to death by *interahamwe* in their midst. But the numbers were only estimates; the thickness of bodies on the ground in some places made it impossible to navigate the camp, and the RPA obstructed full access.

For the next week, the roadways out of Kibeho were clogged with tens of thousands of bedraggled IDPs marching home. Here and there along the way, groups of civilians gathered to taunt and sometimes to beat the returning IDPs. It was a tense time in Rwanda. "Last year, when nobody in the world tried to stop the genocide, and I saw the first RPF coming to liberate Rwanda, these guys were heroes, I went straight to shake his hand," Fery Aalam, a Swiss delegate of the Red Cross, told me. "After Kibeho, I don't know if I'd put out my hand first."

The Kibeho returnees experienced a slightly higher overall rate of arrests and violence than those from other camps. But many of the Hutu Power loyalists from Kibeho were reported to have fled through the bush, making their way across Rwanda's borders to the humanitarian archipelago of UN camps. There was no other safe haven left for the *génocidaires*.

IT WAS ON my fifth day in Rwanda, as I was getting a ride south from Kigali, that I came upon the car wreck in which the young man was killed. There were several injured survivors, and the people I was riding with took them to the hospital in Butare. Some Norwegian Red Cross nurses came out to chat. The nurses were tending to a special emergency wing that had been set up for Kibeho casualties. They had been performing thirty major operations a day, and had discharged a large group of patients that morning. Only the worst cases remained.

"Want to see?" one of the nurses asked, and led the way. Twenty or thirty cots were crowded beneath weak neon light, in a stench of rotting flesh and medicine. "The ones who're left," the nurse said, "are all machete cases." I saw that—multiple amputations, split faces swollen around stitches. "We had some with the brain coming out," the Norwegian said quite cheerily.

"Strange, no? The RPA don't use machetes. They did this to their own."

I felt woozy and moved out to the hall, where I lay down flat on the cool concrete floor beside an open window. The Norwegian followed me. "Strange country," she said. I agreed. She said, "This hospital—last year, big massacre. Hutus killing Tutsis, doctors killing doctors, doctors killing patients, patients killing doctors, nurses, everybody. I'm with the Red Cross—so very Swiss, very neutral. I'm new, just arrived for this Kibeho business. But you think about it. With Kibeho, people say it's starting again. It's the next genocide. I look around. I talk to people. I see what happened. I think maybe it's just ending very ugly and slow."

"How can you tell the difference?" I asked.

"Talk to people. They're scared. They say, What about the Zaire camps, Burundi, Tanzania? What about revenge? What about justice? OK. When people are scared like that they're also hopeful. They're saying they have something to lose—some hope."

I said, "I can see that you'd be a good nurse."

"No, really," she said. "People always say bad things about a government—like with doctors. OK. So, like with doctors, maybe this is because you only need them most when they can't help you enough."

She made me laugh. I said, "You mean, like doctors, they kill some, they can't help some, and they save some."

"Is that so bad?" she said. "Ask people. In a place like this, pretend to yourself like you're a journalist. Talk to everybody."

I told her I was a journalist. "Oh," she said. "Oh la la. I can't talk to you. Red Cross rules. Forget everything I said."

But how could I forget that Norwegian nurse? She was the most optimistic person I ever met in Rwanda.

ONE NIGHT, A few weeks later, I was at a Kigali bistro, sharing a pot of fondue bourguignonne and a pitcher of wine with Annick van Lookeren Campagne and Alexandre Castanias. Annick, who is Dutch, and Alexandre, a Greek, worked as monitors for the UN Human Rights mission in Rwanda. They had both been at Kibeho throughout the catastrophe, and this dinner was the last time they would have together before Annick returned to Holland. That may be why Alexandre spoke about Kibeho. He said it was the first time he did so, and when we finished eating we stayed in the restaurant for hours. We ordered a second pitcher of wine, and sent out for cigarettes, and Alexandre kept standing us rounds of cognac.

The talk about Kibeho had started when Alexandre asked me if I had been to the church at Nyarubuye, to see the memorial there of the unburied dead from the genocide. I hadn't yet, and although when I did go I didn't regret it, I gave Alexandre what I thought—and still think—was a good argument against such places. I said that I was resistant to the very idea of leaving bodies like that, forever in their state of violation—on display as monuments to the crime against them, and to the armies that had stopped the killing, as much as to the lives they had lost. Such places contradicted the spirit of the popular Rwandan T-shirt: "Genocide. Bury the dead, not the truth." I thought that was a good slogan, and I doubted the necessity of seeing the victims in order fully to confront the crime. The aesthetic assault of the macabre creates excitement and emotion, but does the spectacle really serve our understanding of the wrong? Judging from my own response to cruel images and to what I had seen in the hospital ward of Kibeho wounded, I wondered whether people aren't wired to resist assimilating too much horror. Even as we look at atrocity, we find ways to regard it as unreal. And the more we look, the more we become inured to—not informed by—what we are seeing.

I said these things, and Alexandre said, "I totally disagree. I experienced Kibeho as a movie. It *was* unreal. Only afterward, looking at my photographs—then it became real."

When the first wave of shooting began, Alexandre had been at Zambatt, and he said: "I remember there were thousands of people crushing into the parking area. Thousands and thousands of people. I was up on the roof, watching. And I saw this one woman, a fat woman. In thousands and thousands and thousands of people, this one fat woman was the only thing I saw. I didn't see anyone else. They were just thousands. And this fat woman, pressing along with the crowd—while I watched she was like a person drowning." Alexandre brought his hands together, making them collapse inward and sink, and he appeared to shrink within his own frame. "One second she was standing, one second she was falling in the people, and I watched this happening. She disappeared. That was when I wanted only to take photographs. That fat woman, one fat woman, when you say the word Kibeho, she is all I really remember. That will be my one real image of Kibeho forever, that fat woman drowning in thousands and thousands of people. I remember she wore a yellow chemise."

I never saw Alexandre's photographs, but I told him that his description of that moment, and of his own passage from a sense of unreality during the events to the reality of his pictures, was more disturbing, more vivid, and more informative than anything I believed the photographs themselves could tell. In some ways it was quieter; the moment of shock was less concentrated, but it also involved one more and took one along with it.

"I don't know," he said. "I couldn't tell you anything if I wasn't looking."

"You see and you don't see," Annick said. "Mostly you just do things. The pictures come later. When they were crushing on the gate at Zambatt, we were crushing back on it so it didn't fall, and people started throwing babies over. You just catch them. You do things you'd never want to see a picture of."

"Like walking over the bodies," Alexandre said. "I feel very bad about that. It was very unreal and very insane, this decision to walk on dead people. I don't know. I don't know what was right or wrong, or if I feel guilty, but I feel bad. It was necessary. It was the only way to get through."

"We had to pull the live ones out," Annick said. She and Alexandre had collected hundreds of lost and orphaned children from the body piles, and from every crevice where a small person could hide: from the wheel wells of trucks, from under the hoods.

"I don't know why but I didn't care about the people killed by a bullet. I didn't give a fuck about them," Alexandre said. "They were dead, and the people wounded by bullets, they meant nothing to me. It was the people who were crushed."

"Bullets and machetes are supposed to kill," Annick said. "The people who got crushed were just killed by other people, like them, vulnerable, trying to live."

"I got a doctor," Alexandre went on, "I said, 'They just look like they're sleeping, I don't know how to tell if they're dead.' He went through and checked twenty or thirty people, and he said, 'They're dead. They're all dead.' But when I had to walk on them, I felt I might wake them."

"They were like all the luggage," Annick said. I was able to picture that: Kibeho was a ghost town, piled deep with the abandoned belongings of displaced persons, smelling of death—and atop the hill, the charred cathedral that had become a crematorium during the genocide. "When we walked on the luggage," Annick said, "there were probably people underneath. You can't feel guilty, because it's useless, and you walked on them to save lives."

"Walking on them was about being alive," Alexandre said. "After a while it was just about getting on with life. The dead are dead. There's nothing you can do. Even with the living, what could we do? We gave them water. It was our only medicine. It was like a miracle. You'd see the face of a boy, fallen and death-like in the crowd, and you drop a few drops of water on him and he is like —aahhh!" Alexandre's face expanded and he rose a bit in his seat, like a sped-up film of a flower blossoming. "Then you turn around," he said. "And the next minute everyone we gave water to was dead."

"Yah," Annick said.

"Bodies," Alexandre said.

"That guy with the spear in his throat," Annick said. "I just left him. And at one time I was laughing and laughing. I couldn't stop laughing. I was with the wounded, blood everywhere, and a shoulder hanging off from a grenade, or a mouth split open with a machete, and I was just laughing. Me!" she said. "I used to faint with injections, and here I was sewing machete wounds. All I could think was, Do I wrap the bandage this way?"—she whirled a hand in a horizontal orbit—"Or this way?"—vertically.

"Sunday when we drove away, there were people all over the road, bodies, and wounded," Alexandre said. "In a normal time, for people in much less bad shape, you would stop and do anything. We didn't stop. We just left them. I feel very bad about that. I don't know if it's guilt, but it's a very bad feeling."

"Yah," Annick said. "That was bad, eh? We just drove. It was too many people."

"Too many people," Alexandre said. Tears had welled from his eyes, and his nose was running, streaking his lip. He said, "I don't know how my mind works. I just don't know. When people are dead, you expect to see more people dead. I remember in 1973 in Athens, we had cars making a blockade, and the tanks came and crushed the cars. I was eleven or twelve and I saw the people. They're dead, and I expected more and more to see dead people. It becomes normal. We have so many films to see death with bullets, but this is real death, the crushing. At Kibeho, in the second attack, they were just shooting like hell. Shooting like you can't imagine. The RPA was just shooting and shooting, they didn't even look where. I was standing out there, it was raining, and all I could think was I want to get out of the rain. I didn't even think of the shooting, and it was shooting like hell. To get out of the rain—that was all I wanted."

"You shouldn't feel badly," Annick said. "We saved a lot of lives. Sometimes it was useless, there was nothing we could do."

"You know," Alexandre said, "the RPA—they were taking the wounded and throwing them in the pit latrines. They were alive. You know that?"

"Yah," Annick said. "That was bad."

"I don't want to be judged," Alexandre said. "I don't want you to judge me."

He got up to go to the toilet, and Annick said, "I'm worried about Alexandre."

"How about you?" I asked.

"They tell me go to a psychiatrist," she said. "The Human Rights mission. They say I have post-traumatic stress. What will they give me? Prozac? It's stupid. I don't want drugs. I'm not the one with the problem in Kibeho."

LATER, WHEN I did visit Nyarubuye and found myself treading among and on the dead, I remembered my evening with Annick and Alexandre. "You don't know how to think about it," Alexandre had said, when he returned to the table, "who is right and who is wrong, who is good and bad, because the people in that camp were many of them guilty of genocide."

But how do we think about genocide? "I'll tell you how," the American officer with his Jack Daniel's and Coke at the Kigali bar told me. "It's the passenger pigeon. Have you ever seen a passenger pigeon? No, and you never will. That's it. Extinction. You will never see a passenger pigeon." Sergeant Francis, the RPA officer who showed me around at Nyarubuye, understood. "The people who did this," he said, "thought that whatever happened, nobody would know. It didn't matter, because they would kill everybody, and there would be nothing to see."

I kept looking, then, out of defiance. Ninety-five percent of the species of animals and plants that have graced the planet since life began are said to be extinct. So much for providence in the fall of a sparrow. Perhaps even extinction has lost its shock. I saw several hundred dead at Nyarubuye, and the world seemed full of dead. You couldn't walk for all the dead in the grass. Then you hear the numbers—eight hundred thousand, one million. The mind balks.

For Alexandre, all of Kibeho had come down to one fat woman in a yellow blouse drowned by the thousands and thousands of others. "After the first death there is no other," wrote Dylan Thomas, in his World War II poem "A Refusal to Mourn the Death, by Fire, of a Child in London." Or, as Stalin, who presided over the murders of at least ten million people, calculated it: "A single death is a tragedy, a million deaths is a statistic." The more the dead pile up, the more the killers become the focus, the dead only of interest as evidence. Yet turn the tables, and it's clear that there is greater cause for celebration when two lives are saved instead of one. Both Annick and Alexandre said they had stopped counting the dead after a while, although counting was in their job description and tending to the wounded was not.

Still, we imagine it's a greater crime to kill ten than one, or ten thousand than one thousand. Is it? Thou shalt not kill, says the commandment. No number is specified. The death toll may grow, and with it our horror, but the crime doesn't grow proportionally. When a man kills four people, he isn't charged with one count of killing four, but with four counts of killing one and one and one and one. He doesn't get one bigger sentence, but four compounded sentences, and if there's a death penalty, you can take *his* life just once.

Nobody knows how many people were killed at Nyarubuye. Some say a thousand, and some say many more: fifteen hundred, two thousand, three thousand. Big differences. But body counts aren't the point in a genocide, a crime for which, at the time of my first visit to Rwanda, nobody on earth had ever been brought to trial, much less convicted. What distinguishes genocide from murder, and even from acts of political murder that claim as many victims, is the intent. The crime is wanting to make a people extinct. The idea is the crime. No wonder it's so difficult to picture. To do so you must accept the principle of the exterminator, and see not people but *a people*.

At Nyarubuye, tiny skulls of children were scattered here and there, and from a nearby schoolyard the voices of their former classmates at recess carried into the church. Inside the nave, empty and grand, where a dark powder of dried blood marked one's footprints, a single, representative corpse was left on the floor before the altar. He appeared to be crawling toward the confession booth. His feet had been chopped off, and his hands had been chopped off. This was a favorite torture for Tutsis during the genocide; the idea was to cut the tall people "down to size," and crowds would gather to taunt, laugh, and cheer as the victim writhed to death. The bones emerged from the dead man's cuffs like twigs, and he still had a square tuft of hair peeling from his skull, and a perfectly formed, weather-shrunken and weather-greened ear.

"Look at his feet and his hands," said Sergeant Francis. "How he must have suffered."

But what of his suffering? The young man in the car wreck had suffered, albeit for an instant, and the people at Kibeho had suffered. What does suffering have to do with genocide, when the idea itself is the crime?

THREE DAYS AFTER the shooting ended at Kibeho, Rwanda's new President, Pasteur Bizimungu, a Hutu of the RPF, visited the rubble of the camp, paid his respects to a row of bodies that had been laid out for his viewing, and held a press conference, at which he announced that the official body count from the closing operation was three hundred and thirty-four. This absurdly low number suggested a cover-up, and only made the international outcry over the government's handling of the camp closing louder. With an especially vigorous nudge from France, the European Union suspended its already limited aid program for Rwanda, and kept it suspended even after an Independent International Commission of Inquiry on the Events at Kibeho urged foreign donors to continue to support and work with the new RPF-led regime.

The Kibeho Commission was convened at the initiative of that regime, in an effort to signal that the bloody camp closing was not simply business as usual in Rwanda, and it was composed of diplomats, criminologists, jurists, and military and forensic specialists from eight countries, the UN, and the OAU, as well as a Rwandan cabinet minister. In their final report, the commissioners managed to annoy everybody involved at Kibeho—the government, the UN and the humanitarian community, and the *génocidaires*—by distributing blame for the catastrophe fairly evenly among all three parties.

In October of 1994, a similar Commission of Experts, set up by the UN Security Council to investigate the slaughter that had followed Habyarimana's assassination, had found that while "both sides to the armed conflict perpetrated crimes against humanity in Rwanda," the "concerted, planned, systematic and methodical" acts of "mass extermination perpetrated by Hutu elements against the Tutsi group" in Rwanda "constitute genocide," and that no evidence had been found "to indicate that Tutsi elements perpetrated acts committed with intent to destroy the Hutu ethnic group as such." That report marked the first time since the General Assembly passed the Genocide Convention in 1948 that the UN had identified an instance of the crime. So it was striking that the Kibeho Commission's report concluded: "The tragedy of Kibeho neither resulted from a planned action by Rwandan authorities to kill a certain group of people, nor was it an accident that could not have been prevented."

The message was clear: the Commission considered the continued existence of the Kibeho camp "an important obstacle to the country's efforts to recover from the devastating effects of last year's genocide," and found that both RPA personnel and "elements among the IDPs" had subjected people in the camp to "arbitrary deprivation of life and serious bodily harm." If this seems strangely antiseptic language for hacking unarmed children with machetes or shooting them in the back, bear in mind that human rights organizations often describe the entire Rwandan genocide as a single "major human rights violation," which is exactly the same term these organizations use for the death penalty in the United States. The Commission noted that the RPA was a guerrilla army, inept at crowd control and police work, and in its recommendations it urged the government to develop its capacities for a humane and disciplined response to "situations of social tension and emergency." It also found that the international humanitarian agencies, riven by political conflicts, had proved incapable of closing Kibeho peacefully, and urged them to get their own houses in order. Finally, the Commission called on the government to conduct an "investigation of individual responsibilities within its armed forces," but it said nothing about holding the *génocidaires* among the IDPs to account for their crimes at Kibeho.

AROUND THE TIME that the Kibeho Commission released its report, two RPA officers who had been in command during the camp closing were arrested, and about a year later they were tried before a military court. The verdict was a telling indication of how the new regime understood its predicament. The officers were cleared of any responsibility for having presided over, or allowed, a massacre, but they were found guilty of having failed to use the military means at their disposal to protect civilians in danger, which was, of course, precisely the charge the RPF had made against UNAMIR, and the international community as a whole, during the genocide in 1994.

But from whom should the RPA have protected the IDPs if not from itself? The answer implicit in the Kibeho verdict was that the primary danger had been created by the *génocidaires* in the midst of the camp and by the international humanitarian organizations that had been content to let them stay there. In other words, the RPA judged itself to have taken the side of the Hutu masses against the Hutu Power leaders who had caused them so much anguish. The court was asking that the killings at Kibeho be thought of as the Norwegian nurse had suggested when I lay on the hospital floor in Butare—not as a measure of the new order, but as the ugly endgame of the old order.

Mark Frohardt, a veteran of "international emergency response" missions in Chad, Sudan, and Somalia, and the deputy chief of the UN's Human Rights mission in Rwanda, reached a strikingly similar conclusion: "I have no intention of trying to justify the manner in which Kibeho was closed," Frohardt said at the end of two and a half years in Rwanda. "But I do believe that it is important to understand that the inability of the relief organizations to coordinate a successful operation set the stage for the tragedy that followed. Once the army saw that the efforts of relief agencies to move people out of the camps were ineffective, they knew they were the only institution, or force, in the country capable of closing the camps." And, he went on, "the principal reason that we failed to empty the camps and that the RPA operation turned into a disaster was . . . the inability to separate out those who were involved in the genocide, those who are guilty of crimes against humanity, from those who are innocent and who were not involved."

Frohardt was speaking as a human rights and relief worker to an audience composed primarily of fellow professionals in Washington, and he saw that community's failure at Kibeho as symptomatic of a more profound failure of its collective human and political imagination. "I have never worked in a postconflict society in which recent events, recent history, had such an unrelenting influence on the current situation," he said. "Nor have I ever worked in a country where humanitarian and development organizations were so resistant to incorporating the cause and consequence of these events into their analysis of the current situation."

In late 1994, just six months after the genocide, Frohardt recalled, "relief workers in Rwanda were often heard making statements such as 'Yes, the genocide happened, but it's time to get over it and move on,' or 'Enough has been said about the genocide, let's get on with rebuilding the country.'"

I heard such comments, too, and constantly. Frohardt wasn't alone among foreign visitors in recognizing that "everything you do in Rwanda has to be done in the context of the genocide," but he represented a small minority. For most, it was as if the memory of the genocide was a nuisance or, worse, a political gimmick created by the new government as an alibi to explain away its imperfections. After a while, I took to asking, "If, God forbid, a close family member or friend of yours were murdered—or just died—how long would you take to get over the immediate sense of loss, so that a few days or even a week could go by in which you didn't feel its grip? And how about if your entire social universe had been wiped out?" Usually I'd get an answer like "OK, sure, but that doesn't make the genocide an excuse for today's problems."

Sometimes, in Rwanda, I would sit in a hotel dining room watching the news on American satellite television. Among the stories that commanded special fascination between 1995 and 1997 were the O. J. Simpson trial and the coverage of the Oklahoma City bombing. O.J., a football player turned advertising personality, was accused of killing his ex-wife and her friend, and millions of people around the world were galvanized by the quest for truth and justice—and the betrayal of that quest—for a couple of years. In Oklahoma City, a hundred and sixty-eight people were blown to their deaths in a federal building by a couple of crackpots who thought the United States government had embedded computerized tracking chips in their bodies, and the families of the victims became TV household familiars. And why not? Their world had been shattered in a single instant of insanity. The Rwandans in the hotel dining room seemed to understand that sympathetically, though sometimes one or another of them would observe, quietly, that these crimes on American television were comfortingly isolated, and that the "survivors," as victims' families are known in the West, had not themselves been endangered.

Everyone in the hotel dining room would watch, and discuss the details of the trauma, or the legal proceedings, and wonder how it would all turn out. It was an activity that brought us together. And yet here was a society whose soul had been shredded, where an attempt had been made to extirpate an entire category of humanity, where hardly a person could be found who was not related to someone who had either killed or been killed, and where the threat of another round remained intensely real; and here were young foreigners, who had been sent in the name of humanitarianism, saying that Rwandans should quit making excuses.

A YEAR AFTER Kibeho, in May of 1996, I was talking with General Kagame, who had become Rwanda's Vice President and Minister of Defense after the war, about how the UN camps that ringed Rwanda's borders seemed to create more problems than they solved. "I'll give you an example," Kagame said. "Perhaps it's a bad example in that it was tragic. But let's talk about Kibeho, the famous Kibeho. There were hundreds of thousands of people in these camps. Well, unfortunately, in the process of closing the camps, people were killed—very unfortunately—about eight thousand people, to take the highest number. Still we managed to resettle those hundreds of thousands of people. I'm not saying it should have been the cost. But we insisted. We said, 'If you don't want to close them, then we shall close them.' And that's what happened, that tragic situation. But the camps were no more, you see, and you could have had more trouble for the whole country by keeping the camps there."

I was surprised to hear Kagame bringing up Kibeho of his own accord; he might have preferred to forget it. And I was surprised that he used the figure of eight thousand dead. I asked him if he thought that was the accurate number.

"Absolutely not," he said. "It was much less than that."

"But that operation went wrong," I said. "And then nobody was able to stop it, or nobody did stop it."

"They did stop it," he said. "It was stopped, certainly. Maybe you would have lost twenty or even thirty thousand if it wasn't stopped."

"But there were excesses."

"Sure, on the part of individuals."

"On the part of your soldiers."

"Yes," Kagame said. "Yes, yes, and it just proves how it was stopped."

14

I ONCE MET a woman from the southwestern Ugandan town of Mbarara, who had been in secondary school with Paul Kagame in the early 1970s. I asked her what he was like back then. "Skinny," she said, and then she laughed, because calling Kagame skinny was like calling water wet. You couldn't see him without wondering if you'd ever seen a skinnier person. He stood an inch or so over six feet, and his trouser legs hung as if empty—the creases flat as blades. His Giacometti-like stick figure looked as if it had been dreamed up by Hutu Power cartoonists at Kangura, with the fine skeletal fingers that you'd expect of a chief of the cockroaches.

One of the popular cultural myths about Tutsis is that they like to drink milk but don't much like eating, and although I've watched any number of Tutsis eat heartily, the myth has some basis, at least as a comment on manners. "Tutsi wives are lousy cooks because their husbands aren't interested. We just pick a little here and there," a Tutsi told me. He had made something of an informal study of Tutsi arcana. "You've noticed, we'll invite you to drink, and of course later there's some food, but we'll never say, 'Philip, I'm so hungry, let's feast.'" I had noticed. The custom was explained to me as a residual trait of aristocratic refinement, like moving slowly or speaking softly, which are also alleged to be

209

Tutsi manners. The idea was that vulgar people, peasants, are driven by appetite and tend to run around and shout unnecessarily in the confusion of their coarse lives, while people of standing show reserve. Hutus often describe Tutsis as "arrogant," and Tutsis tend to find no cause for apology.

But the Ugandan woman had seen the teenage Kagame differently. When she said he was skinny, she added, "He was a refugee," suggesting that his build told of misfortune, not aristocracy. She also said that he was a top student, and liked music— "I used to see him hang about the record shop until closing time"—but that was about the limit of her recall. "I didn't pay much attention to him," she said. "He was Rwandan."

This was what mattered in Uganda: he was a foreigner. Uganda's population, like that of most African countries, is distributed among so many tribal and regional subpopulations that there is no majority group, just larger and smaller minorities. When Kagame was growing up in Uganda, people of Rwandan descent constituted one of the larger groups. Most are believed to have been Hutu by ancestry, but in the Ugandan context the labels Hutu and Tutsi stood for little more than different historical experiences: nearly all Tutsis were political refugees, while Hutus were primarily descendants of precolonial settlers or economic migrants. Despite the widespread assumption that Hutus and Tutsis carry a primordial germ of homicidal animosity for one another, the exiled Rwandans got along peacefully in Uganda, in Kenya, in Tanzania, and—until Hutu Power politics spilled over in the early 1990s— in Zaire. Only in Burundi did refugees find the politics of Hutu and Tutsi inescapable.

"In exile, we saw each other as Rwandans," Tito Ruteremara, one of the RPF's founders and political commissars, explained. "Living outside Rwanda, you don't see each other as Hutu or Tutsi, because you see everyone else as strangers and you are brought together as Rwandans, and because for the Ugandans, a Rwandan is a Rwandan."

210

So the refugees understood themselves to be as their neighbors imagined them, and they recognized in this identity not only an oppression or humiliation to be escaped but also a value to be transformed into a cause. Here was "the sentiment of national unity" and "the feeling of forming but one people" that the historian Lacger had observed underlying the colonial polarization. And to the founders of the RPF, Rwanda's postcolonial Hutu dictators had, in the name of majority rule, done even more than the Belgians to subvert that idea of the nation. The counterrevolution the RPF eventually proposed followed from this straightforward analysis. To salvage the spirit of Rwandanness for all Rwandans, from the skinniest to the fattest, lest the possibility of solidarity be destroyed forever—that was the idea.

IN 1961, KAGAME watched Hutu mobs torching Tutsi compounds around his parents' home on the hill of Nyaratovu, in Gitarama. He was four years old. He saw a car his father had hired for the family to flee in coming up the road, and he saw that the arsonists saw it, too. They dropped what they were doing and began running toward his house. The car got there first, and the family escaped north to Uganda. "We grew up there," he told me. "We made friends. The Ugandans were hospitable to us, but we were always being singled out. There were always reminders that we'd never be accepted because we were foreigners."

Naturalization is rarely an option in Africa; only a few Rwandan refugees ever acquired foreign citizenship, and those who did often obtained it through bribery or forgery. In Uganda, discrimination and hostility toward Rwandans intensified in the late 1960s and throughout the 1970s under the devastating dictatorships of Milton Obote and Idi Amin. By then, international aid for Rwandan refugees had largely petered out. In contrast to the outpouring of attention for those who fled Rwanda in 1994 after the genocide, Kagame said, "for more than thirty years we were refugees, and nobody talked about us. People forgot. They said, 'Go to hell.' They would say, 'You Tutsi, we know you are arrogant.' But what does arrogance have to do with it? It's a question of people's rights. Do you deny that I belong to Rwanda, that I am Rwandan?"

Refugee politics in the early 1960s was dominated by the monarchists, and thirty years later Hutu Power propagandists loved to point out that Kagame himself was a nephew of the widow of Mutara Rudahigwa, the Mwami who had died in 1959 after receiving an injection from a Belgian doctor. But as the RPF's Tito Ruteremara, Kagame's elder by nearly twenty years, told me: "People of our political generation, whose consciousness was formed in exile, as refugees, despised the monarchists—despised all the old colonial ethnic corruption, with the Hamitic hypothesis and so on." Kagame agreed: being a Tutsi, or a monarchist, was an ancestral problem, and neither identity seemed likely to do anyone much good.

Political leaders often love to tell about their childhoods, those formative years, happy or sad, whose legend can be retroactively finessed to augur greatness. Not Kagame. He was an intensely private public man; not shy—he spoke his mind with uncommon directness—but entirely without bluster. A neat dresser, married, a father of two, he was said to like dinner parties, dancing, and shooting pool, and he was a regular on the tennis courts at Kigali's Cercle Sportif; his soldiers revered and adored him and had put his name in many chants and songs. He was certainly the most discussed man in Rwanda, but he did not care, in his public life, to be charming or, in any conventional sense, charismatic. I mean, he gave off very little heat, and yet his coolness was commanding. Even in a crowded room, he cut a solitary figure. He was a tactician; his background was in military intelligence, reconnaissance, and guerrilla warfare; he liked to study and anticipate the moves of others, and to allow his own moves to carry a surprise.

"I have wanted to be original about my own thinking, especially in regard to my own situation here," he once told me, adding, "Not that I don't realize that there are other people out there to admire, but it is just not my habit to admire anybody. Even if something has worked, I think there are many other things that could work also. If there's anything else that has worked, I would certainly pick a bit from that. But if there could be another way of having things work, I would like to discover that. If I could have some original way of thinking, that would be OK with me."

Except for the phrasing, he sounded like the poet Rilke on love and art, but Kagame was speaking about leadership in governance and in war, and most of all—as always—about being Rwandan. He wanted to find an original way of being Rwandan, and Rwanda clearly needed one. Still, originality is a dangerous enterprise, and Rwanda was a dangerous place. Kagame said he wanted to be "exemplary," so he was careful about his own example, and perhaps it was his quest for an original response to his truly original circumstances that made him wary of allowing others to imagine the lost world of his childhood. There were influences, of course, but the only one he ever seemed inclined to talk about was his friendship with another Rwandan refugee boy named Fred Rwigyema.

"With Fred," Kagame told me, "there was something personal on either side. We grew up together almost like brothers. We were so close that people who didn't know automatically thought we were born of the same family. And even as kids, in primary school, we would discuss the future of the Rwandans. We were refugees in a refugee camp in a grass-thatched house for all this period. Fred and I used to read stories about how people fought to liberate themselves. We had ideas of our rights. So this was always eating up our minds, even as kids."

In 1976, when they were in secondary school, Rwigyema dropped out to join the Ugandan rebels, led by Yoweri Museveni, who were fighting against Idi Amin from bases in Tanzania. Kagame didn't see Rwigyema again until 1979, when Amin fled into exile, and Kagame joined his friend in the Museveni faction of the

213

new Ugandan army. In 1981, when the former dictator Milton Obote again seized power in Uganda, Museveni returned to the bush to fight some more. His army consisted of twenty-seven men, including Rwigyema and Kagame.

As more young Rwandan exiles in Uganda joined the rebel forces, Obote cranked up a virulent xenophobic campaign against the Rwandan population. Mass firings and inflammatory speeches were followed, in October of 1982, by a campaign of murder, rape, and pillage, and close to fifty thousand Rwandans were forcibly expelled and sent back to Rwanda. Habyarimana stuck them in camps, where many died, until they were forced back to Uganda in 1984. Two years later, when Museveni took power, at least twenty percent of his army was of Rwandan origin. Rwigyema was near the top of the high command, and Kagame became director of military intelligence.

It was against this backdrop that Habyarimana had declared, in 1986, that there could be no further discussion of a right of return for Rwandan refugees. The RPF was founded the next year as a clandestine movement committed to armed struggle against the Habyarimana regime. Tito Ruteremara led the political wing, and Rwigyema spearheaded the fraternity of Rwandan officers in the Ugandan army who became the core of the RPF's military force. "We had felt the beginnings of this, fighting in Uganda," Kagame said. "Fighting there was to serve our purpose, and it was also in line with our thinking—we were fighting injustice—and it was perhaps the safest way to live in Uganda at that time as a Rwandan. But deep in our hearts and minds we knew we belonged in Rwanda, and if they didn't want to resolve the problem politically, armed struggle would be the alternative."

I once asked Kagame whether he had ever considered at that point that he could become the Vice President of Rwanda and the commander of its national army. "Not by any stretch of the imagination," he said. "It was not even my ambition. My mind was just obsessed by struggling and fighting to regain my rights as a Rwandan. Whatever that would propel me into was a different matter."

IN EARLIER GENERATIONS, when Africans spoke of "liberation" they meant freedom from the European empires. For the men and women who formed the RPF, and for at least a half dozen other rebel movements on the continent in the 1980s and 1990s, "liberation" meant climbing out from under the client dictatorships of Cold War neocolonialism. Coming of age in an ostensibly free and independent Africa, they saw their predatory leaders as immature, as sources of shame rather than of pride, unworthy and incapable of serving the destiny of their peoples. The corruption that plagued so much of Africa was not just a matter of graft; the soul was at stake. And to this rising generation, the horror was that the postcolonial agony was being inflicted on Africans by Africans, even when the West or the Soviet Union had a heavy hand in it. Museveni, whose example in rebellion and later in building up Uganda from bloody ruin had stimulated the RPF, once told me that Africa's failure to achieve respectable independence could no longer be blamed on foreigners: "It was more because of the indigenous forces that were weak and not organized."

Because Museveni was under intense domestic pressure in the late 1980s to rid his army and government of Rwandans and to strip Rwandan ranchers of much of their land, he has often been accused of organizing the RPF himself. But the mass desertion of Rwandan officers and troops from his army at the time of the invasion in October of 1990 was a surprise and an embarrassment to the Ugandan leader. "I think at one point Museveni even called us treacherous," Kagame told me. "He thought, 'These are friends who have betrayed me, and never let me get involved.' But we didn't need anybody to influence us, and in fact the Ugandans were very suspicious of us. They didn't even appreciate our contribution, the sacrifices we had made. We were just Rwandans—

and really this served us very well. It gave us a push, and it helped some weak people in Uganda feel that they had solved a problem when we left."

More astonishing even than the secrecy of the Rwandans within Uganda's army was the RPF's intensive international campaign to mobilize support in the Rwandan diaspora. "It was funny," an Ugandan in Kampala told me. "In the late eighties, a lot of these Rwandans were becoming very involved with their heritage, organizing family gatherings. They would get everybody together and make a tree, listing every other Rwandan they knew: names, ages, professions, addresses, and so on. Later, I realized they were making a database of the entire community, and well beyond Uganda—through all of Africa, Europe, North America. They were always having fund-raisers here for engagements, weddings, christenings. It's normal, but there was pressure to give a lot, and you couldn't understand the money involved. At one wedding of two big shots, it was fifty thousand dollars. So you'd ask about the great parties they must be having with so much money, but no—everything was bare bones. Well, we didn't get it at the time."

From the start, the RPF leadership was made up of Hutus as well as Tutsis, including defectors from Habyarimana's inner circles, but its military core was always overwhelmingly Tutsi. "Of course," Tito Ruteremara said. "Tutsis were the refugees. But the struggle was against the politics in Rwanda, not against the Hutus. We made that understood. We told people the truth—about the dictator, about our politics of liberation and unity with debate— so we grew strong. Inside Rwanda, they were recruiting by force and coercion. For us it was everyone volunteering. Even the old women went to work on plantations to get some money. Even if you were a sick man who could only afford to say a small prayer —that was good."

The Ugandan who had watched in puzzlement as Rwandans drew family trees and raised funds had a friend whose husband was Rwandan. "The morning of October 1, 1990, this woman's husband said to her, 'This is going to be a very important day in history.' He wouldn't say more, just 'Mark my words.' She and her husband were very close, but it wasn't until she heard on the news that night that Fred Rwigyema had gone over to Rwanda taking his people that she knew what he was talking about."

Museveni responded to the RPF's invasion of Rwanda by ordering the Ugandan army to seal the border and block the mass desertion of Rwandans, who were stealing every bit of equipment they could grab. He also contacted Habyarimana to urge negotiations. "We tried to bring peace," Museveni told me. "But Habyarimana was not willing. He was busy mobilizing Belgium, mobilizing France. Then he started accusing me of starting it all. So then we left the thing to run its course." Tito Ruteremara laughed when he recalled those first days of the war. "Habyarimana was a very stupid man," he said. "When he blamed Museveni, he saved us. Now, instead of stopping us from crossing into Rwanda, Museveni closed the border from the other side—so we couldn't turn back. So Habyarimana actually forced us to keep fighting him, even when we might have felt like we were losing."

KAGAME FOLLOWED THE initial reports of the RPF invasion from Fort Leavenworth, Kansas, where he was enrolled as an Ugandan in an officer training course. On the second day of the war, Fred Rwigyema was killed. A story went around that he was assassinated by two of his officers, who were, in turn, court-martialed and executed. Later, the RPF took to saying that Rwigyema was killed by enemy fire, and that the two officers were killed in an enemy ambush. However that may be, within ten days of Rwigyema's death Kagame quit his course in Kansas and flew back to Africa, where he deserted his Ugandan commission and replaced his murdered friend as the RPF field commander. He was a few days shy of his thirty-third birthday.

I once asked if he liked fighting. "Oh, yes," he said. "I was very annoyed. I was very angry. I will still fight if I have reason to. I will always fight. I have no problem with that." He was certainly good at it. Military men regard the army he forged from the ragtag remnants of Rwigyema's original band, and the campaign he ran in 1994, as a work of plain genius. That he had pulled it off with an arsenal composed merely of mortars, rocket-propelled grenades, and, primarily, what one American arms specialist described to me as "piece of shit" secondhand Kalashnikovs, has only added to the legend.

"The problem isn't the equipment," Kagame told me. "The problem is always the man behind it. Does he understand why he is fighting?" In his view, determined and well-disciplined fighters, motivated by coherent ideas of political improvement, can always best the soldiers of a corrupt regime that stands for nothing but its own power. The RPF treated the army as a sort of field university. Throughout the war, officers and their troops were kept sharp not only by military drill but also by a steady program of political seminars; individuals were encouraged to think and speak for themselves, to discuss and debate the party line even as they were also taught to serve it. "We have tried to encourage collective responsibility," Kagame explained. "In all my capacities, in the RPF, in the government, in the army, my primary responsibility is to help develop people who can take responsibility indiscriminately."

In tandem with political discipline, the RPF earned a reputation for strict physical discipline during its years as a guerrilla force. Across much of Africa, a soldier's uniform and gun had long been regarded—and are still seen—as little more than a license to engage in banditry. During the four years of fighting in Rwanda, marriage and even courtship were forbidden to RPF cadres; thievery was punished with the lash, and officers and soldiers guilty of crimes like murder and rape were liable to be executed. "I don't see the good in preserving you after you have so offended others," General Kagame told me. "And people respected it. It

218

brought sanity and discipline. You don't allow armed people freedom to do what they want. If you are equipped to use force, you must use it rationally. If you are given a chance to use it irrationally you can be a very big danger to society. There's no question about it. Your objective is to protect society."

At the end of the war, in July of 1994, even many international aid workers regarded the RPF with awe and spoke with stirring conviction of the righteousness of its cause and conduct. The RPF had hardly gone to war for humanitarian reasons, but it had effectively been the only force on earth to live up to the requirements of the 1948 Genocide Convention. That RPF elements had carried out reprisal killings against alleged *génocidaires*, and committed atrocities against Hutu civilians, was not in dispute; in 1994, Amnesty International reported that between April and August "hundreds—possibly thousands—of unarmed civilians and captured armed opponents" had been killed by RPF troops. But what most vividly impressed observers in the waning days of the genocide was the overall restraint of this rebel army, even as its soldiers were finding their ancestral villages, and their own families, annihilated.

"The RPF guys had this impressive clarity of purpose about them," James Orbinski, the Canadian doctor who worked in Kigali during the genocide, told me. "They had ideas of right and wrong that were obviously flexible—I mean they *were* an army—but basically their ideas and actions were a hell of a lot righter than wronger. Armies always have a style. These guys—their uniforms were always ironed, they were clean-shaven, and their boots were shined. You'd see them walking around behind their lines, two guys holding hands, sober, proud to be there. They fought like hell. But when they came into a place, you didn't see the usual African looting. I remember when Kigali fell, a guy took a radio from a house, and he was immediately taken out and shot."

A Hutu businessman told me a different story: "They were very organized, very tight, *and* they looted like hell. True, it wasn't just every man for himself. It was mostly quite orderly, with a command structure. But what they needed, or wanted, they took, top to bottom. They came to my shop with trucks, and stripped it. I didn't like it, but at the time I was happy to keep quiet. I considered it more or less a tax for the liberation—at the time."

HEROES, SAVIORS, HERALDS of a new order. Kagame's men—and boys (a lot of them weren't clean-shaven, just too young for a razor)—were all those things in that moment. But their triumph remained shadowed by the genocide, and their victory was far from complete. The enemy hadn't been defeated; it had just run away. Everywhere one went, inside Rwanda and in the border camps, to RPF leaders and to Hutu Power leaders, to relief workers and to foreign diplomats, in the hills, in cafés, even inside Rwanda's packed prisons, one heard that there would be another war, and soon. Such talk had begun immediately after the last war, and I heard it almost every day on each of my visits.

It was strange to be waiting for a war, which is what I felt I was doing along with everyone else during much of the time I spent in Rwanda. The more certain you felt it was coming, the more you dreaded it and the more you wished it would hurry up and get itself over with. It began to feel almost like an appointment. The only way it might be avoided was for a no-nonsense, battle-ready international force to overwhelm and disarm the fugitive Hutu Power army and militias in the UN border camps, and that was never going to happen; instead we were protecting them. So one waited, and wondered what the war would be like, and with time it occurred to me that this anxious expectation was a part of it: if the next war was inevitable, then the last war never ended.

In this climate of emergency and suspense, neither at war nor at peace, the RPF set out to lay the foundations of a new Rwandan state, and to create a new national narrative that could simultaneously confront the genocide and offer a way to move on from

220

it. The Rwanda that the RPF had fought to create—with all Rwandans living peacefully inside the country for the first time since independence—was a radical dream. Now, the existence of a rump Hutu Power state in the UN border camps forced that dream to be deferred, and even before Kibeho, Kagame began saying that if the international community would not sort out the *génocidaires* in Zaire from the general camp population and send the masses home, he would be prepared to do it himself. "We want people back," he told me, "because it is their right and it is our responsibility to have them back, whether they support us or not."

In the meantime, all talk of reconciliation and national unity ran up against the fact that the next war would be a war *about* the genocide. For, while the RPF and the new government required that the genocide be recognized as, in Kagame's words, "the defining event in Rwandan history," Hutu Power still sought to make its crime a success by making it indistinguishable from the continuum of Rwandan history.

KAGAME ONCE TOLD me that after signing the Arusha Accords, in the summer of 1993, he had talked about retiring from the fight—"to go to school, or somewhere, and just have a rest." But, he said, "after a few weeks it turned into a political problem. Some people came from Kigali and said, 'You know, everybody's worried. They think when you mentioned getting out you were planning something.'" Kagame laughed, a high, breathy chuckle. "I said, 'Look, you are really unfair. When I stay in, I'm a problem. When I say I'm getting out, I'm a problem. If I wanted to be a problem, I would actually be a problem. I don't have to dance around weeping, you see.'" Of course, the peace never lasted long enough for Kagame to relax. "My business was to fight," he said. "I fought. The war was over. I said, 'Let's share power.' And it was sincere. Had it not been, I would have taken over everything."

It annoyed Kagame and his RPF colleagues that Rwanda's new

government was routinely described in the international press as *his* government, and labeled "Tutsi-dominated" or, more pointedly, "minority-dominated." A moratorium had been imposed on political party activities, but in the spirit of the Arusha Accords the government included many members of the old anti-Hutu Power opposition parties in top posts. What's more, sixteen of the twenty-two cabinet ministers, including the Prime Minister and the Ministers of Justice and the Interior, were Hutus, while the army, which was quickly doubled in size, to at least forty thousand men, included several thousand former officers and enlisted men from the ranks of Habyarimana's old army and gendarmerie. As President Pasteur Bizimungu, who was Hutu, told me, to speak of Tutsi domination echoed "the slogans or the way of portraying things of the extremists," when, for the first time in the hundred years since colonization, "there are authorities in this country, Hutu and Tutsi, who are putting in place policy so that people may share the same fundamental rights and obligations irrespective of their ethnic background—and the extremists don't feel happy about that."

Kagame, for whom the office of Vice President was specially invented, did not deny that the RPF formed the backbone of the regime, and that as its chief military and political strategist he was the country's most powerful political figure. "He who controls the army controls all," Rwandans liked to say, and following the total destruction of the national infrastructure during the genocide this seemed truer than ever. But Kagame imposed institutional checks on his own power—who else could impose them?—and when he said that he could remove those checks, he was only stating the obvious. He may even have been overstating the case, since it was never clear, after the genocide, that he had complete control of the army, but he was trying to explain what it meant that he had chosen not to be an absolute leader in a country that had no experience of anything else. And he said, "I never had any illusions that these political tasks were going to be simple."

One of the first acts of the new government was to abolish the system of ethnic identity cards, which had served as death tickets for Tutsis during the genocide. But even without identity cards, everybody seemed to know who his neighbors were. In the aftermath of the genocide, the ethnic categories had become more meaningful and more charged than ever before. Rwanda had no police and no working courts; the great majority of its legal professionals had been killed or had themselves become killers, and while suspected *génocidaires* were arrested by the thousands, many Rwandans preferred to settle their scores privately, without waiting for the state to be established.

So there were killings; nobody knows how many, but you heard stories of new killings every few days. As a rule, the victims were Hutus, and the killers were unidentified. The RPA claimed to have jailed hundreds of indisciplined soldiers, but military secrecy tended to shroud these affairs. And it *was* a delicate matter when two soldiers were sentenced to death by an RPA tribunal for reprisal killings, and nobody had yet been brought to trial for crimes during the genocide. Still, from their places of exile, Hutu Power leaders greeted the news of reprisal killings in Rwanda with expressions of outrage that often sounded more like gleeful enthusiasm—as if with each Hutu murdered their own crimes were diminished. Hassan Ngeze had decamped to Nairobi and was again publishing *Kangura*, and he and countless other "refugee" pamphleteers cranked up a relentless campaign, aimed largely at Western diplomats, journalists, and humanitarians, proclaiming more loudly than ever that the RPF was Rwanda's true genocidal aggressor.

"This gang made a genocide, then they say Hutu-Tutsi, Hutu-Tutsi, and everything is a genocide to them," Kagame scoffed, adding, "Johannesburg alone has more crime than the whole country of Rwanda. Nairobi has more. I'm saying we have problems. I'm saying things are ugly. But I'm saying, let's distinguish. If we take everything to be the same, then we are making a mistake."

The paradox was not lost on Rwanda's new leaders that the genocide had brought them greater power and at the same time poisoned their prospects for using it as they had promised. "We were compelled to take on a totally new, different situation—something we had not anticipated," Kagame said. "The twist was so abrupt, and the magnitude of the problems that arose was so immense, that bringing people together and making the country whole became more difficult. You will find that in the army, about a third of the people, maybe slightly more, have lost their families. At the same time the people who are responsible are not being brought to justice effectively. I imagine this undermines one's initial dedication and discipline. This is natural, absolutely natural, and it has its own consequences."

A UNICEF study later posited that five out of six children who had been in Rwanda during the slaughter had, at the very least, witnessed bloodshed, and you may assume that adults had not been better sheltered. Imagine what the totality of such devastation means for a society, and it becomes clear that Hutu Power's crime was much greater than the murder of nearly a million people. Nobody in Rwanda escaped direct physical or psychic damage. The terror was designed to be total and enduring, a legacy to leave Rwandans spinning and disoriented in the slipstream of their memories for a very long time to come, and in that it was successful.

I FELT TEMPTED, at times, to think of Rwanda after the genocide as an impossible country. Kagame never seemed to afford himself the luxury of such a useless notion. "People are not inherently bad," he told me. "But they can be made bad. And they can be taught to be good."

He always sounded so soothingly sane, even when he was describing, with characteristic bluntness, the endless discouragements and continued anguish that surely lay ahead. He spoke of all the woes of his tiny trashed country as a set of problems to be solved, and he seemed to relish the challenge. He was a man of rare scope—a man of action with an acute human and political intelligence. It appeared impossible to discover an angle to the history he was born into and was making that he hadn't already reckoned. And where others saw defeat, he saw opportunity. He was, after all, a revolutionary; for more than fifteen years, his life had consisted of overthrowing dictators and establishing new states in the harshest of circumstances.

Because he was not an ideologue, Kagame was often called a pragmatist. But that suggests an indifference to principle and, with a soldier's stark habits of mind, he sought to make a principle of being rational. Reason can be ruthless, and Kagame, who had emerged in ruthless times, was convinced that with reason he could bend all that was twisted in Rwanda straighter, that the country and its people truly could be changed—made saner, and so better—and he meant to prove it. The process might be ugly: against those who preferred violence to reason, Kagame was ready to fight, and, unlike most politicians, when he spoke or took action, he aimed to be understood, not to be loved. So he made himself clear, and he could be remarkably persuasive.

We always met in his office at the Ministry of Defense, a big room with translucent curtains drawn over the windows. He would fold his antenna-thin frame onto a big black leather chair, I would sit to his right on a couch, and he would answer my questions for two or three hours at a stretch with a quietly ferocious concentration. And what he said mattered, because Kagame was truly somebody of consequence. He made things happen.

Several times, when I was sitting with him, I found myself thinking of another famously tall and skinny civil warrior, Abraham Lincoln, who once said, "It is to deny what the history of the world tells us is true to suppose that men of ambition and talents will not continue to spring up amongst us. And, when they do, they will as naturally seek the gratification of their ruling passion as others have so done before them . . . whether at the expense of emancipating slaves, or of enslaving freemen." Kagame had proven himself quite effective at getting what he wanted, and if Kagame truly wanted to find an original response to his original circumstances, the only course open to him was emancipation. That was certainly how he presented it, and I didn't doubt that that was what he wanted. But the time always came when I had to leave his office. Kagame would stand, we'd shake hands, a soldier with a side arm would open the door, and then I would step back out into Rwanda.

15

BONAVENTURE NYIBIZI AND his family were evacuated to the RPF zone from the Sainte Famille church in mid-June of 1994. Looking out from the convoy, he saw Kigali as a necropolis: "Just blood and"—he made a shivering sound, like a tire deflating—"pfffhhh-h-hh."

In the RPF collection camps for survivors, Bonaventure sought news of his family and friends. It didn't take him long to conclude that "it was unrealistic to hope that somebody had survived." A sister of his was found alive, but three of her five children had been killed, as were his mother and everyone who lived with her. Most of his wife's family and friends had also been wiped out. "Sometimes," he said, "you met someone who you thought had been killed, and you learned that somehow they had managed to stay alive." But the euphoria of such reunions, which punctuated the survivors' gloom for months after the genocide, was tempered by the constant tallying of losses. "Mostly," Bonaventure said, "you didn't even want to hope."

Around July 20, Bonaventure returned home, and sank into despair. "Kigali was difficult to believe," he told me. "The place smelled of death. There were very few people whom you knew from before, and no water or electricity, but the problem for most people was that their houses were destroyed. Most of my house was destroyed. People were finding their furniture and belongings in the homes of neighbors who'd run away, or taking the neighbors' things. But to me that was not important at all. I was not really interested in doing anything."

Bonaventure believed that survival was meaningless until one found "a reason to survive again, a reason to look to tomorrow." This was a widely held view in Rwanda, where depression was epidemic. The so-called survival instinct is often described as an animal urge to preserve oneself. But once the threat of bodily annihilation is relieved, the soul still requires preservation, and a wounded soul becomes the source of its own affliction; it cannot nurse itself directly. So survival can seem a curse, for one of the dominant needs of the needy soul is to be needed. As I came to know survivors, I found that, when it comes to soul preservation, the urge to look after others is often greater than the urge to look after oneself. All across the ghostly countryside, survivors sought each other out, assembling surrogate families and squatting together in abandoned shacks, in schoolyard shanties and burned-out shops, hoping for safety and comfort in hastily assembled households. A shadow world of the severely traumatized and achingly bereft established itself in the ruins. The extent of orphanhood was especially staggering: two years after the genocide, more than a hundred thousand children were looking after one another in homes that lacked any adult presence.

Bonaventure still had his wife and his children, and he began adopting more children. He recovered his car and what remained of his home, and he was receiving back pay from his foreign employer. But even he needed more to live for—a future, as he said. One day, in August, he learned that USAID was sending someone to reestablish its mission in Kigali. Bonaventure picked the man up at the airport and returned to work with a vengeance. "Every day, fourteen hours," he told me. "I was very tired, but it helped a lot." Bonaventure came to dread the idleness and disengagement that he associated with his recent victimization. "In most cases," he said, "with a person who lost his family and friends, when you look—what's he doing?—actually he's doing nothing. So there is no hope for him. To keep busy is very, very important."

EVERYTHING NEEDED DOING—at once. Bonaventure couldn't imagine how Rwanda would be restored to anything resembling working order, and the international disaster experts who began teeming through on assessment missions agreed that they had never seen a country so laid to waste. When the new government was sworn in, there wasn't a dollar or a Rwandan franc left in the treasury; not a clean pad of paper, or a staple, much less a working stapler, left in most government offices. Where doors remained, nobody had keys to the locks; if a vehicle had been left behind, the odds were it wouldn't run. Go to the latrine, it was likely to be stuffed with dead people, and the same went for the well. Electric, phone, and water lines—forget it. All day long in Kigali, there were explosions because somebody had stepped on a land mine or jarred a bit of unexploded ordinance. Hospitals lay in ruins, and the demand for their services was overwhelming. Many of the churches, schools, and other public facilities that hadn't been used as slaughterhouses had been sacked, and most of the people who had been in charge of them either were dead or had fled. A year's tea and coffee harvests had been lost, and vandals had left all the tea factories and about seventy percent of the country's coffee-depulping machines inoperable.

Under the circumstances, one might suppose that the dream of return would have lost some of its allure for the Tutsis of the Rwandan diaspora; that people who had sat in safe homes abroad, receiving the news of the wholesale slaughter of their parents and siblings, their cousins and in-laws, would reckon their prospects for a natural death in exile and stay there. One might suppose that a simple desire not to go mad would inspire such people to renounce forever any hope of again calling Rwanda "home." Instead, the exiles began rushing back to Rwanda even before the blood had dried. Tens of thousands returned immediately on the heels of the RPF, and hundreds of thousands soon followed. The Tutsi returnees and throngs of fleeing Hutus jockeyed past one another at the frontiers.

The returning Rwandans came from all over Africa and from further afield—from Zurich and Brussels, Milan, Toronto, Los Angeles, and La Paz. Nine months after the RPF liberated Kigali, more than seven hundred and fifty thousand former Tutsi exiles (and almost a million cows) had moved back to Rwanda—nearly a one-to-one replacement of the dead. When Bonaventure remarked that he found few familiar faces on returning to Kigali, he was speaking not only of the missing but also of all the people he'd never seen there before. When Rwandans asked me how long I'd been in Rwanda, I often asked the same of them, and after I'd spent a few months in the country it was not unusual to find that I'd been there longer than the Rwandan I was talking to. When I asked people why they had come, I usually got casual answers— to have a look, to see who was alive, to see what they could do to help out—and almost always I'd be told, "It's good to be home."

Once again, strange little Rwanda presented the world with a historically unprecedented, epic phenomenon. Even the RPF leaders, who had been working the refugee diaspora networks for years—consciousness-raising, fund-raising, and recruiting—were astonished by the scale of this return. What possessed these people, a great many of whom had never before set foot in Rwanda, to abandon relatively established and secure lives in order to settle in a graveyard? The legacy of exclusion, the pressures of exile, and the memory of, or longing for, a homeland all played a part. So did a widespread determination to defy the genocide, to stand and be counted in a place where one was meant to have been wiped out. And for many, the sense of belonging was mingled with a straightforward profit motive.

Drawn by empty housing free for the taking and by a demand for goods and services vastly greater than the supply, the returnees rolled into the country hauling loads of dry goods, hardware, medicines, groceries, you name it. If you came with a car, you could immediately claim standing in the transportation industry; if you had a truck, you could become a freight handler; if you had a few thousand dollars you could pretty much pick your niche in a small trade, and with a hundred thousand you might become a captain of industry. There were stories of people who pooled a little cash, hired a vehicle, packed it with cigarettes, candles, beer, fuel, or triple-A batteries, drove to Rwanda, unloaded for a profit of two hundred or three hundred percent, then repeated the process ten or fifteen times, and made themselves rich in the course of a few weeks.

You or I might have done nearly as well if we'd put our enterprising minds to it, and a few foreign carpetbaggers did make out in the Rwandan aftermath. But if fast money was the objective, there was no need for mid-career Rwandan professionals, living in exile with little children whose heads had never been at risk of being chopped off by a neighbor, to move their entire families into the country. The profit motive only explains how return was a viable option and how in the course of a few months minibus taxis were again plying the main routes in Kigali; stores were open for business, public utilities were mostly revived, and new banknotes issued, invalidating the old currency that had been carted off by the fleeing *génocidaires*. The Rwandan franc had suffered a devaluation of at least two hundred fifty percent between the beginning and end of 1994, but with money flowing across the borders, a nightclub had only to switch on the generator and turn up the music to maintain a packed dance floor. The old dictum that it's much easier to destroy than to create remained true, but the speed with which much of Rwanda's basic physical plant was restored to working order was nearly as baffling as the speed with which it had been demolished.

IT WAS IMPOSSIBLE not to be moved by the mass return of the "fifty-niners," and it was impossible not to be troubled by it as well. In 1996 more than seventy percent of the people in Kigali and Butare, and in some rural areas of eastern Rwanda, were said to be newcomers. People who had never left the country—Tutsi and Hutu—often felt displaced in their own homes. Their complaints always came with the caveat "Don't quote me by name." Such requests for anonymity can have many meanings. They suggest an atmosphere of intrigue and fear, and a desire to speak truthfully in circumstances where the truth is dangerous. But they can also bracket secretive moments in a longer conversation, moments in which the speaker seems to doubt what he's saying, or is getting personal, even petty, or is exaggerating wildly, perhaps lying outright, to make a point he knows he cannot fully defend. The recipient of such confidences must try to discern the calculation behind the request. With Rwandans, whose experience had taught them not to underestimate any fear, this could get very tricky. I was especially wary of anonymous remarks that attributed one or another quality to an entire group of people, including the speaker's own. So when people who were speaking openly suddenly asked not to be quoted and then said terrible things about the Tutsi "fifty-niners," as if the whole crowd were one person, I was skeptical. But I heard the same stories and attitudes hundreds of times.

A Tutsi survivor said, "They come here, they see us, and they say, 'How did you survive? Did you collaborate with the *interahamwe*?' They think we were fools to have stayed in the country —and maybe we were—so they disdain us. They don't want to be reminded. It shocks us to the bones."

232

An anti-Habyarimana Hutu said, "The Tutsis were in trouble in last year's massacres, and the army is now dominated by Tutsis. So we thought the survivors would be taken care of, that it would be the first task of the new government. But only those returning from outside are getting homes. And meanwhile, if these people from outside have a problem with a Hutu, they accuse him of committing the genocide they weren't even here for."

A Tutsi said, "We survivors find it very difficult to integrate into the present society and—I hate to say it—into the government, too. They have their own style from outside, and they don't have much trust in us either. When they came they took the country as in a conquest. They thought it was theirs to look after. They said of us Tutsis who were here, 'The smart ones are dead and those who survived are traumatized.' The young RPF fighters all had their parents coming from outside the country and they were tired of the austerity of fighting, so they took homes and goods for their families and they didn't like the survivors getting in the way. And they would say, 'If they killed everyone and you survived, maybe you collaborated.' To a woman who was raped twenty times a day, day after day, and now has a baby from that, they would say this. To a Tutsi who was intermarried or a child who was orphaned they would say this. Can you imagine? For us, it was too hard at first, finding that everyone was dead, that we didn't know anyone. It didn't occur to us to grab better houses, and now it's we who are taking care of most of the orphans."

A Hutu said, "They don't know the country. They trust only each other. They weren't here, and they can't understand. Some of the influence is good. We needed change, fresh ideas. But there are many extremists among them. And many Hutus who were in trouble during last year's killings are in trouble again under this regime. People who were targeted then for being RPF followers are now accused of being *génocidaires*. Some are in prison. Some run to another country. Some are killed. It's the army that controls the government, and inside the army there is not enough control. Truly, if I could afford not to live under plastic sheeting in a camp with *génocidaires*, I would become a refugee."

A Tutsi said, "Our women used to do collections to send Tampax to the women with the RPF when they were up in the mountains, and now when we are with our old Hutu friends, some of the people we're closest to in the world, these people look at us like 'Why are you always with this Hutu?' And we say to ourselves, 'We've lived together with Hutus all our lives, and we speak almost the same language, and we saw our families killed by Hutus, but you're more racist than we are.' It's an enemy in their subconscious. Their idea of cohabitation is really very theoretical. For Hutus now, it's like for us before the RPF came. Even if you live quietly, you can't say many things, you can't criticize a politician, you must live in fear. Of course, all the Hutus now have someone in the camps or in prison, and you can't abandon your brother even if he killed people. So it's a real problem, whom to trust. But the returnees don't even want to discuss it."

Even among the returnees there was a good deal of grumbling about other returnees. They had imagined they were one people engaged in a homecoming, only to discover that they were all kinds of people from all kinds of places. Those who had spent the past three decades in Uganda being called Rwandans were, in fact, deeply Ugandan, and people called Rwandans who had lived in Burundi seemed alien to them. They had no better reason to regard each other as kin than a child of Sicilians born in Argentina would have to feel related to a Milanese who had lived his entire adult life as an immigrant in Sweden. Adapting to life in Zaire under the capricious dictatorship of Mobutu Sese Seko and in Tanzania under the authoritarian socialism of Julius Nyerere had not been comparable experiences. Some of the returnees had lived in Francophone countries, others in Anglophone countries, and although most still spoke at least some Kinyarwanda, many were more at home in Swahili or some other foreign African language which other returnees didn't speak.

Hutu Power created a world in which there was just us and them, and Rwanda was still generally regarded from within and without as a bipolar world of Hutus and Tutsis. But an elaborate grid of subcategories lay just beneath the surface. There were Hutus with good records, and suspect Hutus, Hutus in exile and displaced Hutus, Hutus who wanted to work with the RPF, and anti-Power Hutus who were also anti-RPF, and of course all the old frictions between Hutus of the north and those of the south remained. As for Tutsis, there were all the exiled backgrounds and languages, and survivors and returnees regarding each other with mutual suspicion; there were RPF Tutsis, non-RPF Tutsis, and anti-RPF Tutsis; there were urbanites and cattle keepers, whose concerns as survivors or returnees had almost nothing in common. And, of course, there were many more subcategories, which cut across the others and might, at any given moment, be more important. There were clans and families, rich and poor, Catholics, Muslims, Protestants of various stripes, and a host of more private animists, as well as all the normal social cliques and affiliations, including male and female, who were marrying each other at a fantastic clip, now that the war was over and it was allowed in the RPF, and now that so many had lost any other form of family.

It made one's head spin. Even Rwandans didn't claim to have it all mapped. For the most part, they stuck with the people they knew from before, and didn't care so much if they made no new friends so long as they didn't acquire new enemies. In the long view, it seemed to my American mind that there was some hope in the fact that a country which had been destroyed by a mad wish for every citizen to have exactly the same identity as every other—the identity of a mass murderer, no less—contained more diversity than ever. But that was taking a very long view. Intermarriage rates were at an all-time low, scoring another point for the *génocidaires* in the new, officially ethnicity-free Rwanda;

and not a day went by without a new story going around on *radio trottoir* of an imminent Hutu Power invasion from Zaire.

"THEY SAY THE war was won but for us too much was lost," Odette Nyiramilimo told me. After the genocide, she and Jean-Baptiste had adopted ten children, and took it upon themselves to treat child survivors for free at their clinic. "We feel it's a moral obligation," she said, "but the children are so traumatized that we hardly know how to help them."

After the family was evacuated from the Hôtel des Milles Collines, Jean-Baptiste had gone to work with an RPF medical unit helping survivors, and Odette had taken their three children to Nairobi, vowing never to return to Rwanda. Then she received news that some of her nephews and nieces had survived. "As soon as I heard that, I knew I had to come back," she said. "We began to find them and to take them in, but it's very difficult to satisfy all their needs. One of them—a four-year-old—weighed just seventeen pounds when he was found." Once she told me, "We were in the car, Jean-Baptiste and I, and our three children, and one of the kids said, 'I'm so happy just to be all five of us together again.' We said, 'Aren't you happy to live with your cousins?' But they didn't say anything."

Odette looked over at her children in the pool of the Cercle Sportif. When she turned back to me, she said, "This life after a genocide is really a terrible life." The fluidity and urgency with which she had told the story of her earlier ordeals had given way to a hopscotch, free-associating rhythm as she described life in the aftermath. "When I was still in Nairobi, saying I'd never come back, there was a group of young Rwandan fifty-niners who'd gone to visit Rwanda for the first time," she said. "They got back to Nairobi and said how beautiful and wonderful it all was, and the only problem in Rwanda was the survivors who want to tell you all their stories forever. That really got to me."

She said, "The trauma comes back much more as time

passes—this year more than last. So how can I look forward to next year? We take refuge a bit in our work, but many people become very depressed. I'm afraid it gets worse. I dream more of my sisters and cry through my dreams."

Odette had one nephew who survived the genocide in Kinunu, on the hill where she was born in Gisenyi. She had visited him only once, to help bury the dead, who were numerous, and she did not want to go back. "All the Hutus there watched us come, and some wanted to hug me," she said. "I cried out, 'Don't touch me. Where did you put everyone?' One was married to a cousin of mine. I said, 'Where's Thérèse?' He said, 'I couldn't do anything.' I said, 'What do you mean?' He said, 'It wasn't me who did it.' I said, 'I don't want to see you. I don't want to know you.' Now whenever the Hutus there see a car coming to my nephew's, they all hide. People will say I'm an extremist because I can't accept or tolerate the people who killed my family. So if they're afraid once in their lives—I was afraid since I was three years old—let them know how it feels."

She said it was hard to make new friends among the returnees. "They came with all their things. They can laugh, have a party. Among us it's always tales of genocide, and they don't like to hear about it. If they see I'm married to a Hutu, that I have some old Hutu friends, they don't understand. Really, everyone lives for himself now."

She said, "I was talking to my youngest, Patrick. I said, 'What are you thinking about?' He said, 'Those two guys who came with machetes. It comes back all the time.' The children don't go out —you have to push them—they like to stay home. They think about it a lot. My little Patrick, he goes alone into a room, and he looks under the bed for *interahamwe*. My daughter Arriane was in a very good boarding school in Nairobi, and one night she sat up reliving everything, and she cried. At midnight the dorm monitor came by and they spent nearly the whole night together. Arriane told her what had happened, and the monitor was amazed.

She'd had no idea. And this was a Kenyan. Nobody really knows. Nobody wants to know."

Odette nodded at my notebook, where I was writing as she spoke. "Do the people in America really want to read this? People tell me to write these things down, but it's written inside of me. I almost hope for the day when I can forget."

ONE DAY IN Kigali, I ran into Edmond Mrugamba, a man I had come to know around town, and he invited me to join him for a visit to the latrine into which his sister and her family had been thrown during the genocide. He had mentioned the story before. I remembered that he made a sound—*tcha, tcha, tcha*—and chopped his hand in the air to describe his sister's killing.

Edmond drove a Mercedes, one of the few that remained in Rwanda, and he was wearing a faded denim shirt and jeans and black cowboy boots. He used to work for a German development program in Kigali, and his wife was German; she remained in Berlin with their children after the genocide. As we drove in the direction of the airport, Edmond told me that he was a well-traveled man, and that after many trips in East Africa and Europe, he had always felt that Rwandans were the nicest, most decent people in the world. But now he couldn't recover that feeling. In 1990, after the first RPF attack, he had been threatened because he was Tutsi; he had gone into exile and had only returned after the new government was installed. Edmond was in his late thirties; his father had been a cattle keeper in Kigali. His oldest brother was killed in the massacres of 1963. "And I don't speak of my uncles killed in fifty-nine and sixty-one," he said, "my grandmother burned in the house, my maternal uncle, a nurse, chopped into many pieces. There were many others who were killed, and others luckily went to Uganda." Edmond himself had lived for eleven years in Burundi before returning under Habyarimana and finding work with the Germans. He showed me a snapshot of himself in full camouflage uniform and floppy khaki bush hat. In 1993, he left Germany for Uganda and outfitted himself to join the RPF—"then my appendix burst, and I had to have an operation."

Edmond spoke quietly, with great intensity, and his bearded face was expressive in a subtle, wincing way. Despite his ordeals, he told me, he had never imagined the depth of the ugliness, the meanness—"the disease," he said—that had afflicted Rwanda, and he could not understand how it could have been so well masked. He said, "An animal will kill, but never to completely annihilate a race, a whole collectivity. What does this make us in this world?"

Edmond returned from exile because he had found it intolerable to be living in a strange land thinking that he might be of use in Rwanda. Now he lived alone in a small, dark house with a young boy, a nephew who had been orphaned in the genocide. "And I ask myself sometimes, Is my presence here really of any significance?" he said. "To build a new Rwanda. I dream all the time. I dream of theories of this history of violence. I dream of finding an end to it."

Near the outskirts of Kigali, we turned onto a red-dirt track that narrowed and descended between high reed fences surrounding modest homes. A blue metal gate leading to his dead sister's house stood open. The yard was crackly dry bush strewn with rubble. A family of squatters—Tutsis just returned from Burundi—sat in the living room playing Scrabble. Edmond ignored them. He led me around the side of the house to a stand of dried-out banana plants. There were two holes in the ground, about a foot apart and three feet in diameter—neat, deep, machine-dug wells. Edmond grabbed hold of a bush, leaned out over the holes, and said, "You can see the tibias." I did as he did, and saw the bones.

"Fourteen meters deep," Edmond said. He told me that his brother-in-law had been a fanatically religious man, and on

April 12, 1994, when he was stopped by *interahamwe* at a road-block down the street and forced to lead them back to his house, he had persuaded the killers to let him pray. Edmond's brother-in-law had prayed for half an hour. Then he told the militiamen that he didn't want his family dismembered, so they invited him to throw his children down the latrine wells alive, and he did. Then Edmond's sister and his brother-in-law were thrown in on top.

Edmond took his camera out of a plastic bag and took some pictures of the holes in the ground. "People come to Rwanda and talk of reconciliation," he said. "It's offensive. Imagine talking to Jews of reconciliation in 1946. Maybe in a long time, but it's a private matter." The squatters had come out of the house. They stood together at a short distance, and when they grasped Edmond's story they began sniffling.

On the way back to town, I asked Edmond if he knew the people living in his sister's house. "No," he said. "When I see people who live in a place that isn't theirs, when there are survivors all around who have lost their homes, I know they're miserable people. I want nothing to do with them. All I can think about is the people I've lost." He reminded me that one of his brothers had been killed as well as his sister and her family. Then he told me that he knew who his brother's killer was, and that he sometimes saw the man around Kigali.

"I'd like to talk to him," Edmond said. "I want him to explain to me what this thing was, how he could do this thing. My surviving sister said, 'Let's denounce him.' I saw what was happening —a wave of arrests all at once—and I said, 'What good is prison, if he doesn't feel what I feel? Let him live in fear.' When the time is right, I want to make him understand that I'm not asking for his arrest, but for him to live forever with what he has done. I'm asking for him to think about it for the rest of his life. It's a kind of psychological torture."

Edmond had thought of himself as a Rwandan—he had identified with his people—but after the genocide he lost that mooring.

Now, to prove himself his brother's keeper, he wanted to fix his brother's killer with the mark of Cain. I couldn't help thinking how well Cain had prospered after killing his brother: he founded the first city—and, although we don't like to talk about it all that much, we are all his children.

16

ONE OF THE few things that the fleeing Hutu Power vandals left in ready-to-use condition was Rwanda's central prison system, thirteen red-brick fortifications, built to house a total of twelve thousand inmates. During the genocide, the gates were opened so that convicts could be put to work, killing and collecting corpses, but the jails didn't stay vacant for long. By April of 1995, a year after the killings, at least thirty-three thousand men, women, and children had been arrested for alleged participation in genocide. At the end of that year, the number had climbed to sixty thousand. Some prisons were expanded, new ones were built, and hundreds of smaller community lockups were crammed to overflowing, but the space could not keep up with the demand. By the end of 1997, at least a hundred twenty-five thousand Hutus accused of crimes during the genocide were incarcerated in Rwanda.

A few soldiers usually stood around the periphery of Rwanda's prisons, but there were no guards on the inside. Prisoners and soldiers both considered themselves safer this way. But the government's fear of sending soldiers into the prisons did not extend to foreign visitors, and I was always permitted to bring a camera. This puzzled me. Rwanda's prisons had not elicited favorable press. They were widely viewed as a human rights catastrophe.

Although the tightly packed inmates were all accused of terrible violence, they were generally calm and orderly; fights among them were said to be rare, and killings unheard of. They greeted visitors amiably, often with smiles and with hands extended for a shake. At the women's prison in Kigali, I found three hundred forty women lying around on the floor, barely clad in the stuffy heat of a few cramped cells and corridors; babies crawled underfoot, and two inmate nuns in crisp white habits said mass in a corner. At Butare prison, old men stood in a downpour with bits of plastic over their heads while young boys, scrunched together in a small cell, sang a chorus of "Alouette." In the men's block of Kigali prison, I was conducted past acrobatic and choral groups, a Scout troop, and three men reading *Tintin* by the captain of the prisoners and his adjutant, who wielded a short baton to clear a path through the tangled ranks of prisoners. The captain kept calling out, "Here's a journalist from the United States," and the huddled men, squatting at our feet, clapped mechanically and made little bowing motions. It occurred to me that this was the famous mob mentality of blind obedience to authority which was often described in attempts to explain the genocide.

Rwanda's conventional hierarchies had reconstituted themselves behind the prison walls; "intellectuals," civil servants, professionals, clerics, and merchants had the least uncomfortable cells, while the mass of peasants and laborers made do outdoors, crouching in the bony folds of their neighbors' limbs in unroofed courtyards, and referred all questions to their leaders. Why did they put up with it? Why didn't they riot? Why were attempted escapes so rare in Rwanda, when the guard system was so weak? A rampaging mob of five thousand prisoners could have easily overrun the walls of Kigali's central prison and severely destabilized the capital, sparking a major crisis for the government they despised, even a general uprising if there was support for it. Nobody could entirely explain the passivity in the prisons; the best guess was that, having been assured that they would be slaughtered by the RPF, and finding themselves instead receiving regular visits from friendly international relief workers, reporters, and diplomats, the prisoners were simply astonished to be alive and did not care to push their luck.

Between my visits to the prisons, I stopped by to see General Kagame in his office at the Ministry of Defense. I was wondering why the government exposed itself to bad press about the prisons, and how he interpreted the prisoners' apparent calm acceptance of their horrible conditions. Kagame answered my question with a question of his own: "If a million people died here, who killed them?"

"A lot of people," I said.

"Yes," he said. "Have you found many that admit they participated?"

I hadn't. In the early days after the genocide, it had been easy for visitors to find perpetrators, in the jails and the refugee camps and also on the streets of Rwanda, who admitted to taking part in the killings, and even boasted about it. Yet by the time I began visiting Rwanda, the criminals had recognized that confession was a tactical error. In the prisons and the border camps, I couldn't find anyone who would even agree that there had been a genocide. There had been a civil war and, yes, some massacres, but nobody acknowledged seeing anything. Every one of the scores of prisoners I spoke with claimed to have been arbitrarily and unjustly arrested, and of course, in any given case it was entirely possible. But many prisoners also told me they were confident that their "brothers" in the UN border camps would soon come to liberate them.

I once heard Kagame say that he suspected as many as a million people had particpated directly or indirectly in the genocide. His adviser, Claude Dusaidi, who liked to make extreme pronouncements, put the number at three million, which amounted to proclaiming every other Rwandan Hutu guilty. Such claims—impossible to prove or to disprove—struck many Rwandans and foreign observers as acts of intimidation, carefully calculated to place all Hutus under a cloud of suspicion; and this perception was only hardened when a UN-sponsored effort to honor those Hutus, like Paul Rusesabagina, who had protected Tutsis during the genocide was scuttled by infighting among Rwandan cabinet ministers. But Dusaidi insisted that Rwanda's outrageously packed prisons did not reflect the outrageousness of the crime that had been visited on the country. "Sometimes one person could kill six people, and sometimes three people could kill one person," Dusaidi said. "Pick any single film of the genocide, and just watch how they kill people. You'll find a group killing a person. So there are many more killers still walking the streets than we have in prison. The number in prison is a dot."

Of course, the fact that guilty people remained free didn't mean that those in prison were the right people. I asked Kagame if it bothered him that a good many innocent people might be in jail and that the experience might harden them into oppositionists. "Yeah," he said. "It's a problem. But that was the way to deal with the situation. If we had lost these people through revenge, that would have been an even bigger problem for us. I would rather address the problem of putting them in prison, because that is the best way to do it for the process of justice, and simply because I don't want them out there, because people would actually kill them."

IN JULY OF 1995, Rwanda's National Commission of Triage—a sporadically functioning body charged with identifying prisoners against whom the accusations of genocide were insubstantial—ordered the release of Placide Koloni from the prison at Gitarama. Koloni had held the office of deputy governor before, during, and—until his arrest—after the genocide. This was normal; the majority of provincial and communal officials who had not fled Rwanda, or been jailed as *génocidaires*, had retained their posts. Koloni had spent five months as a prisoner, and upon his release he returned to his office. Three days later, on the night of July 27, a sentry at a UN military observers' post staffed by Malian blue-helmets saw some men enter Koloni's home. A scream was heard, and the house exploded in flames. The blue-helmets watched as the fire burned through the night. Shortly after dawn, they entered the house and found that Koloni, his wife, their two daughters, and a domestic had been killed.

A week later, a Hutu deputy governor in Gikongoro, to the west of Gitarama, and a Catholic priest in Kamonyi parish, not far from Kigali, were shot dead. An edgy mood settled over Rwanda, not because the death toll was especially high, but because the victims were prominent civic leaders. In mid-August, the government was shaken when the Prime Minister, Faustin Twagiramungu, and the Minister of the Interior, Seth Sendashonga, quit in protest over the persistent insecurity in the provinces, for which they blamed the RPA. Both men were Hutus—Twagiramungu, a leader of the anti-Hutu Power opposition under Habyarimana; Sendashonga, a prominent member of the RPF—and both went into exile.

General Kagame, who never tired of reciting the number of RPA soldiers—four hundred, seven hundred; I lost count after a thousand—who had been thrown in military jails for killings and indiscipline, liked to point out that soldiers were not the only Rwandans frustrated to the point of criminality in the aftermath of the genocide and that Rwanda even has apolitical criminals. "But given the situation you have here," he said, "ordinary crimes are not going to be looked at as ordinary crimes." His distinction offered little comfort to frightened Hutus. "When we see how Koloni was killed, we'd rather be in here than out there," a detainee told me at Gitarama prison, which was known as Rwanda's worst prison in the summer of 1995.

At Gitarama, more than six thousand men were packed into a space built for seven hundred and fifty. That worked out to four prisoners per square yard: night and day, the prisoners had to stand or to sit between the legs of those who stood, and even in the dry season a scum of condensation, urine, and bits of dropped food covered the floor. The cramped prisoners' feet and ankles, and sometimes their entire legs, swelled to two or three times normal size. They suffered from an atrophying of their swollen extremities and from rot; infection often followed. Hundreds had required amputations.

When Lieutenant Colonel R. V. Blanchette, a UN military observer from Canada, first learned of the conditions at Gitarama prison, he paid a visit. "I went down in the back with my flashlight," he told me, "and I saw this guy's foot. I'd heard it was pretty bad in there, but this was quite ugly—very swollen, and his little toe was missing. I shined my flashlight up to his face, and he reached down and pulled off the next toe."

A few weeks after Blanchette's encounter, prisoners at Gitarama told me that conditions were much improved. The Red Cross, which supplied the food and cooking fuel for all of Rwanda's central prisons, had installed duckboards underfoot and evacuated the worst medical cases. "We had eighty-six deaths in June, and in July only eighteen," a doctor at the prison clinic told me. The main causes of death, he added, were malaria and AIDS, which was normal for men in Rwanda, and while prison conditions remained grim—atrocious in most of the small community lockups—by mid-1996 mortality rates in the central prisons were reported to be lower than among the Rwandan population at large.

On the day of my visit to Gitarama prison, six thousand four hundred and twenty-four prisoners formed a solid-looking knot, and I had to plan each step I took with care. It was difficult to figure out how the people fitted together—which limbs went with which body, or why a head appeared to have grown three legs without a torso in between. Many of the feet were badly swollen. The bodies were clad in rags.

Yet the faces didn't correspond to the discomfort in which the bodies were confined. They had a clarity and composure and forthrightness of expression that made the people inside the prison nearly indistinguishable from those outside. Here and there, of course, I would catch the electric glint of insane eyes or a ragged leer of unnerving brutality. But, pressing through the throng, I received the usual welcoming smiles, cheers, and handshakes. In the children's cell, sixty-three boys, ranging in age from seven to sixteen, sat in rows on the floor, facing a blackboard where an older prisoner—a schoolteacher by profession—was conducting a lesson. They looked like schoolboys anywhere. I asked one why he was in prison. "They say I killed," he said. "I didn't." Other children gave the same reply, with downcast eyes, evasive, as unconvincing as schoolboys anywhere.

Rwanda's formal arrest procedures were rarely followed, and it was sometimes enough for someone to point a finger and say, "Genocide." But, according to Luc Côté, a lawyer from Montreal who directed the UN Human Rights office in Butare, "most of the arrests were founded on some type of evidence, and a lot of the time there was a whole lot of evidence," which meant that while they might be technically incorrect they weren't necessarily arbitrary. And even if the procedures were followed to the letter, it wasn't clear what difference it would make, since Rwanda's courts were closed, and for more than two and a half years nobody was brought to trial.

The government attributed the judicial paralysis to its lack of financial and human resources. Police inspectors, responsible for assembling the dossiers against the accused, were constantly being recruited and trained, but even then most were amateurs who found themselves with hundreds of complex cases, no transportation, no support staff, and quite often threats coming at them from both accusers and accused. Rwanda pleaded for bicycles, motorcycles, and pencils and pens from foreign donors, but these basic necessities were much slower in coming than expressions of "concern" that not enough was being done to protect the rights of the accused.

NOBODY EVER TALKED seriously about conducting tens of thousands of murder trials in Rwanda. Western legal experts liked to say that even the lawyer-crowded United States could not have handled Rwanda's caseload fairly and expeditiously. "It's materially impossible to judge all those who participated in the massacres, and politically it's no good, even though it's just," the RPF's Tito Ruteremara told me. "This was a true genocide, and the only correct response is true justice. But Rwanda has the death penalty, and—well, that would mean a lot more killing."

In other words, a true genocide and true justice are incompatible. Rwanda's new leaders were trying to see their way around this problem by describing the genocide as a crime committed by masterminds and slave bodies. Neither party could be regarded as innocent, but if the crime was political, and justice was to serve the political good, then the punishment had to draw a line between the criminal minds and the criminal bodies. "With those who masterminded the genocide, it's clear-cut," General Kagame told me. "They must face justice directly. I'm not as worried about these ordinary peasants who took machetes and cut people in pieces like animals." He explained that "long ago" Rwandan justice was conducted in village hearings, where fines were the preferred penalties. "The guy who did the crime can give some salt or something, and that can bring the people back together," Kagame said.

Salt for state-sponsored mass murder? Village justice, as Kagame sketched it, sounded hopelessly inadequate. But as the lawyer François Xavier Nkurunziza explained: "When you speak of justice with our peasants, the big idea is compensation. A cattle keeper or cultivator who loses his whole family has lost his whole economic support system. You can kill the man who committed genocide, but that's not compensation—that's only fear and anger. This is how our peasants think." The problem, as Kagame suggested when he spoke of salt, was that after genocide compensation could, at best, be symbolic.

The government discussed easing the burden on the courts by ranking degrees of criminality among the *génocidaires*, and assigning lesser offenders to public works or reeducation programs. Politically, the RPF was more concerned with what in postwar Germany was called "denazification" than with holding every individual who had committed a crime during the genocide to account. "Actually, we're trying to see how to get as many ordinary people off the hook as possible," Gerald Gahima, an RPF political officer who was the Deputy Minister of Justice, explained. "But that's not justice, is it? It's not the justice the law provides for. It's not the justice most people would want. It's only the best justice we can try for under the circumstances."

But if the guilty could never be fully punished and survivors could never be properly compensated, the RPF regarded forgiveness as equally impossible—unless, at the very least, the perpetrators of the genocide acknowledged that they had done wrong. With time, the quest for justice became, in large measure, a quest for repentance. Where ministers and parliamentarians had once preached the civic virtue of murdering one's neighbors, members of the new government now traveled the countryside to spread the gospel of reconciliation through accountability.

Mass reburial ceremonies for genocide victims were a favorite forum for the new message. I attended such a reburial in the summer of 1995, on a hilltop amid the lush, mist-strewn tea plantations of Gisenyi. In this setting of astonishing tranquillity, the newly grown grass was pulled back to disclose a mass grave. The broken bodies within it were exhumed and laid out on a long rack. On the orders of village leaders, the local peasantry had come to see, and to smell the death smell, and President Bizimungu came with a half dozen cabinet ministers and many other officials. Soldiers distributed translucent plastic gloves among the villagers, and put them to work, placing pieces of the corpses in coffins and wrapping the rest in green plastic sheets. There were speeches and benedictions. A soldier explained to me that the President had used his speech to ask the peasantry where they had been when these dead were killed in their community, and exhorted them to make atonement. Then the dead were placed in new mass graves, and covered up again with earth.

WHEN RWANDANS SPOKE of reconstruction and reconciliation, they spoke of the need to overcome or to liberate themselves from "the old mentalities" of colonialism and dictatorship, and from the perfect pecking order of intimidation and obedience that had served as the engine of the genocide. The systems by which the old mentalities had been implanted had names—impunity, cronyism, ethnicity, feudalism, Hamitism—but the mentalities themselves lay deeper within each Rwandan, internalized in the reflexive habits of a lifetime's experiences and expectations of brutality: us or them; kill or be killed. When Kagame said that people can be made bad, and can be taught to be good, he added, "There are mechanisms within society—education, a form of participation. Something can be achieved." This view was widely shared, with varying degrees of certainty and skepticism, not only within the RPF but among many of the surviving anti-Habyarimana Hutu leaders, and—on a good day, at least—by much of the Rwandan public.

But where was Rwanda to turn for a model? The justice at Nuremberg was helpfully brought by foreign conquerors, and de-nazification in Germany was carried out in a context where the group that had been subjected to genocide would no longer be living side by side with the killers. In South Africa, armed struggle had ended, and the post-apartheid Truth Commission could presume that the country's defeated white masters had accepted the legitimacy of the new order. Rwanda offered no such tidy arrangement. Guerrilla attacks from Hutu Power forces in Zaire escalated steadily throughout 1995, as did attacks on witnesses and survivors of the genocide. "Right now, if you were to give a general amnesty you would be inviting chaos," said Charles Murigande, chairman of Rwanda's Presidential Commission on Accountability for the Genocide. "But if we could put our hands on the leaders, even an amnesty would be very well received."

That was a very big "if." Just as Habyarimana's death had made him a martyr for Hutu Power, it also ensured that the killing which was purportedly carried out in "defense" of his name had never carried a signal signature: a Hitler, a Pol Pot, a Stalin. The list of Rwanda's "Most Wanted" was a hodgepodge of *akazu* members, military officers, journalists, politicians, businessmen, mayors, civil service functionaries, clerics, schoolteachers, taxi drivers, shopkeepers, and untitled hatchet men—dizzying to keep track of and impossible to rank in a precise hierarchy of command. Some were said to have given orders, loudly or quietly, and others to have transmitted or followed orders, but the plan and its execution had been ingeniously designed to look planless.

Still, Rwandan investigators were able to draw up a list of some four hundred top *génocidaires*—masterminds and master implementers. But all of them were in exile, beyond Rwanda's reach. Almost immediately after its installation in 1994, the new government had appealed to the United Nations for help in apprehending fugitive Hutu Power leaders, so that they might stand trial before the nation. Instead, the UN created the International Criminal Tribunal for Rwanda, which was essentially a subset of the tribunal that had been established for the ugly Balkan war of the early 1990s. "We asked for help to catch these people who ran away and to try them properly in our own courts," a Rwandan diplomat told me. "But the Security Council just started writing 'Rwanda' under the name 'Yugoslavia' everywhere."

The Rwandan government regarded the UN's decision to keep its resources to itself as an insult. The very existence of the UN court implied that the Rwandan judiciary was incapable of reaching just verdicts, and seemed to dismiss in advance any trials that

Rwanda might hold as beneath international standards. "If the international community really wants to fight impunity in Rwanda, they should help Rwanda to punish these people," Gerald Gahima told me at the Ministry of Justice. "It makes it harder to forgive the ordinary people if we don't have the leaders here to be tried in Rwandan courts before the Rwandan people according to Rwandan law." But the UN tribunal would not even sit in Rwanda, where the witnesses and concerned audience were; instead it was headquartered on "neutral territory," in Arusha, Tanzania. "The tribunal," Charles Murigande said, "was created essentially to appease the conscience of the international community, which has failed to live up to its conventions on genocide. It wants to look as if it is doing something, which is often worse than doing nothing at all."

In fact, during its first two years, the UN tribunal didn't appear to be doing much. It was understaffed and systematically mismanaged, and its prosecutorial strategy appeared directionless and opportunistic. Most of its indictments followed the chance arrest on immigration charges of Rwandan fugitives in various African countries, and in some high-profile cases, like that of Colonel Bagasora, who was captured in Cameroon, the UN fought a Rwandan extradition request to advance its own. In this way, the tribunal ultimately wound up with an impressive sampler of Hutu Power masterminds in its custody. But it quickly became clear that the prosecutors had no intention of trying more than a few dozen cases. This only served to aggravate the feeling in Kigali that the UN court was not designed to serve Rwanda's national interest, since the message to the vast majority of fugitive *génocidaires* was that they had nothing to fear: the international community would not help Rwanda get them, nor would it pursue them itself. "It's a joke," Kagame's adviser, Claude Dusaidi, said to me. "This tribunal is now acting as a spoiler."

The largest concentrations of Rwanda's most-wanted were settled in Zaire and Kenya—states whose notoriously corrupt Presidents, Mobutu Sese Seko and Daniel arap Moi, had been intimates of Habyarimana and had taken to hosting his widow, Madame Agathe, at their palaces. Mobutu had called Habyarimana his "little brother," and the slain Rwandan's remains, which had been spirited across the border amid the mass flight to Goma, were entombed in a mausoleum on the grounds of Mobutu's primary estate. When I asked Honoré Rakotomanana, a Madagascan who headed the UN's prosecution team in Rwanda, how he expected to indict anybody from Zaire or Kenya, he said, "There are international treaties to which those countries are signatories." But in nearly two years, before he was sacked in 1997, Rakotomanana never bothered to send a single investigator to Zaire. Meanwhile, in October 1995, Kenya's President Moi assailed the tribunal as a "haphazard process," and announced, "I shall not allow any one of them to enter Kenya to serve summonses and look for people here. No way. If any such characters come here, they will be arrested. We must respect ourselves. We must not be harassed."

Watching the old-boy network of African strongmen protect its own, Kagame spoke of "a feeling of betrayal, even by our African brothers," and he added, ominously, "We shall remind them that what happened here can happen elsewhere—it can happen in these other countries—and then I am sure they will run to us. It can happen tomorrow. Things have happened, and they can happen again."

Even when genocidal leaders were eventually turned over to the tribunal, the problem remained that the UN had forbidden the court to recommend a death penalty. The Nazis at Nuremberg and the Japanese war criminals in Tokyo had faced the death penalty after World War II. Were the crimes committed against humanity in Rwanda lesser offenses than those which prompted the Genocide Convention to be written? According to Kagame, when Rwanda protested that the tribunal should carry the death penalty out of respect for Rwanda's laws, the UN advised Rwanda to abolish *its* death penalty. Kagame called this advice "cynical."

"The Rwandan people know this is the same international community that stood by and watched them get killed," Gerald Gahima said. And his RPF colleague Tito Ruteremara, noting that Rwandans convicted by the tribunal were expected to serve their sentences in Scandinavia, told me, "It doesn't fit our definition of justice to think of the authors of the Rwandan genocide sitting in a full-service Swedish prison with a television." As it turned out, even those Hutu Power leaders who wound up in custody at Arusha found the croissants they were regularly served for breakfast a bit rich. After a while, the tribunal prisoners mounted a protest to demand a normal Rwandan breakfast of gruel.

17

"IN YOUR COUNTRY," the RPA colonel said, "I think you have many comedians." We were sitting on his porch, in the cool, drizzling night of the central Rwandan highlands, drinking beer and whiskey and eating boiled potatoes and brochettes of grilled goat. The colonel dragged a chunk of meat off his skewer with his teeth. He chewed on it for a while, then he said, "In my understanding, many of these comedians in America are black. Why do you think that is?"

I suggested that it might have to do with adversity. People who feel up against it sometimes develop a canny take on how the world works—the rawness of it, the absurdities—and sometimes, if they're funny, they make fun of it.

"Those black guys *are* funny," the colonel said.

I said, "The funny ones are."

He coughed out a one-syllable chuckle and the other guys on the porch, his associates, followed him with some laughter. After a while, the colonel said, "No comedians in Rwanda. Plenty of black people, plenty of adversity—no comedians."

"You must have jokes," I said.

He said, "They're not really funny."

I asked him to try one on me. "Another time," he said. There was a woman present, and the colonel poked his chin out in her direction. "Rwandan jokes," he said, "are not decent."

I was disappointed. I didn't expect to have another time with this colonel, and the subject interested me broadly: not just jokes —art of any kind. Next door in the Congo, in Tanzania, in Uganda, there were great artistic traditions: visual arts and music predominated, and a literary culture had developed in postcolonial times. Even Burundi had world-famous drumming ensembles. Rwanda had a few spectacular costume dances, some traditional songs, and an oral literature of poems and tales that followed archaic forms from precolonial times, but no arts to compete with its neighbors. The closest modern Rwanda came to a cultural flowering was in the fascist agitprop of Hutu Power newspapers and radio, and in the ruffian chic of *interahamwe* pageantry and marching songs. New music was mostly imported, and while some Rwandans had written novels almost nobody read them.

I would have liked to ask the colonel about the poverty of Rwandan art, but I didn't want to offend him. So the conversation moved on. Then the woman left, and the colonel said, "OK, I'll tell you a joke." The setup was simple: a Rwandan kid grew up in the hills, did well in school, went to Paris on a scholarship, and returned with a new set of manners—mod clothes, a grandiose vocabulary, a mincing accent, even a different way of walking, "like a little horse," the colonel said. One day, the boy's father, a simple old peasant, said, "Boy, what's got into you? So you went to France. So what? Look at me. I've been screwing your mother for forty-five years, and I don't walk around town like this." The colonel's hands went out, clutching the air in front of him, and he pumped his hips urgently, in the eternal fashion.

I laughed. But the Rwandans on the porch, the colonel's associates, just nodded gravely. "You see," the colonel said, "it's not really a funny joke. It's about logic. Rwandan jokes are like this, kind of intellectual. For instance, a guy gets what we call a French haircut—shaved on the sides, flat on top—and his friends say, 'How can you have a French cut? You don't even speak French.'"

This time the Rwandans laughed, while I nodded. "It's about logic," the colonel said again. "It's a trick. You laugh at the guy with the haircut *and* you laugh at his friends—back and forth."

It seemed to me that both jokes did have a logic, as all jokes must, but that what they were about was provincialism and foreign influence. They were about aspirations to the image and offerings of a broader modern world, and the opposing tug of traditional Rwandan insularity and conformity; about being caught between a past that you reject or at least want to escape and a future that you can only imagine in terms of imported styles, whose imposition you also reject and want to escape. They were jokes that seemed well suited to a country undergoing the most catastrophic decolonization process in Africa. I told the colonel as much, in a groping way, and he said, "Maybe this is why we have no comedians." He sounded quite discouraged.

"But the jokes are funny," I said.

"No," he told me, "it's not funny. It's going to take us a long time to overcome the old mentalities."

SOMETIMES IT SEEMED that instead of fine arts, Rwandans had politics: the arts of statecraft, writ large and small, at the highest echelons of government and in the most basic negotiations of daily life. What, after all, was the struggle between proponents of a "new order" and adherents of the "old mentalities" if not a clash between two fundamentally opposed representations of Rwandan reality? After a century in which Rwandans had labored under the mystification and deceit of the Hamitic fable, whose ultimate perversity took the world-upside-down form of genocide, the RPF and its anti-Hutu Power allies described their struggle against annihilation as a revolt of realists. "Honesty" was among their favorite words, and their basic proposition was that greater truth

258

should be the basis of greater power. Under the circumstances, the last best hope for Hutu Power was to assert—in its usual simultaneous onslaught of word and action—that honesty and truth themselves were merely forms of artifice, never the source of power but always its products, and that the only measure of right versus wrong was the bastardized "majority rule" principle of physical might.

With the lines so drawn, the war about the genocide was truly a postmodern war: a battle between those who believed that because the realities we inhabit are constructs of our imaginations, they are all equally true or false, valid or invalid, just or unjust, and those who believed that constructs of reality can—in fact, must—be judged as right or wrong, good or bad. While academic debates about the possibility of objective truth and falsehood are often rarified to the point of absurdity, Rwanda demonstrated that the question is a matter of life and death.

In the summer of 1995, a man sought me out in Kigali, saying he had heard that I was interested in the problems of his country. He had long been privy to the workings of Rwandan politics—first as an associate of Hutu Power, then as an oppositionist—and he was now attached to the new government. He told me that he wanted to be completely honest with me about the affairs of his country, but anonymously. "If you betray my name," he said, "I will deny everything."

My visitor was a Hutu, who traveled with a Kalashnikov-toting soldier in tow. "Listen," he said, "Rwanda had a dictatorship, Rwanda had a genocide, and now Rwanda has a very serious threat on the borders. You don't have to be RPF to understand what that means. You don't have to fall into the old thinking—that if you're not with these guys you're with those guys." He went on to explain at length his view that Rwandans can never be trusted. "Foreigners cannot know this place," he said. "We cheat. We repeat the same little things to you over and over and tell you nothing. Even among ourselves we lie. We have a habit of secrecy and suspicion. You can stay a whole year and you will not know what Rwandans think or what they are doing."

I told him that this didn't fully surprise me, because I had the impression that Rwandans often spoke two languages—not just Kinyarwanda and French or English, but one language among themselves and an entirely different language with outsiders. By way of an example, I said that I had talked with a Rwandan lawyer who had described the difficulty of integrating his European training into his Rwandan practice. He loved the Cartesian, Napoleonic legal system, on which Rwanda's is modeled, but, he said, it didn't always correspond to Rwandan reality, which was for him an equally complete system of thought. By the same token, when this lawyer spoke with me about Rwanda, he used a language quite different from the language he would speak with fellow Rwandans.

"You talk about this," my visitor said, "and at the same time you say, 'A lawyer told me such and such.' A Rwandan would never tell you what someone else said, and normally, when you told a Rwandan what you heard from somebody, he would immediately change the rhythm of his speech and close himself off to you. He would think that what he said to you might be passed on later. He would be on his guard." He looked up and studied me for a moment. "You Westerners are so honest," he said. He seemed depressed by the notion. "You say what you think, and you say what you've seen. You say, 'A lawyer told me.' Do you think there are many lawyers here?"

I said I'd met several and that the one whom I'd referred to had told me I was free to quote him by name. "Fine," my visitor said. "But I'm telling you, Rwandans are petty." I wasn't entirely sure of the French word that he used for "petty," which was *mesquin*. When I asked him to explain it, he described someone who sounded remarkably like Iago—a confidence man, a cheater and betrayer and liar, who tries to tell everyone what he imagines they want to hear in order to maintain his own game and get what he's after. Colonel Dr. Joseph Karemera, a founding officer of the RPF and Rwanda's Minister of Health, told me that there is a Kinya-rwanda word for such behavior. Having described the legacy of thirty-four years of Hutu ethnic dictatorship as "a very bad mentality," Karemera said, "We call it *ikinamucho*—that if you want to do something you are deceitful and not straight. For example, you can come to kill me"—he clutched his throat—"and your mission is successful, but then you cry. That is *ikinamucho*."

My visitor liked the word *mesquin*. He used it repeatedly. I remarked that he didn't seem to have a very high opinion of his people. "I'm trying to tell you about them without lying," he said.

Shortly after our meeting, I learned that he had left Rwanda to join the leaders of Hutu Power in exile. I also learned that *ikinamucho* means "theater."

DURING HER LAST year in medical school, in the early 1980s, Odette Nyiramilimo's professor of pediatrics was a doctor named Théodore Sindikubwabo. "I was hugely pregnant when I took my exam with him, and he saw that I was suffering," Odette recalled. "He took me to his office to drink a Fanta, then he drove me home. These were very human qualities, the genuine responses of a father. But he was a false man. During the First Republic, under President Kayibanda, he was the Minister of Health. When he saw Habyarimana taking power and imprisoning all the ministers, he went straight to Kigali Central Hospital, grabbed a stethoscope, and began practicing pediatrics. Then he became a deputy in the parliament. He loved to be important. He came from the south, he had a big house in Butare, which was anti-Power, and he was a Power man with the MRND—so very useful. He had this mentality like a chameleon. But I never thought he could be a killer."

Three days after Habyarimana's assassination, Sindikubwabo was installed as Rwanda's interim President by Colonel Bagasora's crisis committee. At that time, Butare was the only province with a Tutsi governor, and while other civic and political leaders led their constituencies to massacre, this governor, Jean-Baptiste Habyalimana, urged restraint. For the first twelve days of the killing, Butare was a haven of virtual calm, and Tutsis fleeing massacres elsewhere flocked to the region. Then, on April 19, 1994, Théodore Sindikubwabo visited Butare. He fired the governor (who was subsequently killed) and held a rally, where he delivered a call to arms that was broadcast throughout the country. The day after Sindikubwabo spoke, soldiers of the Presidential Guard were flown into Butare, buses and trucks carrying militia and arms arrived, and the slaughter began. The killings in Butare included some of the most extensive massacres of the genocide: in just two or three weeks, at least twenty thousand Tutsis were killed in Cyahinda parish and at least thirty-five thousand in Karama parish.

Sindikubwabo's old villa in Butare had been smashed into a heap of stones by the time I visited it, but he had a nice new one in an exclusive enclave of Bukavu, Zaire, where he lived as president of the government in exile. The property sat just behind the governor's mansion in Bukavu and commanded a stunning view of the hills of Rwanda across the southern tip of Lake Kivu. Two black Rwandan government Mercedes sedans stood in the drive when I stopped by in late May of 1995, and several young Rwandans hung around the gate. An amiable man in a red sports shirt greeted me and introduced himself as Sindikubwabo's chief of protocol. He said that the press was always welcome because Rwanda was terribly misunderstood in the world: yes, the country had suffered a genocide, but it was carried out by the RPF, and Hutus had been the victims. "Look at us, in exile," he said, adding, "Even as we speak, Paul Kagame is killing all the Hutus in Rwanda, systematically." Then he volunteered the opinion that Sindikubwabo was an innocent man and asked whether I believed in the idea of innocence until guilt is proven. I said that I didn't know that Sindikubwabo had been charged with any crimes in any courts of law, and he told me that all Rwandan refugees were waiting for the judgment of the international tribunal. "But who is this tribunal?" he asked. "Who is influencing them? Who are they serving? Are they interested in the truth or only in avoiding reality?"

The chief of protocol told me to wait where I was, and after a while André Nkurunziza, Sindikubwabo's press attaché, took his place. Nkurunziza cut a slightly tattered figure; he had broken teeth and an ancient jacket, and he spoke in an injured, plaintive tone. "This is a government hurt by a media conspiracy that labels it a government of genocide," he said. "But these are not people who killed anyone. We hear them called planners, but these are only rumors planted by Kigali. Even you, when you go to Kigali, they could pay you money to write what they want." He put out a hand to touch my forearm soothingly. "I don't say that they did pay you. It's just an example."

Nkurunziza told me that in 1991 he had visited Washington. "They didn't know there was a war in Rwanda," he said. "They didn't know of Rwanda. I said, 'It's a little country next to Zaire.' They said, 'Where is Zaire?' Now, how can they say they know what happened in my country last year?"

We were standing in Zaire, looking at Rwanda. I said, "What happened last year?"

"This is a long war," Nkurunziza said. "And there will be another war. This is what we think here. There will be another war."

Eventually, I was taken in to Sindikubwabo, who was in his mid-sixties, an old man by Rwandan standards. He sat in a low armchair in his modestly furnished living room. He was said to be ill, and he looked it: gaunt, with pale eyes filmed by cataracts and a strikingly bony, asymmetrical face, divided by a thick scar—the result of a motorbike accident in his youth—that drew his mouth up in a diagonal sneer. He told me that, in keeping with the Arusha Accords, he would welcome "a frank and sincere dialogue about the management of Rwanda" with the RPF. When I asked why anybody should negotiate with the man who was considered to have instigated the massacres at Butare, Sindikubwabo began to laugh, a dry, raspy chuckle that kept up until he was out of breath.

"The moment has not yet come to say who is guilty and who is not guilty," he said. "The RPF can bring accusations against it doesn't matter whom, and they can formulate these accusations it doesn't matter how—reassembling, stitching together, making a montage of the witnesses. It's easy. You're a journalist and you don't know how this is done?" His face began to twitch around his scar. "This becomes a sort of theater piece"—"*une comédie*," he said—"that they're performing right now in Kigali, and it will be sorted out before the tribunal. I come from Butare, and I know what I said in Butare, and the people of Butare also know what I said."

But he refused to tell me what he had said. Even if I found a tape of the speech, he instructed me, I would have to bring it back to him for an interpretation—"every word, what it means, every phrase, what it means, because to interpret the ideas and thoughts of others, it's not easy and it's not fair." Later, when I repeated his words to Odette, she said, "There was nothing to interpret. He was saying things like 'Eliminate those who think they know everything. Work on without them.' I trembled when I heard it."

Sindikubwabo's speech was one of the most widely remembered moments of the genocide, because once the killing began in Butare it was clear that no Tutsi in Rwanda was to be spared. But he insisted that he had been misunderstood. "If the mayors of Butare affirm that the massacres began under my order—*they* are responsible, because it was their responsibility to maintain order in their communities. If they interpreted my message as an order, they executed an order against my words." I wondered why he hadn't corrected them, since he was a doctor and had been President while hundreds of thousands of people were being murdered in his country. He said that if the time came he would answer that question before the international tribunal.

Sitting with Sindikubwabo as he offered what sounded like a

rehearsal of the defense-by-obfuscation he was preparing for the tribunal, I had the impression that he almost yearned to be indicted, even apprehended, in order to have a final hour in the spotlight. But perhaps he knew that in Zaire he was beyond the reach of the UN tribunal. He maintained that a "truly impartial" investigation could not but vindicate him. By way of an example, he handed me what he regarded as a definitive account of recent Rwandan history, an article clipped from the *Executive Intelligence Review*, a publication put out by the crypto-fascist American conspiracy theorist Lyndon LaRouche. I scanned it briefly; it appeared to demonstrate that the British royal family, through its Ugandan puppets, and in collusion with several other shadowy outfits including the World Wildlife Fund for Nature, had sponsored the extermination of Rwanda's Hutu majority.

A PORTRAIT OF President Habyarimana stood behind Sindikubwabo's chair. The dead leader, buttoned up in military dress and draped with braid, looked much happier than the exiled leader, and it seemed to me that as a dead man he did have the happier position. To his people, Habyarimana was the true President—many people in the UN camps told me so—whereas Sindikubwabo was regarded as a nobody who had filled the job for only a brief, unfortunate moment. "He is President of nothing," several refugees said. To his enemies, too, Sindikubwabo was a nobody; RPF leaders and genocide survivors saw him as an attendant lord, plucked from the lower echelons of Hutu Power at the moment of crisis precisely because he was content to play the puppet. Sindikubwabo's own son-in-law was Minister of Agriculture in the new government, and during a mass reburial ceremony in Butare he had denounced his father-in-law as a murderer, and urged Rwandans to avoid ascribing guilt or protecting the guilty on the basis of familial association.

Yet even in his spurned and discredited state, Sindikubwabo remained of use to the Hutu Power machine—as a scapegoat.

With time, the leaders of the ex-FAR, who kept their headquarters at the northern end of Lake Kivu, ten miles west of Goma, had distanced themselves from the government in exile and created an assortment of new political front organizations, whose operatives were not known to have distinguished themselves in the genocide and could be presented to the world as "clean." Chief among these was the Rassemblement Democratique pour la Retour (RDR), whose propaganda, blaming the refugee crisis on the RPF and calling for a blanket amnesty as a precondition for repatriation, won it a great following among relief workers and journalists. Field officers of the United Nations High Commissioner for Refugees often made a special point of introducing me to RDR leaders when I visited the camps. I couldn't understand it. They sounded exactly like Sindikubwabo, and yet the humanitarians who promoted them seemed convinced that they were sensible and legitimate voices of the excluded. RDR spokesmen in Zaire, Kenya, and Brussels were frequently cited on the BBC as "leading representatives of the refugees." That the RDR might be associated with the génocidaires—that it was, in fact, a shadow Hutu Power regime chartered by the ex-FAR command in Goma, and that RDR agents micromanaged the camps, extorting monthly taxes, in cash or a cut of food-aid rations, from every refugee family in Zaire, and intimidating refugees who wanted to go home—was rarely even hinted at.

This was one of the great mysteries of the war about the genocide: how, time and again, international sympathy placed itself at the ready service of Hutu Power's lies. It was bewildering enough that the UN border camps should be allowed to constitute a rump genocidal state, with an army that was regularly observed to be receiving large shipments of arms and recruiting young men by the thousands for the next extermination campaign. And it was heartbreaking that the vast majority of the million and a half people in those camps were evidently at no risk of being jailed, much less killed, in Rwanda, but that the propaganda and brute force of the Hutu Power apparatus was effectively holding them hostage, as a human shield. Yet what made the camps almost unbearable to visit was the spectacle of hundreds of international humanitarians being openly exploited as caterers to what was probably the single largest society of fugitive criminals against humanity ever assembled.

Aid agencies provided transportation, meeting places, and office supplies to the RDR and paramilitary groups that masqueraded as community self-help agencies; they fattened the war coffers of the Hutu Power elites by renting trucks and buses from them, and by hiring as refugee employees the candidates advanced through an in-house patronage system managed by the *génocidaires*. Some aid workers even hired the Hutu Power pop star Simon Bikindi—lyricist of the *interahamwe* anthem "I Hate These Hutus"—to perform with his band at a party. In the border camps in Tanzania, I met a group of doctors, recently arrived from Europe, who told me how much fun the refugees were. "You can tell by their eyes who the innocent ones are," said a doctor from —of all places—Sarajevo. And a colleague of hers said, "They wanted to show us a video of Rwanda in 1994, but we decided it would be too upsetting."

ONCE THE CHOLERA outbreak in Goma had been contained, the camps had ceased to offer a solution to the refugee crisis and became a means of sustaining it; for the longer the camps remained in place, the greater was the inevitability of war, and that meant that rather than protecting people, the camps were placing them directly in harm's way.

Throughout 1995 and 1996, the Hutu Power forces in exile continued their guerrilla war against Rwanda, with raiders from the camps slipping over the borders to mine a road, blow up a power pylon, or attack genocide survivors and witnesses. In addition, the ex-FAR and *interahamwe* from the Goma camps fanned out through the surrounding province of North Kivu, which was home to a sizable population of Zaireans of Rwandan ancestry, and began recruiting, training, and arming Zairean Hutus to fight with them for ethnic solidarity on either side of the Rwanda-Zaire border. Reports soon circulated of Hutu Power raiders getting on-the-job training—attacking Tutsi ranchers and pillaging their cattle—in the rich highland pastures of the Masisi region of North Kivu. By mid-1995, as Zairean tribal militias mounted a resistance, Masisi became known as a combat zone. "This is a direct conse-quence of the camps," a security officer at UNHCR headquarters in Goma told me, "and there's nothing we can do but watch."

Such expressions of helplessness were common among the re-lief workers who maintained the camps. The UNHCR's Jacques Franquin, a former theater director from Belgium who supervised camps that held more than four hundred thousand Rwandan Hu-tus in Tanzania, told me that he knew a number of *génocidaires* among them. "But don't ask me to sort them out," he said. "Don't ask me to take the criminals out of the camps and put humani-tarian workers in danger." What he meant—and what I heard repeatedly—was that so long as the major powers that sat on the Security Council and funded most humanitarian aid lacked the will to act against Hutu Power, humanitarians could not be blamed for the consequences.

"Food, shelter, water, health, sanitation—we do good aid," a relief agency boss in Goma told me. "That's what the international community wants, and that's what we give it." But if the faults of the international response did not originate within the relief in-dustry, they quickly took up residence there. Even if not taking sides were a desirable position, it is impossible to act in or on a political situation without having a political effect.

"The humanitarian mind-set is to not think—just to do," said a French UNHCR officer at the Rwandan camps in Burundi. "We're like robots, programmed to save some lives. But when the contracts are up, or when it gets too dangerous, we will leave and maybe the people we saved can get killed after all." Humanitarians didn't like to be called mercenaries, but "not to think—just to do," as the UNHCR worker put it, is a mercenary mind-set. As a Swiss delegate for the International Committee of the Red Cross told me, "When humanitarian aid becomes a smoke screen to cover the political effects it actually creates, and states hide behind it, using it as a vehicle for policymaking, then we can be regarded as agents in the conflict."

ACCORDING TO ITS mandate, the UNHCR provides assistance exclusively to refugees—people who have fled across an international border and can demonstrate a well-founded fear of persecution in their homeland—and fugitives fleeing criminal prosecution are explicitly disqualified from protection. The mandate also requires that those who receive UNHCR's assistance must be able to prove that they are properly entitled to refugee status. But no attempt was ever made to screen the Rwandans in the camps; it was considered far too dangerous. In other words, we—all of us who paid taxes in countries that paid the UNHCR —were feeding people who were expected to try to hurt us (or our agents) if we questioned their right to our charity.

Nobody knows exactly how many people were in the Zaire camps because no thorough census was ever attempted, and piecemeal efforts were programmatically, often violently, sabotaged by the *génocidaires*, who had a political interest in keeping numbers radically inflated, and liked the extra rations. The birth rate in the camps was close to the limit of human possibility; breeding more Hutus was Hutu Power policy, and the coerced impregnation of any female of reproductive age was regarded as a sort of ethnic public service among the resident *interahamwe*. At the same time, roughly half a million people had succeeded in returning to Rwanda from Zaire of their own accord in the first year after the genocide. Thereafter, the UNHCR claimed that the camp population stabilized at about a million and a quarter Rwandans, but a number of UNHCR staffers told me that its estimates were at least twenty percent too high.

The one sure statistic about the Zaire camps was that they cost their sponsors at least a million dollars a day. A dollar per person per day may not sound like much, especially when one considers that at least seventy percent of that money went right back into the pockets of the aid teams and their outfitters, in the form of overhead, supplies, equipment, staff housing, salaries, benefits, and other assorted expenses. But even if just twenty-five cents a day was being spent on each refugee, that was nearly twice the per capita income of most Rwandans. The World Bank found that Rwanda after the genocide had become the poorest country on earth, with an average income of eighty dollars a year. Since thousands of people in Rwanda were making thousands of dollars a year, at least ninety-five percent of the population was probably living on an average income closer to sixty dollars a year, or sixteen cents a day.

Under the circumstances, living in a refugee camp was not a bad economic proposition for a Rwandan, especially for one plugged into the Hutu Power patronage network. Food was not only free, but ample; malnutrition rates in the camps were far lower than anywhere else in the region, on a par, in fact, with those of Western Europe. General medical care was also as good as it got in central Africa; Zaireans who lived in Goma spoke enviously of refugee entitlements, and several told me they had pretended to be refugees in order to gain admission to camp clinics. After having all essential living expenses covered by charity, camp residents were free to engage in commerce, and aid agencies frequently provided enticements—like agricultural supplies—to do so. The major camps in Zaire quickly became home to the biggest, best-stocked, and cheapest markets in the region. Zaireans came for miles to shop *chez les Rwandais*, where at least half the trade appeared to be in humanitarian-aid stuffs—beans, flour, and oil, spilling from sacks and tins stamped with the logos of foreign donors. And, as the *interahamwe* and ex-FAR stepped up their attacks on the Tutsi herdsmen of North Kivu, the Goma camp markets became famous for incredibly cheap beef.

The camps were cramped, smoky, and smelly, but so were the homes many Rwandans had fled; and unlike most Rwandan villages, the main thoroughfares of the big camps were lined with well-stocked pharmacies, two-story video bars powered by generators, libraries, churches, brothels, photo studios—you name it. Humanitarians showing me around often sounded like proud landlords, saying things like "Great camp," even as they said, "These poor people," and asked, "What are we doing?"

The profits from refugee commerce went in many directions, but large slices went straight through the political rackets into the purchase of arms and munitions. Richard McCall, chief of staff of the United States Agency for International Development, described Zaire as "an unfettered corridor for arms shipment" to the *génocidaires*. The UNHCR, more cautiously, made similar statements, but that never stopped it from asking for more money to keep the camps going.

Officially, the UNHCR's policy in the border camps was to promote "voluntary repatriation." At first, this was done by having people sign up a day or two in advance for buses that would take them back to Rwanda. When a number of the people who did that got beaten or killed before their departure date, it was decided simply to station idling buses in the camps every morning, and let those who wanted make a run for them. Not surprisingly, that program, too, was soon judged a failure. "What is voluntary?" General Kagame once asked me. "It normally means that somebody has to think and make a decision. I don't think that even staying in the camps is a voluntary decision for the innocent people. I believe there is some influence. So how can we speak of them leaving voluntarily?"

In fact, influence against returning to Rwanda often came from within the very humanitarian community that was ostensibly promoting repatriation. "It's not safe for them to go home," I was told by one aid worker after another. "They could get arrested." But what if they deserved to be arrested? "We can't judge that," I was told, and then, to finish the discussion, it was usually said, "Anyway, the government in Kigali doesn't genuinely want them back." Of course, very few of the people working in the camps had ever spent any time in Rwanda; their organizations did not encourage it. So, with time, there developed among them an epidemic of what diplomats call clientitis: an overly credulous embrace of your clients' point of view. As soon as I crossed back over the border to Rwanda, I felt that I'd passed through a looking glass. At UNHCR Goma, I would be told that Rwanda was determined to prevent repatriation and that returnees were frequently harassed just to ensure that the rest of the refugees stayed away. But at UNHCR Kigali, I would be regaled with statistics and arguments demonstrating not only that Rwanda wanted the refugees home but that those who had come back were received with all due propriety.

In June of 1995, Zaire's Prime Minister, Kengo Wa Dondo, visited Goma, and delivered a speech in which he said that if the international community wouldn't shut down the camps, Zaire would be obliged to send the Rwandans home. That August, Zairean soldiers did move on the camps, and in traditionally roughshod manner—lots of shakedowns, and torched huts—they hustled about fifteen thousand Rwandans across the border in less than a week. That was more than the UNHCR had accomplished in the preceding six months. But the UNHCR opposed forced repatriation—unless, as Gerald Gahima at Rwanda's Justice Ministry reminded me, you happened to be a Vietnamese boat person in Hong Kong. The UN refugee commissioner herself, Sadako Ogata, persuaded President Mobutu to call off his boys—it was widely rumored that he was paid cash—and the repatriation "deadlock" that she often decried to the Security Council promptly resumed.

Press coverage of the Zairean action stressed the numerous violations of international humanitarian law that the refugees—mostly older people, women, and children, who were unable to run away—had suffered. There were almost no follow-up stories from the Rwandan side of the border, and events there *were* rather dull: the refugees were smoothly resettled in their communities, arrest rates were below average, and the Kigali office of the UNHCR, impressed by the government's handling of the matter, proclaimed it an auspicious demonstration of Rwanda's sincerity in calling its people home.

"THERE'S NO WAY you can stop the international community from coming, given a situation like a genocide," General Kagame once said to me. "But they may provide the wrong remedies to our problems. On the one hand, they admit that a genocide took place in Rwanda, but they don't seem to understand that someone was responsible for it, that someone planned and executed it. That's why we get confused when there are insinuations that we should negotiate. When you ask, 'With whom?' they cannot tell you. They can't quite bring themselves to say that we should negotiate with the people who committed genocide. Of course, in the long run they create a bigger problem, because the genocide can be made to seem less and less visible as a very big crime that people should be hunted for and prosecuted." What's more, Kagame said, "there are some directly innocent people in those camps, and this has been a very bad situation for them. At least here in Rwanda, although some incidents may take place, there is some level of sanity. It may not be pleasant, it may not be the best, but it is the best in these circumstances."

I told him I kept meeting Rwandans who said that Rwandans never tell the truth, that Rwanda has a culture of dishonesty, that to understand Rwanda one has to get inside that realm of mystification. I wondered what he thought.

"Maybe even those who're saying that are not speaking the truth," he said, and let out an unusually hearty laugh. Then he said, "I don't think it's our culture, especially since I don't see a lot of honesty in politics in many other countries. But in some other countries, when you try to tell lies you are exposed by strong institutions that work to know what exactly has been happening." He fell silent for a moment. Then he said, "Personally, I have no problem with telling the truth, and I'm Rwandan, so why don't people also take me as an example of a Rwandan? People have even told me that perhaps, in politics, sometimes there are certain things you don't say that I have been saying publicly. The more they tell me that, the more I get convinced I am right."

In Kagame's view, lying was not a Rwandan trait but a political tactic, and he thought it a weak one. That didn't mean that you shouldn't keep secrets; but secrets, even if they involve deception, aren't necessarily lies—just truths you don't tell. In a world where politicians were presumed to be liars, Kagame had found that one could often gain a surprise advantage by not being false. "Sometimes," he said, "you tell the truth because that is the best way out."

If there is one thing sure in this world, it is certainly this: that it will not happen to us a second time.

—PRIMO LEVI, 1958
Survival in Auschwitz

It happened, therefore it can happen again: this is the core of what we have to say. It can happen, and it can happen everywhere.

—PRIMO LEVI, 1986
The Drowned and the Saved

18

IN THE FOOTHILLS of the Virunga volcanoes, in the Masisi zone of North Kivu, Zaire, on a rise overlooking a lakeside peasant village called Mokoto, there stood the ruin of a monastery which might have been taken for a relic of medieval Europe. But this ruin was new. Until early May of 1996, Mokoto operated very much like an ancient cathedral town. While the villagers lived below, in huts made mostly of mud brick and thatch, Trappist monks on the hill lived in an imposing compound of masonry and fine woodwork, with a large church, a library, a hostel for visitors, a dairy with nearly a thousand cows, a motor-vehicle repair shop, and an electrical plant powered by a waterwheel. The monastery was the chief provider of social services to Mokoto and neighboring villages; the monks ran six schools and a dispensary, and they had designed a waterworks for the villagers, who had previously spent much of their time carrying buckets. In January and February of 1996, when hundreds of people began showing up at the monastery, seeking sanctuary from bands of attackers who had chased them from their homes, Father Dhelo, the Zairean superior at Mokoto, did not hesitate to take them in.

Father Dhelo knew that the displaced people were Tutsis fleeing the attacks of Hutus led by the ex-FAR and *interahamwe* from the UN camps in Goma, which lay about thirty rugged miles

southeast of Mokoto. Since early 1996, as some Western governments began to tire of paying for the camps, rumors had prolif-
erated about aid being shut down or the camps being forced to
close, and the resident *génocidaires* and their Zairean Hutu allies
had intensified and expanded their war in North Kivu. The effort
now appeared to be to "ethnically cleanse" the mountainous agricultural heartland of North Kivu, with the objective of creating
a more permanent Hutu Power base, which was already being
informally referred to throughout the region as Hutuland.

Father Dhelo knew all this, and he knew that in 1994 the
génocidaires had not hesitated to violate the sanctuary of churches
in Rwanda. But when local Hutu leaders threatened to kill him
for giving sanctuary to the displaced Tutsis at Mokoto, he refused
to be intimidated. "I said to them that if they thought my death
could solve the problem and I would die alone, I would be content
to die," Father Dhelo told me. "After that, they didn't come for
me." Then, in early May, Father Dhelo went away on business.

Close to a thousand Tutsis were camped around the monastery
at the time. According to Father Victor Bourdeau, a French monk
who had lived at Mokoto for seventeen years, a Hutu mob assembled around the camp on the evening of Wednesday, May 8. Shots
were fired in the air, and hundreds of Tutsis took refuge inside
the church. On Friday, the monastery received warning that a major attack was planned. There was no safe way to move the Tutsis
out, but most of the monks were evacuated; Father Victor was one
of six who stayed until Sunday, May 12. That morning, Hutu fighters forced their way into the church, dragged some Tutsis outside,
and executed them with machetes. "There was nothing to be
done," Father Victor said. He and his fellow monks fled on a
tractor.

When I met the Mokoto monks nine days later, they were
displaced people themselves, living in temporary quarters in
Goma. Father Victor, a tall, slender man with the anxious look of
an ascetic, sat in his khaki cassock on a cot in a small stuffy room.

"Everybody in the village was an accomplice, by silence or by looting, and it is impossible to divide the responsibility," he said. "It's like in Rwanda—one can't say all of them are guilty, but to sort it out is impossible." Father Victor had been in Kigali on April 7, 1994, the day after Habyarimana's assassination, and he told me, "It was exactly the same scenario."

MOKOTO'S ISOLATION WAS such that it took three days for news of the monastery massacre to reach Kigali, where I was staying at the time. The story fit the pattern of recent events. In the preceding month and a half, at least ten thousand Tutsis had been chased out of North Kivu and forced to take refuge in Rwanda. The Rwandan government had accused Zaire of complicity in their expulsion, since its troops had often trucked Tutsis to the border, then confiscated or ripped up their Zairean citizenship papers. Zairean officials responded by invoking a much disputed and never enforced nationality law, passed in 1981 in violation of Zaire's own constitution and a host of international legal conventions, that stripped Zaireans of Rwandan ancestry of their citizenship, rendering them stateless. "These refugees from North Kivu are Zaireans," General Kagame's adviser, Claude Dusaidi, told me. "We ask for our citizens to return from the camps, and they send us theirs. They must take them back and give us ours."

As reports of the Mokoto massacre began to circulate in Kigali, similar expressions of outrage greeted me at every Rwandan government office I visited. If Zaire had it in for ancestral Rwandans, I was asked, why were Zairean Tutsis being singled out while Zairean and Rwandan Hutus killed them with impunity? "It's really a genocide going on again," Dusaidi said, "but supported by Zaire against its own citizens." I was repeatedly reminded that Zaire's President, Mobutu Sese Seko, had backed Habyarimana's fight against the RPF, facilitated arms shipments to Rwanda during the genocide, provided bases for the French forces of *Opération Turquoise*, and abetted the resurgent Hutu Power forces in the

279

border camps. A UN investigative team had just published a report showing that the infamous Colonel Bagasora of the ex-FAR traveled under Zairean military papers to the Seychelles to purchase weaponry and munitions. In the first half of 1996, as the war in North Kivu grew fiercer, attacks against Rwanda by the Hutu Power forces in Zaire had also intensified and infiltrators killed hundreds of genocide survivors in an effort that the organization African Rights described as "killing the evidence." So it particularly galled Rwandan officials that the international community kept pouring money into Zaire by way of the camps, but did nothing to hold Mobutu accountable for the actions of his genocidal guests.

Mobutu was the longest-ruling despot in Africa. His ascent to power, between 1960 and 1965, had been accomplished with the careful assistance of the CIA and various bands of white mercenaries through the violent suppression of the popularly elected Congolese national movement, and his endurance was due, in large measure, to his genius for turning the misery of his neighbors to his own advantage. During the Cold War, the United States and its allies propped him up as a bulwark against Communist forces in central Africa. Then the wall came down in Berlin, and Mobutu was no longer of use. Promoting democracy was the new dispensation, and when Mobutu failed to produce anything but a violent parody of multiparty reforms, his erstwhile Western patrons cut him loose. His immense country—the size of Western Europe or the United States east of the Mississippi—was loaded with cobalt, diamonds, gold, and uranium, and he was rumored to be one of the wealthiest men in the world. But by the end of 1993, as his unpaid army ran riot, murdering, looting, and raping its way through the land, Zaire was enduring ten thousand percent inflation, and Mobutu, ostracized, and unable to get a visa to the United States or Europe, appeared headed for ruin. Then the Rwandan genocide put him back in the spotlight—this time as the man who had to be dealt with if you wanted to deal with the refugees.

Once again, Western leaders turned to Mobutu as a power broker in regional affairs; emissaries of the United States, the European Union, and the UN Secretariat shuttled in and out of Gbadolite, the vast jungle palace where Mobutu held court and where Habyarimana was entombed. France, ever eager to bail out Hutu Power, broke ranks with the rest of what in Cold War parlance used to be called "the free world," and unilaterally restored aid to Zaire—which meant, of course, to Mobutu, who shoveled the money directly into his Swiss bank accounts. "That genocide," a European diplomat told me, "was a gift from God for Mobutu." The Rwandan officials I spoke with believed that Mobutu, by tolerating and even encouraging the creation of a highly militarized Hutuland in Zaire, was seeking to ensure that this gift would keep giving.

"If anybody thinks Mobutu can continue to fool people, I don't think it's going to take very long to show people that we're not fools," Colonel Karemera, Rwanda's Minister of Health, warned. The last battalions of UNAMIR had finally withdrawn from Rwanda in April of 1996, and one month later it seemed that the war everyone had been waiting for was getting underway. "Zaire is just provoking and provoking," Claude Dusaidi told me at the Ministry of Defense. "If Zaire wants to expel its citizens and give them to us, let Zaire give them with their land." I heard this line so often from officials in Kigali that I asked Dusaidi, who was famously blunt, if Rwanda was preparing to invade Zaire. "We have enough problems," he said. "We don't have to go beyond our borders to get frustrated. But if we wanted North Kivu, we would go take it."

FOLLOWING THE MASSACRE at the Mokoto monastery, hundreds of Tutsi survivors managed to flee and take refuge in a nearby Zairean village. I wanted to know what was to become of them there. On my way to the border, I stopped at a camp in northwestern Rwanda where thousands of Zairean Tutsis recently expelled from North Kivu were being held. I spoke to about a dozen men, who said that when the Hutu Power attacks began early in 1996, Zaire had sent troops. The Tutsis had expected that the troops would defend them, that Zaire would protect its own people. Instead, most of the soldiers had joined in robbing them, and then forcing them across the border. "They made us pay them for transport to the frontier," said a man, whose outfit—a pair of heavy-duty cross-country ski boots and an Icelandic sweater—testified to his sudden dependence on handouts.

The Tutsi refugees from Zaire were convinced that Mobutu was behind their troubles. "He's a very strong man," said a refugee who had been a Zairean civil servant for decades. "He's been there thirty years, and every time he has domestic opposition he allows a civil conflict, then puts it down, and says, '*Voilà*, peace.'" The refugees also believed that Mobutu could restore order if he chose to. After all, his full, self-given name, Mobutu Sese Seko Kuku Ngbendu Wa Za Banga, has been translated as "the all-powerful warrior who, by his endurance and will to win, goes from conquest to conquest, leaving fire in his wake," and also as "the cock who leaves no hen alone." Nobody seemed to doubt that everything that happened in his realm was his doing, by dint of his actions or inactions, and that the end result would be just what he intended.

But Mobutu didn't want outsiders to see the work in progress. When I arrived at the border, I learned that Zaire was not admitting journalists. "They want to camouflage the total disorder," said a Rwandan mechanic, returning from a day trip to Goma. "That country is finished. Businesses are pulling out." But the border guards didn't know me, and the customs men who grabbed my bag never even looked in it: what they wanted was ransom, a little drinking money, and three dollars sufficed.

Zaire, as a state, had long been considered a phantom construct. Its very name, which Mobutu had conjured up as part of a program of "authenticity," was a bit of make-believe: "Zaire" was an antique Portuguese bastardization of a local word for river. And Mobutu, who liked to appear on television in clips that showed him walking among the clouds in his trademark leopard-skin hat and dark glasses, had gone further, claiming the Adamic power of renaming all of his subjects—or, at least, requiring them to abandon their Christian names and take up African ones. In pursuit of the "authentic" he also nationalized all foreign businesses, put in place a constitution granting himself absolute power, prescribed a national dress code (neckties and suits were outlawed in favor of a snappily modified Mao shirt known as an *abacos*— short for *à bas les costumes*, "down with suits"); he replaced crucifixes with his portrait, struck Christmas from the holiday calendar, and purged every vestige of political opposition. "We are resorting to this authenticity," he once said, "in order to rediscover our soul which colonization had almost erased from our memories and which we are seeking in the tradition of our ancestors."

Mobutu's principle, then, was a double negative: to erase the corrupt memory that had erased the genuine national memory, and thus to restore that original chain of memory. The idea was romantic, nostalgic, and fundamentally incoherent. The place Mobutu called Zaire had never been a nation before the rapacious King Leopold II, King of the Belgians, drew its map, and the very word "authenticity"—an import from the French existentialism that had been the vogue during Mobutu's youth—was blatantly at odds with his professed Africanism. One is reminded of Pol Pot, who returned to Cambodia after studying in Paris, changed his country's name to Kampuchea, chucked out the calendar, proclaimed "Year Zero," and slaughtered a million or more of his countrymen to eradicate Western influences.

Mobutu, to magnify his own grandeur, systematically reduced Zaire to rot, and—despite the defiantly determined spirit of the great mass of Zaireans, who went on procreating, schooling, praying, trading, and debating with some eloquence their prospects for political emancipation—an alarming number of Western commentators took cynical solace in the conviction that this state of affairs was about as authentic as Africa gets. Leave the natives to their own devices, the thinking went, and—*Voilà!*— Zaire. It was almost as if we *wanted* Zaire to be the Heart of Darkness; perhaps the notion suited our understanding of the natural order of nations.

Of course, Mobutu was never more than a capricious puppet of his Western patrons, and ultimately even the idea of authenticity was abandoned to decay, as he shed any pretext of ideology in favor of absolute gangsterism. Zaireans—who used to be obliged to gather and chant Mobutist slogans like "It is better to die of hunger than to be rich and a slave to colonialism!"—watched Mobutu grow richer while they grew hungrier. With time, some even dared to modify Mobutu's pet mantra about the "Three Z's"—Zaire the country, Zaire the river, and Zaire the currency —by privately adding a fourth Z: Zaire the Zero.

All that remained of the state were the chief, his cronies, and his troops—a vampire elite, presiding over nearly a million square miles of decay. The so-called eleventh commandment of Mobutism was *"Débrouillez-vous"*— "Fend for yourselves"—and for at least a generation it had been the only absolute law of the land. Foreign visitors to Zaire were forever marveling that the place managed to survive at all. How did the center hold? A better question might have been whether there was a center. Having allowed his country to unravel, Mobutu liked to pretend that he alone kept it together, and as the war in North Kivu began to heat up, what worried many Zaireans and foreign diplomats even more than Zaire under Mobutu was the thought of Zaire after Mobutu.

"Tribal war and disaster," my cabdriver said as we tooled into Goma, traveling in the oncoming lane of a divided boulevard because it was the side with shallower potholes. "In the end we'll all

284

pay for it." A tour of the humanitarian agencies produced no better news. A convoy of three trucks belonging to CARE had been shot up the week before by machine guns and rocket-propelled grenades on the road near one of the UN camps. Thirteen Zaireans had been killed, and I found several Western aid workers with lakefront houses checking on the condition of their inflatable Zodiac boats, in case—or in hope—of an evacuation.

Everyone had stories of fighting in the hills, but little concrete information. At UNHCR headquarters, I found the repatriation officer sitting before a spanking clean desk. "Forget repatriation," he told me; he was applying for a new post.

ONE WEEK AFTER the killings at Mokoto, I drove into the combat zone of North Kivu. The road ran west from Goma across the lava field, skirting the giant Mugunga refugee camp, where about a hundred and fifty thousand Rwandans lived in a sea of shanties draped with UN-issue blue plastic sheeting. A few miles on lay Lac Vert, the ex-FAR headquarters. The paved road ended in the town of Sake, a derelict settlement crammed with about thirty thousand people of the Hunde tribe, who had been chased out of the hills by Hutu fighters. Hundes, like Hutus, were mostly subsistence farmers, and the two groups' rivalry was entirely economic and political. "Morphologically, we are the same," one Zairean Hutu observed, employing the vocabulary of European "race science" to assert that there was no ethnic animus in the Hutu-Hunde conflict.

Beyond Sake, a dirt road rose sharply through the dense vegetation of the rain-soaked volcanic massif. We soon came to a clearing, and my driver gave me the name of a village. But there was no village, only plots of land where a village once stood, some charred beams, bits of smashed crockery, and sometimes a few bright flowers in a row that implied a human hand. We drove for an hour without seeing anyone—past the sacked homes of Hundes and the abandoned homes of Hutus, many of whom were said to have taken refuge with the Rwandans in the camps. Masisi was known as the breadbasket of Zaire, a zone so fertile, so temperate, and so moist that some crops would yield four harvests a year. Now the devastation appeared complete, except for occasional carefully tilled fields of vegetables, their greenery iridescent beneath low dark clouds that sporadically dumped a few minutes of bright rain.

Along steep, rutted switchbacks, the irregular hills tilted at obscure angles, opening at times into deep ravines with tumbling cataracts, then closing in with a forest of eucalyptus. It was a landscape well worth fighting for, but I couldn't understand the endless procession of desolated villages. When you expel people and conquer territory, don't you occupy it? Weren't these hills supposed to be packed with Hutus? Or was the land just being prepared for the day when the money ran out in the camps? When at last we came to a village with a few people—Hutus and Zairean soldiers—my driver didn't think it advisable to stop and ask what their long-term strategy was.

At the top of the escarpment the forests fell back and the vast alpine pastures of Tutsi herdsmen opened out, rolling over the domes of the hills and folding into the valleys. But there weren't any Tutsis, and there weren't any cattle. After four hours on the deserted road, we had covered about fifty miles and reached Kitchanga, a village where the Tutsis who fled from the Mokoto monastery had found temporary refuge. A large crowd stood outside a shack to buy pieces of a freshly butchered cow. The cow had also come from Mokoto—"rescued," villagers said, from the monastery's dairy; there was suddenly so much beef in town that ten dollars could buy almost thirty pounds of it.

But ten dollars wasn't enough to buy a Tutsi his life: the going rate for transport to the border was between twelve and fifteen dollars. Eight hundred of the Tutsis who had been attacked at Mokoto were now packed into a sodden and steaming thatch schoolhouse in Kitchanga, and they were too poor to pay for their own "ethnic cleansing."

A FEW DAYS before I arrived in Kitchanga, a relief team from Doctors Without Borders had driven up to the Mokoto monastery and found the road blocked by two charred, naked corpses; the hands, feet, and genitals had been cut off, the chests had been opened, and the hearts had been removed. The relief workers counted ten corpses and smelled many more; they estimated the dead to number at least a hundred. While they were at the monastery, some wounded Tutsis came out of the bush where they had been hiding. One was a naked boy who had contrived to cover only the back of his neck. When he let the covering fall away, they saw that his head had been cut almost halfway off, exposing his spine and a patch of cranium. A doctor had sewed the boy back together, and I saw him walking tentatively around an emergency field hospital at Kitchanga.

A barefoot man in a tattered raincoat and shorts at the village school, who identified himself as "the captain of the Mokoto refugees," said that many of the attackers had come from the UN camps. It was easy to identify them, he said, because "they spoke excellent Kinyarwanda and were well dressed," while "we Zaireans are hill people, and feel more at home in Swahili." He explained that some of his people had been able to flee when "the attackers, seeing others pillage, forgot killing to steal, and only came back later." The Mokoto survivors had straggled into Kitchanga empty-handed, and a few old men were wrapped only in blankets because their attackers had stripped them naked, intending to kill them. No one could count on being so lucky again. The captain told me that the Hutu Power militias at Mokoto had chanted, "Kill, kill, kill," and "This is how we fled our country." Unlike the Zairean Tutsi refugees I had met in Rwanda, who said their only hope was to return to Zaire, the captain of the Mokoto Tutsis had given up.

When he told me, "We want to go home," he meant Rwanda. "We have no nationality here," he said.

The Mwami of Kitchanga, the hereditary Hunde chief, a stout man in a brown velvet shirt, wire-rimmed spectacles, and a white baseball cap, agreed. "Truly," he said, "the Hutus want to exterminate all the Tutsis." His own people, too, were having a hard time protecting themselves: their fighters included boys of six and seven, and their arsenal consisted largely of spears, bows and arrows, and homemade rifles that fired nails. "It's not an automatic," the Mwami said of such a gun, "but it kills." Kitchanga, which was formerly home to a mixed population of about two thousand people, was now an exclusively Hunde stronghold whose ranks had been swollen by an influx of thirty-six thousand displaced people. The Red Cross and the UN estimated that about half the population of Masisi, some three hundred thousand people, were displaced from their homes. Even the Mwami was living in temporary housing; his estate five miles out of town had been destroyed. I found him drinking banana beer in his "office"—a gazebo made of UN plastic sheeting—and he told me that Kitchanga was a very hospitable place, but that by giving shelter to Tutsis, it was making itself a magnet for a Hutu attack. He wanted the Tutsis out of there.

The Tutsis had to be evacuated or they would be killed. The problem was that the way to the Rwandan border ran through Hutuland and past the camps. The word in Kitchanga was that the International Organization for Migration, an intergovernmental agency, had promised to come with a convoy of trucks, accompanied by hired Zairean soldiers for security, to take the Tutsis away. But nobody really trusted that this would happen.

DURING THE NIGHT in Kitchanga, I heard the distant pop of gunfire, and in the morning heavy fighting between Hutus and Hundes was reported north of the village. I was told to return to Goma. As I left, three fat pillars of smoke were rising across the valley where Hunde fighters were sacking a Hutu village. Along the road, displaced Hundes were marching toward Kitchanga—women with armchairs bound to their backs, men toting troughs for brewing banana beer, and a slender young man with a spear in one hand and a double bed on his head.

On my return to Goma, I learned that it was true that the International Organization for Migration had planned an evacuation convoy to rescue the Tutsis in Kitchanga, but the plan had been scrapped. The IOM mandate did not permit it to assist "internally displaced" people in crossing international borders. The UNHCR and dozens of other humanitarian organizations that had the lucrative catering contracts for the camps in Goma all had similar limitations in their mandates, which prevented them from saving the Mokoto survivors. Most aid organizations prohibited themselves from transporting anybody anywhere, and could provide relief only on the spot; many refused to conduct operations that involved armed security, lest their "neutrality" should be compromised; still others maintained that it would violate their humanitarian principles to further the aims of "ethnic cleansing" by removing Tutsis just because Hutus threatened them. Individual aid workers I spoke with agreed that it was more humane to "ethnically cleanse" people than to leave them to be murdered. But it became clear that their organizations' first commitment was not to protecting people but to protecting their mandates. "Everything is lies here," Father Victor, the Mokoto monk, told me in Goma. "All these organizations—they will give blankets, food, yes. But save lives? No, they can't."

Twelve days after the Mokoto massacre, Rwanda's ambassador to the United Nations called on the Security Council to "take immediate action to prevent genocide in eastern Zaire." Rwanda's request referred specifically to Mokoto and to the Tutsis who remained at Kitchanga. The Zairean mission to the UN countered that the conflict in North Kivu was "a completely internal situation" and was therefore none of the Security Council's business.

The government of Zaire denied any problem pertaining to "Kinyarwanda-speaking Zairean nationals," maintaining, absurdly, that "of the languages spoken in Zaire, Kinyarwanda is not one of them." Zaire also advised the Council that "the word 'genocide' is not a part of Zaire's political landscape." The Security Council did nothing; it didn't even register one of its boilerplate "expressions of concern."

When I returned to Kigali, I learned that some Tutsi businessmen in North Kivu were organizing an evacuation to rescue the Mokoto survivors at Kitchanga, and at the end of May more than a thousand of them were brought to the Rwandan border. Throughout June and July, Tutsi refugees continued to arrive in Rwanda, and as the fighting spread in eastern Zaire, Tutsis from much farther north began fleeing to Uganda. By late August, the eradication of Tutsis from North Kivu was believed to be nearly complete.

19

ON MY RETURN to Kigali from visiting the survivors of the Mokoto massacre in May of 1996, I had asked Kagame what he thought would become of the Tutsi refugees who were being expelled from Zaire into Rwanda. "Perhaps, if the young men have to fight, we shall train them," he said. A year later, he told me that the training had already been under way. Kagame had concluded that he could not fully dismantle the threat of the Hutu Power camps in Zaire unless "the kind of support they were getting from the Zairean government and the international community" was also brought to an end.

The world powers made it clear in 1994 that they did not care to fight genocide in central Africa, but they had yet to come up with a convincing explanation of why they were content to feed it. The false promise of protection represented by the camps placed Hutu civilians, as well as Tutsis and everyone else in the region, in mortal peril, and it was no comfort that this state of affairs was not brought about by a malevolent international policy in central Africa but by the lack of any coherent policy. In Washington, where 1996 was a presidential election year, one Clinton administration official was reported to have told a meeting of the National Security Council that the main policy concern in Rwanda and Zaire was that "we don't want to look like chumps." In Kigali, where the main concern was the threat of a Hutu Power invasion, Colonel Joseph Karemera, Rwanda's Minister of Health, asked me, "When the people receiving humanitarian assistance in those camps come and kill us, what will the international community do—send more humanitarian assistance?" Sometimes, Karemera said, he couldn't help feeling that "this international community is looking at us like we're from a different generation of human evolution."

In July of 1996, General Kagame visited Washington and explained once again that if the international community could not handle the monster it was incubating in the camps, he would. It was assumed that Kagame was bluffing; the thought of Rwanda invading Zaire was a bit like Liechtenstein taking on Germany or France. Mobutu sponsored invasions of his neighbors, not the other way around, and Mobutu was still Washington's hope for the region. "Occasionally," an American diplomat explained to me, "you have to dance with the devil to do the Lord's work." And in this, at least, Paris agreed. France remained Hutu Power's biggest advocate. The attitude toward Kagame's warnings among the Africa hands at the Quai d'Orsay seemed to be: let him try. (In 1995, the new French President, Jacques Chirac, had refused to invite Rwanda's new President, Pasteur Bizimungu, to an annual conference of Francophone African leaders in Biarritz, which opened with Chirac presiding over a moment of silence to honor the memory of President Habyarimana—and not the dead of the genocide that had been committed in Habyarimana's name.)

Shortly after Kagame's visit to Washington, Burundi's army moved to close all the camps for Rwandans on its territory. The UNHCR protested, but when Burundi refused to back down the refugee agency began to cooperate. Soon the refugees were jockeying to get on the trucks that shuttled back and forth across the border. In the course of a few weeks, two hundred thousand people were sent home, and the UN even took to describing the repatriation as voluntary. The Rwandan government broadcast the message that the returnees were to be welcomed in their communities and that they should get their homes back—and, as a rule, that was what happened. UN observers told me that arrest rates were lower than anticipated; in some cases notorious *génocidaires* were even denounced by fellow returnees.

I spent several days watching the convoys rolling in from Burundi. When I asked returnees if the repatriation was forced, they all said no. But when I asked why they had suddenly volunteered to come home, they said they'd had no choice. The answer was almost always the same: "Everybody was coming. We left together, so we returned together." One man, a bricklayer, who stood barefoot in ragged clothing amid his six children, said, "There are superiors"—he turned his eyes skyward—"who concern themselves with politics and affairs of humanity, and there are the simple people like us"—his eyes rolled down to stare at his feet—"who know nothing of politics and merely work with our hands to eat and live." The mass return from Burundi made it clearer than ever that the only obstacle to a comparable repatriation from Zaire was Hutu Power's ability to intimidate not only the camp populations but also the entire international community.

"I think we've learned a lot about the hypocrisy and double standards on the part of the people who claim they want to make this world a better place," General Kagame told me. "They turn it into a political problem, and say we cannot have the refugees back unless we forgive these fellows who committed the genocide." Kagame was indignant. "I say to them, 'We told you to separate those groups. You have failed. If you—the whole world put together—are unable to do this, how can you expect us to do much better? You hold us to a standard that has never existed on this earth. You want us to wake up one morning and have everything right—people walking hand in hand with one another, forgetting about the genocide, things moving smoothly. It sounds nice to talk about it.'"

At first, Kagame told me, he had assumed that dealing with

"people who had committed serious crimes against humanity" would be "the responsibility of the entire international community." He still thought it should be. "But that hasn't happened," he said. "So what remains is to turn around and fight another war."

SHORTLY AFTER THE RPF took Kigali in 1994, Kagame's old associate, President Museveni of Uganda, had introduced him to a Zairean named Laurent Désiré Kabila, who had been an anti-Mobutu rebel throughout the 1960s and 1970s, and who hoped to revive that struggle. Kagame, Museveni, and Kabila began establishing networks with Zaireans and other Africans who regarded Mobutu as a menace to stability and progress on the continent. "We used to say to the Zaireans, 'We know you are brewing trouble for us, but we shall brew trouble for you,'" Kagame told me. "We said, 'You need peace, we need peace, let's work together, but if you do not work with us—well.'"

Of course, there was no peace and no prospect of it, and by the middle of 1996, Kagame started assembling a seed force to mount a rebellion in Zaire. Zairean Tutsis, faced with the immediate threat of elimination, were ripe for recruitment, and they offered the added convenience of appearing and speaking enough like Rwandans so that if RPA soldiers mingled with them it would be difficult to tell them apart. But soldiers and political cadres were sought from throughout Zaire, and Kigali soon became the clandestine hub for all sorts of anti-Mobutists eager for armed struggle in Zaire.

After the destruction of the Tutsi communities of North Kivu, Kagame assumed that South Kivu would be the next target of the Mobutist–Hutu Power alliance, and he was not mistaken. About four hundred thousand Zairean Tutsis lived in South Kivu; they were known as the Banyamulenge—the people of Mulenge—because Mulenge was the place where their ancestors first settled after migrating from Rwanda in the seventeenth and eighteenth centuries. Since the establishment of the UN camps for Rwandan Hutus in 1994, the Banyamulenge had fallen prey to extensive cattle raids and to a mounting campaign of harassment and hostile propaganda. Before long Zairean officials were speaking openly of the Banyamulenge as "snakes" and taking measures to strip them of their land; local radio stations and newspapers sounded more and more like the Hutu Power media of Rwanda.

Programmatic violence against the Banyamulenge began in early September of 1996. Hutu Power and Mobutist forces, working together with locally recruited militias, sacked Tutsi homes, businesses, and churches and attacked their residents—arresting or executing some and expelling others to Rwanda. When Banyamulenge were lynched in the streets, government officials expressed approval. Although the UN and humanitarian agencies had teams throughout the area, there was no international outcry. But unlike the Tutsis of North Kivu, who went to their deaths and into exile without resistance, many Banyamulenge were armed and they fought back when attacked, inflicting substantial damage on their attackers. At the same time, hundreds of newly trained and well-equipped resistance fighters began to filter into Zaire from Rwanda. As the fighting intensified and spread, aid workers fled from much of South Kivu, abandoning those they had purported to protect to their own devices.

Then, on October 8, Lwasi Ngabo Lwabanji, deputy governor of South Kivu, proclaimed that all Banyamulenge residents of the province had one week to get out. He didn't say where they should go, only that those who remained would be considered to be rebels in a state of war with Zaire. No doubt Lwasi was a bit overexcited; even in Zaire, deputy governors did not customarily declare war. But the spirit of his ultimatum was firmly in line with official Zairean attitudes and practices. Although Mobutu himself had just been diagnosed with prostate cancer and was undergoing treatment in Switzerland, he had been running Zaire as an absentee landlord for so long that his court continued to function as ever.

Two days after Lwasi's decree, a government spokesman in Kinshasa, the capital of Zaire, announced, "It's true that we all want the Banyamulenge to leave."

Kagame had been preparing for just such a moment. "We were ready to hit them," he later told me, "hit them very hard—and handle three things: first to save the Banyamulenge and not let them die, empower them to fight, and even fight for them; then to dismantle the camps, return the refugees to Rwanda, and destroy the ex-FAR and militias; and, third, to change the situation in Zaire." He was only waiting for the sort of massive provocation from Zaire that he presumed was inevitable. "And of course," he said, "this stupid Zairean deputy governor gave us the opportunity."

So tiny Rwanda hit enormous Zaire; the Banyamulenge rose up; RPA commandos and Laurent Kabila's rebel seed force—the Alliance of Democratic Forces for the Liberation of Congo/Zaire (ADFL)—swept into South Kivu and began pushing north; Mobutu's famously cowardly army fled ragtag; aid workers were evacuated, and the camps were dispersed. On November 2, 1996, three and a half weeks after Deputy Governor Lwasi had declared civil war, the ADFL and the RPA marched into Goma, and Kabila proclaimed an area of at least a thousand square miles to be "liberated territory." (While the Rwandan government was openly enthusiastic about these developments, it categorically denied that any RPA troops had entered Zaire until early June of 1997, several weeks after the ADFL forces took Kinshasa and drove Mobutu from power, at which point Kagame told me, "Everywhere it was our forces, our troops—they've been walking for the last eight months.")

Thousands of Rwandans from the camps returned to Rwanda during the first weeks of fighting in Zaire, but by early November the great mass of them—at least three-quarters of a million people, from both North and South Kivu—were assembled on the vast lava field in and around the Mugunga camp, about ten miles west

296

of Goma. They had been herded there by the ex-FAR and the *interahamwe*, by the pressure of the advancing Alliance, and even, incredibly, by some UNHCR officers, who had directed them away from Rwanda and toward Mugunga before themselves fleeing the country. After capturing Goma, Kabila declared a cease-fire, and called on the international humanitarian community to come and get the refugees out of his way so that he could continue his advance westward. Of course, Mugunga was completely inaccessible, behind a powerfully armed front line composed of tens of thousands of Hutu Power and Mobutist fighters. And that was precisely the point that Kabila and his Rwandan sponsors were trying to make: to get the refugees out of harm's way, you had to be prepared to fight. What was needed was not a relief mission, but a rescue mission, because the noncombatants at Mugunga weren't so much refugees as hostages, being held as a human shield.

It was another very strange time. During the first nine and a half months of 1996, the fact that the Mobutist–Hutu Power alliance in eastern Zaire was slaughtering thousands of people and forcing hundreds of thousands more from their homes did not seem to excite the international press. During that period, exactly one dispatch on the subject, reported from Rwanda, appeared in my local paper, *The New York Times*, and in its competition, *The Washington Post*, coverage had been limited to two freelance "opinion" pieces. Perhaps the idea that people called refugees not only suffer and require aid but also are capable of systematic crimes against humanity, and may require direct confrontation by military force, was considered too technical or confusing in an age of radically reduced foreign coverage. But, in early November, the prospect of three-quarters of a million refugees dying en masse, under siege or in battle on the lava fields, once more drew a pack of hundreds of reporters to the Rwanda-Zaire border. Goma was again the world's leading international story—and nothing was happening.

Nobody could get to Mugunga, and nobody knew what condition the people gathered there were in. Relief agency press officers assured reporters that the refugees had to be suffering from mass starvation and cholera. Possible death tolls were invented and announced—tens of thousands of dead, perhaps a hundred thousand. It was terribly upsetting to be sitting at a lakefront hotel in the Rwandan border town of Gisenyi, surrounded by reporters, and to think that just a dozen miles to the west, out of sight and out of reach, people were dying the most preventable sorts of deaths at a record-breaking clip. And it made one feel even worse to wonder if maybe the situation over there wasn't really so bad. If you asked the relief agency press officers when, in history, previously well-fed people had starved to death in a few weeks, you either got no answer or you were told that most of the people at Mugunga were *women and children.*

From New York, the Secretary-General of the United Nations, Boutros Boutros-Ghali, pronounced that "genocide by starvation" was taking place at Mugunga. Boutros-Ghali had no evidence that anybody was even hungry, and he certainly could not say who was committing this alleged genocide, since refugees could only be hungry because they were being blocked from leaving, and the only people blocking them were other so-called refugees. Still, with reports of famine and mass death among the invisible refugees filling the television news, the Security Council started to draw up plans to deploy a humanitarian, military intervention force to Goma, ostensibly to liberate the refugee masses at Mugunga. This sounded promising, until it emerged that the proposed force might be proscribed by its mandate from doing the one thing that it was needed to do, which was to *use* force to confront, to disarm, or, if necessary, to overwhelm the Hutu Power army and militias.

AT NINE IN the morning on November 15, 1996, I sat in a house on a hill in Gisenyi overlooking Goma, taking notes from the BBC radio news:

Canadian UN-force commander stresses force will *not* disarm or separate militants at Mugunga. Late night UN resolution leaves vague how feeding refugees and at the same time encouraging them to return to Rwanda will work. There's talk of soldiers fanning out from bases in Goma to find and feed refugees. But UN says it won't reestablish camps. Canadian commander says, "In order to separate militias, the level of violence would be too high and not only soldiers but innocents would be killed."

I also wrote my impressions of this news:

Another lame UN force. Innocents are getting killed, have been getting killed, and will get killed however this plays out. And how can you feed hundreds of thousands, dig them holes to shit in, give them plastic sheets to sleep under, and say you haven't established a camp? Anyway, why use an army in a place you don't care enough to kill and die for? Total paralysis.

Then I switched stations to Radio Star, the rebel "voice of the liberated Congo" from Goma, and took more notes:

The road to Mugunga and west is open. The *interahamwe* have fled. Announcer says, "The whole problem is cleaned up." Refugees are marching home to Rwanda. The rebellion continues on to Kinshasa.

This time, my impressions were briefer: "Huh? Can it be?"
I ran out the door, drove to the border and across, into Goma, where I turned onto the Mugunga road, heading west toward the camp, and found myself inching along against a stream of hundreds of thousands of Rwandans heading east, trudging steadily home. Over the preceding days, it turned out, the ADFL and the

RPA had again taken the offensive, encircling Mugunga, and attacking it from the rear, in such a way as to draw the armed elements away from the border while pushing the refugee masses homeward. The main evidence of the battle lay nearly twenty miles beyond the camp itself—a line of blown-up trucks, buses, and cars that had been headed toward the Zairean interior. Fluttering around them on the road were heaps of papers, including much of the archive of the ex-FAR high command: receipts for arms shipments from dealers all over Europe, charters for the creation of political front organizations among the refugees, tax collection tables for the camps, accounts of financial transactions with humanitarian agencies, correspondence with Mobutu and his generals—even meticulously handwritten lists of Tutsis in North Kivu.

As the return got under way, it was widely reported that the ex-FAR and the *interahamwe* had retreated deeper into Zaire with the remnants of Mobutu's army, allowing the so-called ordinary refugees to head home. The reality was not so perfect: among those who fled west into Zaire's jungles—perhaps a hundred and fifty thousand people, perhaps twice as many; nobody knows—there were many noncombatants; and inside Rwanda, it quickly became clear that a great number of people with crimes to answer for had melted into the flood of returnees. But the immediate threat to Rwanda of a renewed total war had been removed, and—happily—it appeared that the refugees had not starved in the process.

All along the road to Mugunga and in the rat-infested wreckage of the camp itself, I found aid workers shaking their heads and marveling at the fact that most of the refugees still had at least a few days' rations and the strength to walk as much as fifteen or twenty miles a day at a brisk clip, carrying impressive loads under a fierce sun. In just four days, some six hundred thousand Rwandans marched back across the border from Goma. By the end of November, the total number of returnees was said to be around seven hundred thousand, and thousands more kept straggling in. Although the Rwandan government continued to issue adamant denials of military involvement in Zaire, General Kagame himself was less guarded. "Because we are not necessarily unhappy about what's happened—and, on top of that, what has happened is what we would have wished to have happened—I'm sure people would be right to suspect our involvement," he told me. What's more, he added, "We have the satisfaction that, on our part, we have always tried to do what we thought was right. There can never be greater satisfaction for me than this. I think it's a good lesson for some of us. We can achieve a lot by ourselves for ourselves, and we've got to keep struggling to do that. If people can help, that's all well and good. If they can't, we should not just disappear from the surface of this earth."

DURING THE DAYS I spent on the road amid the returning six hundred thousand, I was repeatedly visited by an image—remembered or imagined from various paintings and movies—of the Napoleonic armies straggling home from Russia: limping hussars and frozen horses, blood on the snow, the sky a blackness, mad eyes fixed forward. The weather was kinder in Africa, and the people on the road were mostly in good health, but that recurrent image of another time and place made me wonder why we in the West today have so little respect for other people's wars. The great homeward trundling of these Rwandans marked the rout, at least for the moment, of an immense army dedicated to genocide, yet the world had succored that army for years in the name of humanitarianism.

"To you we were just dots in the mass," one returnee observed, after I had spent the first days of the migration driving through the boiling swarm on the road from Mugunga. They had always sworn, in the camps, that they would go home as they had left—en masse, as one. To be dots in the mass was precisely the point: it was impossible to know who was who. They came at a rate of twelve thousand an hour (two hundred a minute), a human battering ram aimed at the frontier. But this wasn't quite the triumphant invasion long promised by the extremist Hutu leaders; rather, it was a retreat from exile conducted in near-silence. At one point, through the men and women and children pouring over fifty miles of blacktop, pushing bicycles, wheelbarrows, motorbikes, even automobiles, dragging wooden crates like sleds, balancing enormous bundles on their heads, toting babies in slings and cradling them in their arms, carrying steamer trunks and empty beer bottles, and sometimes carrying nothing but the burden of their pasts, there came four men shouldering a blanket-draped figure on a stretcher. As they pushed through the knotted thousands, one kept saying, "A cadaver, a cadaver." What made this man singular was his need to declare himself. Except for the knock of cooking pots, the swish of bare feet and rubber sandals, and the bleat of a stray goat or a lost child, the homecoming throng, as a rule, was ominously mute.

Back in Rwanda, thousands stood for hours along the roads watching the influx with the same wordless intensity. Never before in modern memory had a people who slaughtered another people, or in whose name the slaughter was carried out, been expected to live with the remainder of the people that was slaughtered, completely intermingled, in the same tiny communities, as one cohesive national society.

20

"A CERTAIN GIRUMUHATSE is back," an old woman in the highlands of central Rwanda told me a few weeks after the mass return from Goma. She spoke in Kinyarwanda, and as she spoke her right hand described a graceful chopping motion against the side of her neck. Her full statement was translated like this: "A certain Girumuhatse is back, a man who beat me during the war with a stick, and from whom I received a machete blow also. This man threw me in a ditch after killing off my whole family. I was wounded. He's now at his house again. I saw him yesterday at the community office after he registered. I told him, 'Behold, I am risen from the dead,' and he replied, 'It was a human hell,' and he asked my pardon. He said, 'It was the fault of the authorities who led us in these acts, seeking their own gains.' He said he regretted it, and he asked my pardon."

The woman gave her name as Laurencie Nyirabeza. She was born in 1930, in the community of Taba, a few minutes' walk from where we met in the shade of an empty hilltop market above a small commercial center—two short rows of derelict concrete and adobe storefronts on either side of a sandy red-dirt road. Twice a week, on market days, the center was teeming; otherwise, it had the air of a ghost town. The rusting hull of a burned-out bus lay on the road's shoulder and thick bushes sprouted from the prom-

303

inent ruins of a large home that had belonged to Tutsis, killed in 1994.

Most of Taba's Tutsis were killed then. Those who remained, like Nyirabeza, were quite alone, and nearly all had lost their homes. With no means to rebuild, and afraid to stay amid neighbors whose conduct during the killings they remembered too well, many survivors had moved to this center to squat in the stores left vacant by dead Tutsis or by Hutus who had fled to Zaire. Now they feared eviction. In the preceding two weeks, more than two thousand people had returned to Taba from the camps in Zaire, and among them was the man, Girumuhatse, who Laurencie Nyirabeza said had massacred her family and left her, too, for dead.

Nyirabeza was a small woman with eyes set deep in a face that thrust forward. She wore her hair combed straight up from the slope of her forehead in a crown nearly six inches high. The effect was at once imposing and witty, which was in keeping with her manner. More than a dozen survivors had responded to my invitation to meet in the market, but most said nothing. The voices of those who did speak rarely rose above a furtive murmur, and whenever a stranger approached, they fell silent. Nyirabeza was different. She did not whisper or shrink. She seemed to feel she had little left to lose. Even as she told me about Girumuhatse, her lips occasionally twitched in a smile, and more than once the other survivors responded to her speech with edgy laughter. Nyirabeza described herself as "a simple peasant"; her schooling had ended after the third grade. But she had a way with words—spirited and wry, and barbed with the indignation of her injury. Still, she said she had been shocked speechless when Girumuhatse, her former neighbor, with whom she used to share food and drink, claimed that his acts were not his fault. Girumuhatse had killed ten members of her family, she told me, mostly her children and grandchildren.

"This man who is responsible for his acts," Nyirabeza said, "lives now with all his family and gets his property back, while I remain alone, without a child, without a husband." Then she said—and this was one time there was a ripple of laughter—"Maybe he will continue these acts of extermination." She scoffed at Girumuhatse's request for her pardon. "If he can bring back my children whom he killed and rebuild my house," she said, "maybe." There was more laughter from the survivors.

Then a man said wearily, "We'll live together as usual," and Nyirabeza walked away. A moment later a woman began weeping, hiding her face in her dress. Another woman, very old and leaning on a long, thin staff, held out her hands and flapped them up and away from her body. "We're just like birds," she said with a distant smile. "Flying around, blown around."

As I walked back down the hill, I found Nyirabeza crouched on a stone, staring out over the valley. She did not look up when I said goodbye. A young civil servant, a survivor himself, who had been helping me as a translator, told me that people generally don't like to visit the center. "It's sad," he said, "and the survivors there ask for things."

It was true that the survivors made heavy demands. At one point Nyirabeza had said, "I wait only for justice."

I WAS SURPRISED when Laurencie Nyirabeza said that Girumuhatse had not denied attacking her. In my time in Rwanda, I had never encountered anyone who admitted to having taken part in the genocide. I wanted to hear what Girumuhatse had to say for himself, and two days later I returned to Taba with a French-speaking Rwandan named Bosco, an unemployed florist who had agreed to come along as a translator. We stopped first to see Nyirabeza, because she had suggested that Girumuhatse might still want to kill her. But she refused to be intimidated; she sent a young woman with us to point out Girumuhatse's place—an adobe compound that stood at the edge of a steep hill planted with bananas, about a hundred yards from the abandoned shop where Nyirabeza was living.

A man sat in the doorway. He had just returned from Zaire with his family, and said he had lived in this house in 1994, when, as he put it, "there were many killings." On his return, he found a family of Tutsi survivors living there. He knew that government policy allowed returnees fifteen days to evict squatters, but the survivors had nowhere to go, so the two families were living together. The young man said his name was Emanuel Habyarimana. I asked if there were any other men around who had come back from Zaire. He said, "None living in these houses here."

As Bosco and I walked back to the road, a pack of children crowded around us, and we asked them if they knew Girumuhatse. They laughed and said he lived in the house where we'd just been visiting and was probably inside. "No," a girl said. "That's him down there." She pointed into the valley at a figure climbing toward us along a path. Bosco quickly produced a few banknotes and dispatched the kids to buy themselves sodas.

For a moment, the man appeared to be trying to get away. He cut off into a field, but Bosco hailed him and waved, and he turned back up the path, moving with a long, swinging gait. He wore a sort of soiled canvas lab coat, open over a thin blue shirt, and shabby brown pants and sandals cut from old tires. His eyes were narrow and heavily bloodshot, and his mouth was bunched up tight. He stood freely before us, but he had the aspect of someone cornered. His chest heaved, and although the day was cool, sweat kept beading at his temples and trickling down his forehead.

Bosco struck up a conversation. The man said that Emanuel, whom we'd just met, was his son, and that it was good to be back. We talked about life in the camps, and I said that when I'd visited Zaire, every Rwandan I spoke with had denied the genocide, and insisted instead that since the end of the war all the Hutus in Rwanda were being systematically killed. For instance, according to one rumor circulating in the Zairean camps, women who returned to Rwanda had their breasts cut off, and men were put in the equivalent of doghouses with floors of wet plaster that would then harden around their feet. The man said, "It sometimes happens that some people tell lies and others tell the truth. There were a lot of dead here."

He introduced himself as Jean Girumuhatse. I told him that his name was familiar to me because it was said in the community that he had killed a whole family. "It's true," Girumuhatse said. "They say I killed because I was the leader of the roadblock right here." He pointed to the road where it passed closest to his house. "Right now, all is well," he told me. "But then, at that time, we were called on by the state to kill. You were told you had the duty to do this or you'd be imprisoned or killed. We were just pawns in this. We were just tools."

Girumuhatse, who said he was forty-six years old, could not recall any specific cases of Hutus who had been executed simply for declining to kill; apparently, the threat—kill or be killed—had been enough to ensure his participation in murder. But Girumuhatse had run a roadblock, and to be the chief of a roadblock was to be not a pawn but a mid-level figure in the local chain of command—a mover of pawns. Girumuhatse said he had no choice, and at the same time, he told me, "In most cases with the killing it's my responsibility, because I was the leader, and now that I'm back I will tell all to the authorities."

WHEN THE MASS repatriation from Zaire began on November 15, 1996, the government of Rwanda ordered a moratorium on arrests of suspected genocide perpetrators. In a month of extraordinary developments, this was surely the most unexpected. But just as in 1994 the radio had rallied the masses to kill, so once again the radio explained how things stood. Everyone heard, for instance, that President Pasteur Bizimungu had gone to the border to welcome the returnees as brothers and sisters. A version of the President's message was repeatedly broadcast on Radio Rwanda, and throughout the country his words were being studied for guidance.

After calling the mass return "a tremendous joy for all Rwandans," the President said, "The Rwandan people were able to live together peacefully for six hundred years and there is no reason why they can't live together in peace again." And he addressed the killers directly: "Let me appeal to those who have chosen the murderous and confrontational path, by reminding them that they, too, are Rwandans. I am calling upon you to abandon your genocidal and destructive ways, join hands with other Rwandans, and put that energy to better use." Then he said, "Once again welcome home."

But why should survivors be asked to live next door to killers—or even, as happened in Girumuhatse's house, under the same roof? Why put off confronting the problem? To keep things calm, General Kagame told me. "You don't necessarily just go for everyone you might think you should go for," he said. "Maybe you create an atmosphere where things are stabilized first, then you go for those you must go for. Others you can even ignore for the sake of gradually leading a kind of peaceful coexistence." Kagame recognized that this was asking a lot of his people; and, following the return, there were numerous reports of soldiers rescuing alleged killers from angry mobs and placing them in "protective custody." It would not be easy to balance the demands for justice and the desire for order, Kagame told me. "In between these two intentions there are problems, there are the feelings of people."

AS SOON AS Girumuhatse told me he was a killer, he stopped sweating. His breath came more easily. His eyes even looked clearer, and he seemed eager to keep talking. A storm had blown in, dumping rain, so we moved into my jeep, which was parked right where Girumuhatse's roadblock had stood during the genocide. As we settled in, he announced that one reason he had been under pressure during the genocide was that he had been told to kill his wife, a Tutsi.

"I was able to save my wife because I was the leader," he said, adding that he had feared for his own life, too. "I had to do it or I'd be killed," he said. "So I feel a bit innocent. Killing didn't come from my heart. If it was really my wish to kill, I couldn't now come back." Girumuhatse's voice was unnervingly cozy beneath the thrum of the rain. Did he feel at least a bit guilty? He remained unmoved when he told me, "I knew many of the people that I ordered killed." I asked how many deaths he had ordered. He was slow in answering. "I know of six people who were killed before my eyes by my orders."

"Did you never kill with your own hands?"

"It's possible I did," Girumuhatse said. "Because if I didn't they'd have killed my wife."

"Possible?" I said. "Or true?"

Bosco, the translator, said, "You know what he means," and didn't translate the question.

Girumuhatse reiterated his wish to explain everything to the authorities. As he understood it, he was being allowed to recover his property and his health—"and then they will call me." He wasn't afraid. If he told all, he believed, he would get "a limited punishment." He said, "The authorities understand that many just followed orders."

Girumuhatse had the government's policy almost right. Three months earlier, after nearly a year of debate, Rwanda's parliament had adopted a special genocide law, which categorized responsibility for the crime according to the perpetrator's position in the criminal hierarchy, and offered sentence reductions for lower-level criminals who confessed. Although all murderers were liable to the death penalty under Rwanda's standard penal code, the genocide law reserved execution only for the elites defined in Category One: "Planners, organizers, instigators, supervisors, and leaders . . . at the national, prefectural, communal, sector, or cell level," as well as "notorious murderers who, by virtue of the zeal or excessive malice with which they committed atrocities, distinguished themselves" and perpetrators of "acts of sexual torture." For the vast remainder of rank-and-file killers and their accomplices—the followers—the maximum penalty of life imprisonment could be whittled down, with a valid confession and guilty plea, to as little as seven years. Penalties for nonlethal assault and property crimes were comparably reducible.

Girumuhatse had absorbed the spirit of the new law. "If it can end that way, and after being punished I can return to my home and recover my life, I would accept that," he told me. "If this vengeance can end in this country and wrongdoers can be punished, that would be best." What he didn't seem to grasp was that his leadership position during the genocide placed him firmly in Category One, where the death penalty could not be staved off with a confession.

Even as Girumuhatse prepared to tell all, he laid the blame for his crimes on the former mayor of Taba, Jean Paul Akayesu, who was remembered as a famously avid hunter of Tutsis and who had installed Girumuhatse as the roadblock leader. In 1995, Akayesu was arrested in Zambia, and in 1997 he was brought to trial for genocide before the International Tribunal for Rwanda, where, after countless delays in the proceedings, a verdict was expected in the summer of 1998. In court, Akayesu himself blamed his political superiors for any killings of innocent Tutsis in Rwanda in 1994.

The genocide "was like a dream," Girumuhatse told me. "It came from the regime like a nightmare." Now, it seemed, he had not so much waked up as entered a new dream, in which his confession and his pat enthusiasm for Rwanda's reform—"The new regime is quite good. There are no dead. We were surprised by the welcome. There is a new order"—did not require any fundamental change of politics or heart. He remained a middleman, aspiring to be a model citizen and to reap the rewards. When the authorities said kill, he killed, and when the authorities said confess, he confessed.

BETWEEN VISITS TO Taba, I talked to an aid worker in Kigali who had just returned from western Tanzania, where close to five hundred thousand Rwandan Hutus still remained in refugee camps. (A month later, in mid-December of 1996, Tanzania closed the camps and repatriated the Rwandans, bringing the total number of returnees to nearly a million and a half in six months.) During his visit to the camps, the aid worker had heard that children there had a game of making clay figures and placing them in the road to be run over by passing vehicles. The clay figures represented Tutsis, and each time one was crushed the children cheered, because they believed they had just caused a Tutsi to die in Rwanda. The aid worker told me this story as a sort of parable. It make him wonder whether it wasn't Rwanda's inevitable destiny to endure another round of mass butchery.

That possibility was all too obvious. Rwanda's government since the genocide had staked its credibility on proving that systematic murder between Hutus and Tutsis was avoidable. The mass return from the camps, which the government presented as a triumph, was the great test of that claim. Yet Kagame, as always, regarded the victory as incomplete. "Yes, people have come back," he said. "That's one problem solved, and it has created another problem, which we also have to solve." He then proceeded to name a lot of problems—housing, justice, the economy, education, the demobilization of thousands of ex-FAR soldiers returning from exile, and, above all, "this issue of ethnicity."

A few months earlier, shortly before the fighting began in South Kivu, Kagame had told me two stories about men in his army. One soldier, he said, had recently written a letter, "telling me how he was left alone in his family, and how he knew that some people killed his family during the genocide, and how he has chosen not to hold anybody else responsible for that. Instead, he has decided to take his own life because he doesn't see what his life means anymore." The letter was found after the soldier's suicide. As Kagame understood it, "he had somebody in mind to kill but instead of doing that he decided to kill himself." The second story was about an officer who killed three people and wounded two in a bar. Some soldiers were about to kill him for his crimes, but he said, "Let me tell you what the problem is and then you can kill me." So the soldier arrested the officer, and he explained, "I've been seeing killers who've been allowed to live and just roam around and nobody takes action against them. Well, I decided I cannot take any more of that, so I killed them. Now, go ahead and do whatever you want with me."

Kagame said, "Imagine what is going on in the mind of that person. I don't know. He could have gone to a market and shot a hundred people. He could have killed anybody—such a person who does not even fear being killed. It means there's some level of insanity that has been created." He said, "People think this is a matter that we should have got over and forgotten, and—no, no, no, no, we are dealing with human beings here."

I heard many such stories, of the temptations of revenge, the release of revenge, the dissatisfactions of revenge. Obviously, many survivors did not share Kagame's view that it was possible to re-habilitate a human being who had followed the logic of the gen-ocide. So after the return from Zaire, I asked him whether he still believed that killers could be successfully reintegrated into society. "I think you can't give up on that—on such a person," he said. "They can learn. I'm sure that every individual, somewhere in his plans, wants some peace, wants to progress in some way, even if he is an ordinary peasant. So if we can present the past to them and say, 'This was the past that caused all these problems for you, and this is the way to avoid that,' I think it changes their minds quite a bit. And I think some people can even benefit from being forgiven, being given another chance."

Kagame also said, "We have no alternative."

DRIVING BACK TO Taba a few days after we met Girumuhatse, Bosco asked me if I'd heard about the girl who'd been burnt alive in Kagili recently. I hadn't, so he told me. There was a girl—a woman, really—about Bosco's age, an acquaintance of his. She was at a disco, and a guy came on to her. She turned him down. He said she'd be sorry. She laughed. He persisted. She told him to go away, to quit bothering her; she said he was crazy. He went away, then came back with a jug of petrol and a match. Four people were killed. The rejected suitor himself wound up hospitalized with burns. When he was asked why he killed four people, he said it was nothing to him after what he'd done in 1994—he could kill as many as he liked.

Bosco was surprised that I, a journalist, hadn't heard this story before. I think I responded rather dully, less as a journalist than as a consumer of American journalism, where the tabloid curiosity of psycho killers who go berserk in public spaces poses only a distant sense of random menace to the public at large—like lightning, drunk drivers, or falling chunks of tall buildings. A great-grandmother of mine was finished off in her ninety-sixth year by a potted geranium plunging from a window ledge, and although it could happen to me, too, I don't consider it a nearer danger because it happened to her. But Bosco's story was different. In Rwanda, he was telling me, a person who says, "The genocide made me do it," leaves everyone in the entire society with a sense of total jeopardy.

Laurencie Nyirabeza's granddaughter, Chantalle Mukagasana, told me much the same thing. I had wanted to hear Nyirabeza's reaction to Girumuhatse's account of himself, but she was in a quiet mood when I returned to Taba, and Chantalle, a lank thirty-three-year-old who was widowed during the genocide and lost four of her five children—Marie, Marthe, Marianne, and Jonathan—filled the silence. "Even if he confesses, he's an impostor," she said of Girumuhatse. "He's lying if he says he just followed orders." According to Chantalle, the man was an unreserved Tutsi killer. She said he had overseen the murder of his wife's parents, "just to have the pleasure of watching them killed," and when he found his Tutsi wife feeding her brother, Girumuhatse had tried to kill his brother-in-law, too.

Nyirabeza had accused Girumuhatse of killing ten members of her immediate family. Chantalle held him personally responsible for the massacre of twenty-seven members of her extended household. He had been the leader, she said, and he also partook in the massacre, using a small hoe. Chantalle had escaped with her one-month-old daughter, Alphonsine, on her back, only because on the morning of the killings she had seen Girumuhatse murder a cousin of hers named Oswald with a machete. After that, Chantalle sought refuge at the nearby home of her godmother, a Hutu. While she was there, she heard Girumuhatse come and ask for tea—to give him strength, he said, to kill Chantalle's father. She also said that her godmother's son, who was one of Girumuhatse's accomplices, "went behind the house to sharpen his machete, but his mother forbade him to kill me." Later, the godmother told Chantalle that her son had killed Chantalle's mother. And now the godmother and her son had come back from Zaire.

All the killing Chantalle described had happened within a few days in one small cluster of houses, on the hill that was under Girumuhatse's command. She laughed when I told her that Girumuhatse said he only saw six people killed on his orders. "Oh, if I could confront him," she said at one point, but in another moment she said, "Even if I denounced him, what can it change?"

After the genocide, Chantalle said, "I had to find my own clothes alone, and I had to find my food alone, and now these people return and are given food and humanitarian aid." It was

314

true; while the international community had spent more than a billion dollars in the camps, devastated Rwanda had gone begging for a few hundred million, and the tens of thousands of survivors, squatting in the ruins, had been systematically ignored. Once, Chantalle told me, someone had handed out hoes to Taba's survivors. "That's all," she said. "Period."

IT WAS IMPOSSIBLE to give survivors what they really wanted—their lost world as it was in the time they called "Before." But did it have to be that those who were most damaged by the genocide remained the most neglected in the aftermath? Bonaventure Nyibizi was especially worried about young survivors becoming extremists themselves. "Let's say we have a hundred thousand young people who lost their families and have no hope, no future. In a country like this if you tell them, 'Go and kill your neighbor because he killed your father and your seven brothers and sister,' they'll take the machete and do it. Why? Because they're not looking at the future with optimism. If you say the country must move toward reconciliation, but at the same time it forgets these people, what happens? When they are walking on the street we don't realize their problems, but perhaps they have seen their mothers being raped, or their sisters being raped. It will require a lot to make sure that these people can come back to society and look at the future and say, 'Yes, let us try.'"

That effort wasn't being made. The government had no program for survivors. "Nobody wants to help them," Kagame's adviser, Claude Dusaidi, told me. He meant no foreign donors, no aid agencies. "We say, 'Give us the money, we'll do it.' Nobody is interested." Bonaventure, who was later appointed Minister of Commerce, explained the lack of foreign help as a consequence of Rwanda's lack of investment opportunities. "You cannot count on the international community unless you're rich, and we are not," he said. "We don't have oil, so it doesn't matter that we have blood, or that we are human beings." For his part, Dusaidi had concluded that the international community didn't want to recognize that the genocide had really taken place. "They wish we would forget it. But the only way we are going to get to forget it is to help the survivors to resume normal life. Then maybe you can establish the process of forgetting."

A surprising phrase—"the process of forgetting." Since the Holocaust, discussions of genocide have become almost inextricably bound up in a discourse about the obligations of memory. But in Rwanda—where Pacifique Kabarisa, who worked for the organization African Rights, told me that many genocide survivors "regret that they weren't killed"—forgetting was longed for as a symptom of minimal recovery, the capacity to get on with life. "Before this return," Chantalle told me, "we were beginning to forget, but now it's as if you had a wound that was healing and then someone came and reopened it."

There could be no complete closing of the wound for the generation that suffered it. Instead, while survivors charged that the government should—and could—do more for them, and while foreigners impatient for reconciliation accused the government of using the genocide as an excuse for its shortcomings, Rwanda's new leaders were asking their countrymen to be stoical. "We cannot bring things to a halt just because we want to emphasize justice and make sure everyone who was involved at every level is held accountable," Kagame told me. It was essential, he said, to maintain a forward momentum, not "to fall back and say, 'Well, these Hutus killed, so they must be killed, and these Tutsis were the victims, so they must now get the better of what there is in this situation.'" After a moment, he added, "I think there has got to be some serious thinking on the question of being rational."

Within a few weeks of the mass return from Zaire, the moratorium on arrests was rescinded to allow for the detention of suspects who fit Category One of the genocide law, and the moratorium was soon abandoned altogether. Yet Gerald Gahima, Deputy Minister of Justice, told me that most killers would probably remain at large. In Taba alone, where the return from the camps had been relatively light, the judicial police inspector said that at least sixty Category One suspects had come back. The inspector had Girumuhatse's name on his list, but he didn't know much about him. "It's said he killed people," he told me, and he read off some names of Girumuhatse's alleged victims, including the same Oswald whose murder Chantalle said she had witnessed, and one of her uncles whom she'd named.

Jonathan Nyandwi, one of six hundred and forty genocide prisoners at the community lockup in Taba, was better informed. He used to keep a bar near Girumuhatse's roadblock, and although he professed at first not to know whether Girumuhatse was a killer, when I mentioned Oswald, he said, "He was my godson," and "He was killed by one Jean Girumuhatse." Nyandwi confirmed that Chantalle's father had met the same fate, but he disputed her claim that Girumuhatse had killed his own wife's parents. According to him, Girumuhatse had only tried to kill his wife's brother, Evariste.

I found Evariste a few days later. He said that his parents had been killed by "accomplices of Girumuhatse" and that he himself had fled during the attack. Later, he had sought refuge with his sister, Girumuhatse's wife. "The moment I arrived, Girumuhatse cried out and called others," Evariste recalled. "They took me, stripped me, and began to beat me with sticks, and my sister began crying like a madwoman, saying, 'You can't kill my brother like that!'" Girumuhatse, he said, "tried to take me to the roadblock of my neighborhood, so I could be killed in my place. I was totally nude, and they were leading me toward a mass grave to throw me in." Somehow, Evariste had slipped free, and managed to escape into the night.

Evariste believed that Girumuhatse had killed more than seventy people. He hadn't seen the man since his return, but he had seen Girumuhatse's wife and their son Emanuel—his sister and nephew—and he told me that both of them feared Girumuhatse and wanted him arrested. Yet Evariste, a Tutsi and a town councillor, was afraid to denounce the man who had tried to kill him. "I'm sure that there could be death for my sister and her children," he explained, and he told me that since Girumuhatse's return his own nights were again filled with fear. "People can't say out loud that they want revenge," Evariste said. "But truly many people have the wish."

THE MORNING AFTER I met Evariste, I found the streets of Kigali lined with people carrying hoes and machetes. It was a day of public work service; everywhere vacant lots were being transformed into brickyards, a first step toward constructing homes for people displaced by the return. At one such site, I saw General Kagame in a crowd of ragged laborers, spading mud into a wooden brick frame. "This is soldier's work, too," he told me. A few feet away, a man was down on his knees, swinging a big machete, chopping up straw to mix into the mud. He had just come back from Zaire, and he said he was rather astonished, after hearing "Monsieur le Vice-Président" demonized in the camps, to see him there. "But it's normal," he added, "because every authority who wants to work for the country must set the example for the people."

The speed with which the doctrines of genocide had been displaced by the order to live together was exhilarating, but it also served as an eerie reminder that Rwanda's old balance of authority and compliance remained perfectly intact. The system was useful for the overwhelming demands of the moment; you put in a new message, and—presto!—revolutionary change. But wasn't it only a change of complexion? Shortly before I came across Kagame making bricks, I had told the story of Girumuhatse to Gerald Gahima, at the Justice Ministry. At first, he had been inclined to favor the man for confessing, but as the details piled up he became increasingly glum.

"For values to change," Gahima said, "there has to be an

acknowledgment of guilt, a genuine desire for atonement, a willingness to make amends, the humility to accept your mistakes and seek forgiveness. But everyone says it's not us, it's our brothers, our sisters. At the end of the day, no one has done wrong. In a situation where there has been such gross injustice and nobody is willing to seek forgiveness, how can values change?"

It was a good question, and I wanted to give Girumuhatse one more chance to help me answer it. He received Bosco and me in a tiny parlor at his home, and this time his son Emanuel joined us. On my first visit, Emanuel had steered me away, saying there were no other men around who had returned from Zaire, and later his uncle, Evariste, had told me that he wanted his father arrested. I wondered if Emanuel knew what his uncle had said, and I was pleased when he sat down in a position that placed him out of his father's line of sight but where I could watch him directly, on a ledge, a bit behind and above Girumuhatse.

When I asked Girumuhatse about the young man named Oswald, whom many people said he had killed, Emanuel began to grin so widely that he had to suck in his lips and bite them to contain himself. All Girumuhatse would say about Oswald was "He was killed during the war." Emanuel rolled his eyes, and when I asked by name about Chantalle's father he kept grinning. Chantalle's father was also killed, Girumuhatse said, and he would not elaborate.

Girumuhatse was suffering from a nasty cough, and he sat doubled forward over his knees on a low stool, staring unhappily at the floor. When he told me that he had commanded people from about fifty families during the killings, Emanuel let out a little snort. "Did you direct all of that?" he said in a mocking tone. "Just you?"

Finally, I asked Girumuhatse if it was true that he had tried to kill his wife's brother. Only then did I realize that Emanuel understood French, because his expressions lurched out of control. But Bosco refused to relay the question; Girumuhatse, he said, was shutting down with embarrassment. A few minutes later, Emanuel stepped outside, and at that point Girumuhatse told me he had tried to save his wife's brother, explaining, "I tried to take him to his neighborhood to protect him, so that he wouldn't be killed here before my eyes."

When I got up to leave, Girumuhatse walked outside with me. "I'm glad to have spoken," he said. "To tell the truth is normal and good."

21

UNSOUND OF BODY—his prostate cancer spreading—in his final days as President of Zaire, Mobutu Sese Seko was incontinent. Trophy seekers who scoured the military camp where he played out his endgame in Kinshasa found little of greater interest than the Big Man's diapers. It was said that Mobutu's mental grip was also rather weak. Several people who boasted impeccable access to the gossip of the old court assured me that by the end he was barking mad—pharmaceutically and characterologically unmoored, sometimes maundering and sometimes vivid with rage—and steadfast only in his delusion that he was on the brink of battering Laurent Kabila's rebel Alliance, which had in fact conquered his immense land almost to his doorstep in just seven months.

And yet, Mobutu's last completed act as President suggested that, at least in broad terms, he grasped what was happening. On May 11, 1997, he ordered that the remains of Rwanda's assassinated Hutu Power President, Juvénal Habyarimana, be exhumed from their mausoleum on his estate at Gbadolite and brought to Kinshasa aboard a transport plane. Mobutu was said to fear that Kabila's cohort might rip Habyarimana from his rest and make mischief with him, and he wanted the Rwandan disposed of. Through four days and four nights, the dead President of Rwanda remained in the plane, on the tarmac at Kinshasa, while the dying President of Zaire made his satraps scurry, one last time, to figure out what to do with the ghoulish cargo. The verdict was cremation, not a normal Congolese rite. Improvising a little over the body of a man who had been a practicing Catholic, Mobutu's fixers impressed a Hindu priest into service, and Habyarimana went up in smoke. The next morning, Mobutu, too, had flown away—to Togo, then Morocco, where he soon died—and within twenty-four hours of his departure the first soldiers of the RPA marched into the capital of Zaire at the head of Kabila's Alliance.

IN FRETTING OVER Habyarimana's last rites, Mobutu had really staged a funeral for a generation of African leadership of which he—the Dinosaur, as he had long been known—was the paragon: the client dictator of Cold War neocolonialism, monomaniacal, perfectly corrupt, and absolutely ruinous to his nation. Six months earlier, when the Rwandan-backed rebel Alliance first captured Goma, I had driven directly to Mobutu's lakeside palace at the edge of town. The gates stood open and unguarded. The Zairean flag lay in a lump in the driveway. Munitions abandoned by Mobutu's Special Presidential Division littered the grounds—heaps of assault rifles and cases marked "TNT" packed with sixty-millimeter mortar rounds. Five mint black Mercedes sedans, a shiny Land Rover, and two ambulances were parked by the garage. Inside, the house was a garish assemblage of mirrored ceilings, malachite-and-pearl-inlaid furniture, chandeliers, giant televisions, and elaborate hi-fis. Upstairs, the twin master bathrooms were equipped with Jacuzzis.

Goma was largely a shantytown. Its poverty was extreme. One day I stopped by the house of an acquaintance who had gone away, leaving his dogs. Their snouts stuck out beneath the locked gate. I was feeding them some United Nations high-protein biscuits when three men came around the corner and asked for some, too. I held out the box to the first man, who was clad in rags, and said, "Take a few." His hands shot out, and I felt the box fly from my grip as if it were spring-loaded. The man's companions immediately pounced on him, tussling, cramming biscuits into their mouths, snatching biscuits out of one another's mouths, and along what had seemed a deserted street people came running to join the fray.

Mobutu's Jacuzzis were lined with bath oils and perfumes in bottles of Alice in Wonderland magnitude; they must have held about a gallon apiece. Most were quite full. But one appeared to have enjoyed regular use: a vat of Chanel's Egoïste.

He bathed in the stuff.

That was Zaire, and in the spirit of Louis XIV's "*L'état c'est moi*," Mobutu was fond of boasting, "There was no Zaire before me, and there will be no Zaire after me." In the event, Kabila—who used to call Zaire "*le Nowhere*"—made Mobutu's word good; on May 17, 1997, he declared himself President, and restored to the country the name Mobutu had scrapped: the Democratic Republic of the Congo. The speed with which he had swept to victory owed much to the fact that, as a rule, the Zairean army had preferred to flee than to fight, raping and looting its way through town after town ahead of the rebel advance. The only forces that truly made a stand for Mobutu were tens of thousands of fugitive fighters of Rwanda's Hutu Power and a couple of dozen French-recruited Serbian mercenaries.

Kabila, too, had required foreign help to accomplish his march so efficiently, and not only from Rwanda. Behind his Alliance there had formed a pan-African alliance representing the political or military enthusiasm of at least ten governments across the continent. After the initial rebel victories in North and South Kivu, as Congolese recruits flocked to Kabila's cause, support also poured in from neighboring states—Angola, Burundi, Tanzania, Uganda, Zambia—and from as far afield as Eritrea, Ethiopia, South Africa, and Zimbabwe.

Had the war in the Congo happened in Europe, it would

probably have been called a world war, and to Africans the world *was* at stake. For this was the war about the Rwandan genocide. As Uganda's President Museveni told me shortly after Kabila was sworn in: "The big mistake of Mobutu was to involve himself in Rwanda. So it's really Mobutu who initiated the program of his own removal. Had he not involved himself in Rwanda, I think he could have stayed, just like that, as he had been doing for the last thirty-two years—just do nothing to develop Zaire, but stay in what they call power, by controlling the radio station, and so on."

Mobutu had certainly been warned, and not only by those who dethroned him. In the study of his abandoned palace in Goma, I found a long memorandum about the Rwanda conflict addressed to Mobutu by one of his counselors. From its contents it appeared to have been written in 1991, not long after the RPF first invaded Rwanda, at a time when Mobutu was presiding over the negotiation of a series of short-lived cease-fires. The memo described Habyarimana's court as "composed for the most part of intransigent extremists and fanatics," and predicted that the RPF rebels would "in one manner or another realize their final objective, which is to take power in Rwanda." The memo urged Mobutu to serve as "a moral umbrella" and "the Spiritual Father of the negotiation process" without alienating the RPF or Uganda's President Museveni, and above all to protect the "primordial interests of Zaire" regardless of who should prevail in Rwanda.

Standing there—as a looter, really—in Mobutu's "liberated" study, reading this banal document that had been rendered remarkable only by the enormity of intervening events, I was struck again to think how completely the world was changed by the genocide in Rwanda. It wasn't necessarily a nicer or a better world, just a few years and a million deaths ago, before the genocide. But in central Africa it was a world in which the very worst was still unknown.

In 1994, during the height of the extermination campaign in

Rwanda, as Paris airlifted arms to Mobutu's intermediaries in eastern Zaire for direct transfer across the border to the *génocidaires*, France's President François Mitterrand said—as the newspaper *Le Figaro* later reported it—"In such countries, genocide is not too important." By their actions and inactions, at the time and in the years that followed, the rest of the major powers indicated that they agreed. Evidently, it did not occur to them that such a country as Rwanda can refuse to accept the insignificance of its annihilation; nor had anybody imagined that other Africans could take Rwanda's peril seriously enough to act.

The memory of the genocide, combined with Mobutu's sponsorship of its full-scale renewal, had "global repercussions, wider than Rwanda," Museveni told me, "and here in Africa we were determined to resist it." Just as Mobutu was what Museveni called an "agent" of his Western puppeteers, so the Rwandan *génocidaires*, who had once again threatened to reduce the entire region to blood, owed their sustenance to the mindless dispensation of Western charity. The West might later wring its hands over the criminal irresponsibility of its policies, but the nebulosity known as the international community is ultimately accountable to nobody. Time and again in central Africa, false promises of international protection were followed by the swift abandonment of hundreds of thousands of civilians in the face of extreme violence. Against such reckless impunity, the Congolese rebellion offered Africa the opportunity to unite against its greatest homegrown political evil and to supplant the West as the arbiter of its own political destiny.

I OFTEN FOUND it helpful to think of central Africa in the mid-1990s as comparable to late medieval Europe—plagued by serial wars of tribe and religion, corrupt despots, predatory elites and a superstitious peasantry, festering with disease, stagnating in poverty, *and* laden with promise. Of course, a key process that had helped European peoples pull toward greater prosperity and saner governance was colonialism, which allowed for the exporting of their aggressions and the importing of wealth. Ex-colonies don't enjoy such opportunities as they tumble into the family of modern nation-states; whatever forms of government they come up with, in their struggles to build sustaining political traditions, are likely to be transitional.

Long before Rwanda became a case study in international negligence, Museveni once said, "A little neglect would not be so bad. The more orphaned we are, the better for Africa. We will have to rely on ourselves." And the extent to which the Congolese revolution took the outside world by surprise exposed a stubborn misconception that had dominated Western attitudes toward post-Cold War Africa—that Africans generate humanitarian catastrophes but don't really make meaningful politics.

Appeasement had been the wrong policy toward Nazi Germany, and so it had been in Goma, too. Yet the very vacuum of responsible international engagement at Goma had created an unprecedented need and opportunity for Africans to fix their own problems. Although Kabila's foreign backers were openly skeptical about his capacities to serve as more than a temporary leader of the Congo—and even in that role he would quickly disappointment them—the Alliance's swift sweep to victory inspired Uganda's President Museveni, speaking at Kabila's inauguration, to proclaim that the war had "liberated not only the Congo but also all of Africa."

As the political godfather of the new central African leadership, Museveni was listened to closely. He called for national and international solidarity, and for economic order and physical security as the basis for political development. Hearing him, one could almost forget that central Africa's prospects remained terribly bleak. What was left of much of the region looked a lot like this:

The infrastructure of the country, especially the roads, had almost totally collapsed. Most of the country was inaccessible . . . There was a critical shortage of trucks . . . Utilities, such as water and power supply, had severely deteriorated . . . Manufacturing plants were either closed or operating at very low rates . . . There was a total lack of basic consumer goods such as sugar, soap, and paraffin. Goods were being smuggled into and out of the country, and sold on the parallel ("black") market. The economy had become completely informal and speculative.

This passage from Museveni's autobiography described Uganda in 1986, when he installed himself as President after more than a decade of armed struggle. When I told him I thought I was reading about the Congo—or, for that matter, much of Rwanda after 1994—he said, "Same situation, exactly."

Uganda's annual economic growth in the early 1990s averaged close to five percent, and in 1996 it exceeded eight percent. Decent roads laced the country. There were good state schools, improved medical care, an independent judiciary, a rather feisty parliament, a boisterous and often contrarian press, and a small but growing middle class. Insecurity remained, especially in the rebellion-plagued north and west of the country. But Uganda, a decade after the ravages of Idi Amin and Obote, set a standard of promise that had to make anyone who called the Congo or Rwanda "impossible" or "hopeless" think again.

MUSEVENI WAS A heavy-handed manager, technocratic, pragmatic, accustomed to having things very nearly his way. He was a man of enormous energy, not only as a politician but also as a cattle breeder, and he possessed a frontiersman's inventiveness. On the morning that I visited him, the state-owned *New Vision* newspaper announced: "Yoweri Museveni has disclosed that a local grass species he recently introduced to Egyptian researchers has been processed into a highly effective toothpaste which has been called Nile Toothpaste."

The item about the toothpaste unfolded as a classic Muse-venian parable of African self-reliance. As a child in the bush, Museveni had learned to chew a grass called *muteete* and found that it left his teeth perfectly clean and smooth. Then, at a British colonial secondary school, he was introduced to Colgate, to cure him of his bumpkin ways. "But," he said, "when you use this Colgate and you pass the tongue over your teeth you feel these 'roadblocks.'" The white man's toothpaste was inferior. As President, he remembered the *muteete*, and modern science confirmed his memory. The grass, he said, possessed "the best toothpaste agents ever found." Nile Toothpaste would soon be on the market, and Uganda would collect royalties. Museveni urged his compatriots to pursue similarly market-oriented research. He thought banana juice might make a hit in the soft-drink industry. He noted that Ugandan flower exports to Europe were soaring, and exporters elsewhere were running scared. The message was clear: seek the value in a devalued Africa; we are on a roll.

Uganda's capital, Kampala, was just an hour's flight north of Kigali, near the shore of Lake Victoria, yet it seemed another world entirely: a boom town with an air of promise. Of course, it was easy to find people who complained about the government, but the problem that animated them most—whether the regime was moving toward becoming a liberal democracy too slowly, too quickly, or not at all—was the sort of problem that Rwandans, whose chief preoccupation was their physical security, could only yearn to discuss without fear.

Museveni received me in a pavilion on the immaculate grounds of State House, at the end of Kampala's Victoria Avenue. He sat behind a desk on a plastic lawn chair, wearing an untucked brown plaid short-sleeved shirt, corduroys, and sandals. Tea was served. On a shelf beneath his desk were a book on the Israeli war in Sinai, the Washington journalist Bob Woodward's book *The Choice*, about Bill Clinton's election campaign, and a volume called *Selected Readings on the Uses of Palm Oil*. Museveni appeared tired; he did not try to hide his need to yawn. Even in the official portrait photographs that hung in most shops and offices around the capital, his round face and nearly shaved pate had an uncharismatic, everyman look that was part of his appeal. His speech, like his writing, was lucid, blunt, and low on bombast.

Toward the end of the war in the Congo, when Kabila's victory appeared inevitable, *The New York Times* ran an editorial headed "Tyranny or Democracy in Zaire?"—as if those were the only two political possibilities, and whatever was not one must be the other. Museveni, like many of his contemporaries among the leaders of what might be called post-postcolonial Africa, sought a middle ground on which to build the foundations for a sustainable democratic order. Because he refused to allow multiparty politics in Uganda, many Western pundits were inclined to join with his Ugandan critics in withholding admiration for his successes. But he argued that until corruption was brought under control, until a middle class with strong political and economic interests developed, and until there was a coherent national public debate, political parties were bound to devolve into tribal factions or financial rackets, and to remain an affair of elites struggling for power, if not a cause of actual civil war.

Museveni called his regime a "no-party democracy," based on "movement politics," and he explained that parties are "uni-ideological," whereas a movement like his National Resistance Movement or the Rwandese Patriotic Front is "multi-ideological," open to a polyphony of sensibilities and interests. "Socialists are in our movement, capitalists are in our movement, feudalists—like the kings here in Uganda—are members of our movement," he said. The movement was officially open to everyone, and "anybody who wants" could stand for election. Although Museveni, like most African leaders of his generation, was often described as a former Marxist guerrilla, he was a staunch promoter of free enterprise, and he had come to favor the formation of political groupings along class lines, in order to produce "horizontal polarization," as opposed to the "vertical polarization" of tribalism or regionalism. "That's why we say, in the short run, let political competition not be based on groups, let it be based on individuals," he told me, adding, "We are not likely to have healthy groups. We are likely to have unhealthy groups. So why take this risk?"

Museveni's complaint was with what might be called cosmetic democracy, in which elections held for elections' sake at the behest of "donor governments" sustain feeble or corrupt powers in politically damaged societies. "If I have got a heart problem and I try to appear healthy, then I will just die," Museveni told me. We were speaking of the way that the West, having won the Cold War and lost its simple template for distinguishing bad guys from good guys around the world, had found a new political religion in promoting multiparty elections (at least in economically dependent countries where Chinese is not widely spoken). Museveni described this policy as "not only meddling but meddling on the basis of ignorance and, of course, some arrogance also." He said, "These people seem to say that the developed parts of the world and the undeveloped parts of the world can all be managed uniformly. Politically this is their line, and I think this is really rubbish—to be charitable. It's not possible to manage radically different societies exactly in a uniform way. Yes, there are some essentials which should be common, like universal suffrage, one person one vote, by secret ballot, a free press, separation of powers. These should be common factors, but not the exact form. The form should be according to situations."

IT ANNOYED MUSEVENI and Kagame equally that Rwanda's RPF-led government was widely viewed as a puppet regime of Uganda's, and that Kabila had in turn been tagged by opponents as a pawn of "Rwando-Ugandan" imperialism. "They were puppets of the French," Museveni said of his Rwandan and Congolese critics, "so they think that everybody else is looking for puppets or masters." He considered it obvious that other countries in the region should look to Uganda's example. "When Martin Luther published his criticism of the papists, it spread because it struck a chord in different places," he said. "And when the French Revolution happened there were already local republican elements in different European countries. So when there were changes in Uganda against the dictatorship of Idi Amin—yes, there was some attraction to those ideas."

That Museveni should present himself in the light of early modern European history was a measure of his determined optimism. He was a student of how the great democracies emerged from political turmoil, and he recognized that it did not happen quickly, or elegantly, or without staggering setbacks and agonizing contradictions along the way. I often heard it said, even by Museveni's admirers, that he was, alas, no Jeffersonian democrat. But the traditions and particular circumstances which produced Jefferson are unlikely to be found afresh in Africa, and it's doubtful that those who yearn for such a man again would be prepared to tolerate the fact that Jefferson's leisure to think and write as grandly as he did was financed in large measure by his unrepentant ownership of slaves.

Still, in addition to the stories of Luther and the French Revolution, Museveni had no doubt also read about the American Revolution, which required eight years of fighting, four more years to get the Constitution ratified, and another two years before elections were held—a total of thirteen years after the Declaration of Independence proclaimed, with "a decent respect to the opinions of mankind," not only the causes of the anticolonial struggle but also the divine, and universal, legitimacy of waging such struggles by force of arms. The story would appeal to Museveni. The Yankee general who had led the Revolutionary army in from the bush won America's first two presidential elections.

Museveni got himself elected for the first time in 1996, a decade after taking power, and could run for another five-year term in 2001. But until Uganda experienced a smooth transfer of power to an elected successor, "no-party democracy" could not be said to have met the ultimate test of its institutions. In the meantime, nearly everything depended on the goodwill and the capacities of the leader—but not, Museveni assured me, on the wishes of the international community. The Euro-American architects of the old postcolonial order were welcome to work with Africa, he said, but on Africa's terms, as joint-venture investors both of capital and of technical expertise. "I really don't think the Europeans have the capacity to impose their will again. I don't think that America or anybody will dominate Africa anymore," he told me. "They may cause destabilization, but they cannot reverse the situation if the indigenous forces are organized. By the sheer force of Africa we shall be independent of all foreign manipulation."

A FEW WEEKS after Mobutu's abdication, Bill Richardson, the United States ambassador to the United Nations, flew to the Congo to see President Kabila. His presence, he told me, reflected a "renewed U.S. interest in Africa," sparked by the awareness that the countries that had formed the alliance behind Kabila's Alliance constituted a "regional strategic and economic power bloc, through shared experience," that "needs to be dealt with seriously." He spoke of the attraction of market economies, and "a lot of improvement" in social and political conditions, and he expressed admiration for both Kagame and Museveni.

But Richardson had come to the Congo not only to offer American help but also to threaten to withhold it. Since midway through the war, international aid workers, human rights activists, and journalists in the eastern and northern Congo had been reporting that Rwandan Hutus who fled into the jungle after the

332

breakup of the UN border camps were being killed, piecemeal and in massacres, by Kabila's forces. The UN wanted to send a human rights investigation team, and Kabila was stonewalling. Richardson's message was: Let the team come, or face international isolation and forget about the foreign aid you desperately need.

Kabila's people were understandably prickly about the question of massacres. On the one hand, they denied the charges; on the other hand, they insisted that any killings of Hutus had to be placed in the proper context. A great many Rwandans from the camps who had remained in the Congo were not only fugitive *génocidaires* but active-duty fighters for Mobutu. Even during the pitch of battle, these combatants had, as always, kept themselves surrounded by their families and followers—women, children, and the elderly, whom they used as a human shield and who suffered accordingly. What's more, the Hutu Power fighters themselves were reported to have committed massacres of Congolese villagers and of their own cohorts as they retreated westward. (I saw the aftermath of such a massacre at the Mugunga camp during the mass return in November of 1996: two dozen women, girls, and babies, chopped to death and left to rot in the middle of the camp—"because they came from another camp, looking for food," according to a Mugunga resident, who seemed to think such killing unremarkable.)

At times, the UNHCR had managed to establish temporary camps for tens of thousands of Rwandan Hutus as they fled westward. One of the largest was at the village of Tingi-Tingi, in the eastern Congo. On television, it looked like any camp for war-dispossessed refugees, but offscreen it was also a major Hutu Power military installation. Disgusted aid workers and bush pilots later told me that the ex-FAR and *interahamwe* maintained a regime of terror in the camp, killing noncombatants seemingly at random. The same forces controlled the airfield, where, mingled in among genuine aid agency flights, planes plastered with the logos of aid organizations regularly landed arms and took off carrying prominent *génocidaires* to Nairobi. Of course, much of the aid that did get through was appropriated and consumed by Hutu Power forces.

In mid-April of 1997, the front page of *The New York Times* carried an unusually ambivalent article about the refugee crisis in the Congo, which described a camp for Rwandan Hutus near the city of Kisangani: "While thousands of small children in the camps have distended bellies and limbs like twigs and seem near death by starvation, there are also a considerable number of strapping young men who look fit and healthy and well-fed."

"When we get food, I eat first," a "husky thirty-five-year-old father of three starving children" told the *Times*, and "aid workers said his situation was not uncommon."

It was strange to read such a story, and at the same time to hear that Emma Bonino, the European Union's Minister of Humanitarian Affairs, was accusing Kabila's troops of committing genocide against the refugees, in part by obstructing "humanitarian access." Even as she spoke, the UN was flying daily planeloads of Rwandan Hutus—many of them fit young men—to Kigali, for repatriation and resettlement, in a program sanctioned by Rwandan and Alliance officials. At least fifty thousand former camp residents were brought back to Rwanda in this fashion, while as many made their way over the borders to areas of Angola held by Mobutist-backed rebels, to the Central African Republic, and to the other Congo—the Republic of the Congo—where they were once again accommodated in camps, which were once again heavily militarized.

On the other hand, many Rwandan Hutus were clearly disappearing in the Congo, and many of the killings that were being attributed to Kabila's backers appeared to have occurred in noncombat situations. Several appalling death-squad-style massacres were reported in detail. These killings dominated the international coverage of the Congo war and its aftermath, and the blame was directed primarily at Tutsi troops from the Congo and from Rwanda. Not long after the *Times* article about killer refugees at Kisangani appeared, the camp it was reported from was attacked and disbanded by a mixture of Alliance forces and local Zaireans. Stories circulated that thousands of its residents had been massacred—but nobody could be sure exactly what had happened because Kabila's forces barred access to investigators.

AMBASSADOR RICHARDSON EMERGED from his meeting with good news: Kabila had promised to give the UN human rights probe unlimited access. In high spirits, Richardson flew on to visit a camp for Rwandan Hutus at Kisangani, not far from where some of the largest refugee massacres were reported to have occurred. The people in the camp were mostly women and children who had been straggling through the jungle for months, and they were in bad shape, some barely alive—crumpled skin clinging to skeletons. After a leisurely tour, Richardson stood near the camp gate, surrounded by camp residents, and read a prepared statement, which described the "humanitarian crisis in the Congo" as "a tragedy that dates back to the 1994 genocide in Rwanda." What's more, he said:

> The failure of the international community to respond adequately to both the genocide and the subsequent mixing of genocidal killers with the legitimate refugee population in the former eastern Zaire only served to prolong the crisis. This climate of impunity was further exacerbated by ethnic cleansing and conflict in the [North Kivu] region—and also by former President Mobutu's policies of allowing these genocidal forces to operate, recruit and resupply on his territory. Tragically, this chapter is not yet closed. Reports of widespread killings continue. All of

us, the new government of the Democratic Republic of Congo, its neighbors and the international community, have the responsibility to stop the killing of innocent civilians. We must also protect legitimate refugees, continue repatriation efforts and work to bring the genocidal killers to justice.

This was the highest-level official acknowledgment of reality and responsibility by an international statesman to date, and it was delivered before reporters of *The New York Times, The Washington Post*, the *Los Angeles Times*, and several international television, radio, and wire services. Yet not one of those papers reported it. General Kagame later told me that he'd seen a typescript of the statement and wondered if it was a hoax. When I assured him that Richardson had really said those words, he called it an "important admission" and "something great in the whole situation," adding, "Maybe somebody should slip it into the Internet or something."

A few weeks after Richardson's visit, the UN massacre investigation team arrived in Kinshasa, right on schedule. But it was never able to go about its business. Kabila threw up one hurdle after another, and even after Secretary-General Kofi Annan agreed to find a new team leader and to expand the investigation's scope to cover not only the eight months of the Congo war but the preceding four years—since Rwanda's *génocidaires* first began filling the eastern Congo with mass graves—Kabila continued to stonewall. A great many African heads of state closed ranks behind him. Their feeling was that after sitting out the Rwandan genocide, the so-called international community had little credibility as moral referees in the war against the *génocidaires*.

Such was the mood on much of the continent in the early summer of 1997. In July, Kenya's aging strongman, Daniel arap Moi, who had broken off relations with Rwanda after the genocide, received General Kagame for a state visit. Two days later, Kenya arrested and turned over to the UN tribunal at Arusha seven of the most-wanted masterminds of the genocide. Moi denounced these former friends of his as "foreign spies and criminals," and arrests continued. Among those caught were General Gratien Kabiligi of the ex-FAR, who had until recently commanded the Hutu Power forces in the Congo; Georges Ruggiu, the Belgian broadcaster for the genocidal radio RTLM; and Hassan Ngeze, who had published the Hutu Ten Commandments and forecast President Habyarimana's death in the newspaper *Kangura*.

ONCE, WHEN WE were talking about the genocide and the world's response to it, General Kagame said, "Some people even think we should not be affected. They think we are like animals, when you've lost some family, you can be consoled, given some bread and tea—and forget about it." He chuckled. "Sometimes I think this is contempt for us. I used to quarrel with these Europeans who used to come, giving us sodas, telling us, 'You should not do this, you should do this, you don't do this, do this.' I said, 'Don't you have feelings?' These feelings have affected people." Kagame aimed a finger at his skinny body and said, "Maybe that's why I don't put on a lot of weight—these thoughts keep consuming me."

In early June of 1997, just after Richardson's visit to the Congo, I went to Kigali for a day to see Kagame, and ask him about the reported massacres of Rwandan Hutus in the Congo. "I think there is a bit of exaggeration," he said, "in terms of systematic extermination, systematic killings of refugees, or even possible involvement of high authorities of different countries." Then he added, "But let's go back a little bit, if people are not to be hypocrites. . . . First of all, again, I want to bring out the involvement of some countries in Europe. Remember the *Zone Turquoise*?"

Kagame spent more than an hour describing the resurgence of Hutu Power after the RPF's victory in 1994, starting with the arrival of French forces during the last weeks of the genocide, and running through the activities of the *génocidaires* in the camps—

the rearming, the training, the alliance with Mobutu, the killings and expulsions in North Kivu, the constant attacks against Rwanda, and the campaign to eradicate the Banyamulenge Tutsis from South Kivu. He rattled off the names of towns in the Congo where major battles had been joined during the Alliance's march to Kinshasa, and described the massive troop involvements of Hutu Power forces. "It becomes extremely difficult for me to imagine that the whole world is so naive as not to see that this was a real problem," he said. He could only conclude, he added, that "there was some high-level conspiracy" in the international community to protect the killers and, perhaps, to assist them toward an ultimate victory.

But why would any of the major powers have pursued such an insane policy? "To fight off their guilt after the genocide," Kagame said. "There is a great amount of guilt."

This was the same conversation in which, at the outset, Kagame told me that Rwanda had had no troops in the Congo, as he had been telling everyone for eight months, and in which he wound up telling me that in fact he had initiated the whole campaign, and his troops had been there all along. The total reversal surprised me more than the information, and I was left to wonder why one of the shrewdest political and military strategists of our times was taking credit for the war at just the moment when he was being heaped with blame for war crimes.

Reviewing the tapes of our conversation, I realized that Kagame's reasons were clear. He was not denying that many Rwandan Hutus had been killed in the Congo; he told me that when revenge was the motive, such killings should be punished. But he considered the *génocidaires* responsible for the deaths of those they traveled with. "These are not genuine refugees," he said. "They're simply fugitives, people running away from justice after killing people in Rwanda—*after killing*." And they were still killing.

The brief period of calm in Rwanda that followed the mass

return from the UN camps at the end of 1996 had quickly broken down, and since February the systematic killing of Tutsis had been steadily on the increase. Much of the northwest was in a state of low-level war. The eastern Congo, too, remained in turmoil, and sizable concentrations of Hutu fighters who had refused every chance for repatriation continued to operate across the area. Kagame was especially concerned about the tens of thousands of *génocidaires* who had fled to the Central African Republic, Congo-Brazzaville, and rebel-held areas of Angola.

"Even now, these fellows are crossing our borders, ex-FAR and militias, mixed with maybe some of their family members," Kagame said. "They are armed with rocket-propelled grenades, with machine guns, they are killing people as they move, and this is nothing to the international community. What is a thing is that Tutsis were killing refugees. There's something extremely wrong here. This is why I think there's this terrible guilt on the part of some people, which they are trying to fight off by always painting a picture of Tutsis being on the wrong side and Hutus being victims. But there is no amount of intimidation or distortion that can defeat us on this. It will cause us problems, but we are not going to be defeated." He sounded angrier than I had ever heard him. "There are a lot of them left," he said of the *génocidaires*, "and we will have to keep dealing with that situation for as long as it lasts. We are not really tired of dealing with that at all—it's they who will get tired, not we."

A grim prospect, but Kagame was trying to explain why the war in the Congo had happened as it had happened—in order, he said, that Rwanda should not "be rubbed off the surface of the earth." That was how he saw his choice, and it explained the startling coolness of his speech. But although his voice and his manner were as contained as ever, he was clearly indignant to find his troops accused of destroying what he regarded as an army bent on Rwanda's annihilation. Kagame's defiance and his sense of injury added up to an Ahab-like wrath. He didn't just want the world to see things his way; he seemed to believe that the world owed him an apology for failing to accept his reasoning.

Ideally, he told me, an investigation would be the best way to clear up the story of massacres in the Congo. "But," he said, "because of this background, which I have already described to you, because of this partisan involvement, because of these politically motivated allegations even at the high levels in the international community, you see here that we are dealing with judges who cannot be judged. And yet they are terribly wrong. This is the bad thing about the whole thing. I have lost faith. You see, the experience of Rwanda since 1994 has left me with no faith in these international organizations. Very little faith.

"In fact," Kagame went on, "I think we should start accusing these people who actually supported the camps, spent a million dollars per day in these camps, gave support to these groups to rebuild themselves into a force, militarized refugees. When in the end these refugees are caught up in the fighting and they die, I think it has more to do with these people than Rwanda, than Congo, than the Alliance. Why shouldn't we accuse them? This is the guilt they are trying to fight off. This is something they are trying to deflect."

It was true that the victory of the pan-African alliance Kagame had put together in the Congo had constituted a defeat for the international community. The major powers and their humanitarian representatives had been pushed out of the way, and, he said, "they are angered, and the guilt is exposed by the defeat." He said, "they have not determined the outcome, so again this is something they cannot stomach." He said, "Kabila emerges, alliance emerges, something changes, Mobutu goes: things happen, the region is happy about what is happening, different people have had different ways of supporting the process. And they are left out, and everything takes them by surprise. They are extremely annoyed by that, and they can't take it like that."

As Kagame understood it, "The African and the Western worlds are so many worlds apart." Yet he seemed to recognize that a defeat for the international community could not be translated into a victory for anybody. He had spent his life in central Africa, not fighting against what used to be called the "civilized world," but fighting to join it. Yet he had concluded that that world was trying to use "the refugee issue" to destroy his progress. "That really is their purpose," he said. "It's not so much the human rights concerns, it's more political. It's 'Let's kill this development, this dangerous development of these Africans trying to do things their own way.'"

22

THE FIRST IN-FLIGHT movie on my second-to-last trip to Rwanda, in February of 1997, was *A Time to Kill.* It is set in Mississippi, in the atmosphere Faulkner celebrated as "miasmic." A couple of worthless white-trash rednecks are out drinking and driving. They abduct a young black girl, rape her, torture her, and leave her corpse in a field. They get caught and thrown in jail. The girl's father doesn't trust the local judiciary to do adequate justice, so he waits for the men to be brought in chains to the courthouse, steps out of the shadows with a shotgun, and blows them away. He is arrested for first-degree murder and put on trial. His culpability is never in question, but a clever young white lawyer— risking his reputation, his marriage, his life and that of his children—appeals to the jury's sentiment, and the girl's father is set free. That was the movie. It was pitched as a tale of racial and social healing. Triumph for the protagonists, and catharsis for the audience, came with the acquittal of the vigilante killer, whose action was understood by a jury of his peers to have achieved a higher degree of justice than he could have expected from the law.

The second in-flight movie was *Sleepers.* It is set in New York, in the tough midtown neighborhood of Hell's Kitchen. Four kids play a prank that results in the accidental death of a passerby. They are sent to a reform school, where they are repeatedly gang-raped by the wardens. Then they are released. Years pass. One day, two of the original quartet encounter the warden who had been their chief tormentor in reform school, so they draw their handguns and blow him away. They are arrested. To the viewer, their culpability is never in question. But in court they deny everything; they say they were in church at the time of the murder. This alibi requires the cooperative testimony of a priest, who is also an alumnus of the terrible reform school. The priest is a man of great honesty. Before testifying, he swears on the Bible that he will tell the truth. Then he lies. The men are acquitted and released. It was another tale of the triumph of justice over the law; the priest's lie was understood to have been an act of service to a higher truth.

Both movies had been quite popular in America—seen by many millions of citizens. Apparently, the questions they raised struck a chord with their audiences: What about you? Can you condemn these vigilante killers after such violations? Can you grieve for the scum they killed? Might not you do the same? These are fine issues to ponder. Still, I was troubled by the premise the two movies shared: that the law and the courts were so incapable of fairly adjudicating the cases in question that it wasn't worth bothering with them. Perhaps I was taking my in-flight entertainment too seriously, but I was thinking of Rwanda.

Six weeks earlier, in mid-December of 1996, shortly after the mass return from the border camps, Rwanda had finally begun holding genocide trials. This was a historic event: never before had anybody on earth been brought to court for the extraordinary crime of genocide. Yet the trials received sparse international attention. Even the government seemed reluctant to make much fanfare about them, since the courts were crude and inexperienced and had little prospect of meeting Western standards of due process. At one of the first trials, in the eastern province of Kibungo, a witness with machete scars across his scalp identified the defendant as his attacker. The defendant dismissed the charge as nonsense, saying that if he had struck a man such a blow he would

343

have made sure that his victim did not live to talk about it. He was found guilty and sentenced to death. So it went. Defense counsel was rarely available, and trials rarely lasted more than a day. Most ended with sentences of death or life imprisonment, but there were some lighter sentences and there were acquittals, which was the only way to determine that the judiciary exercised any independence.

In late January of 1997, the highest-ranking *génocidaire* in Rwandan custody—Froduald Karamira, who had been Bonaventure Nyibizi's friend in prison before becoming an extremist and giving Hutu Power its name—was brought to court in Kigali. Karamira had been arrested in Ethiopia; he was the only suspect Rwanda had succeeded in extraditing from abroad. For his trial, he appeared in a prisoner's suit—pink shorts and a pink short-sleeved shirt—and many Rwandans later told me that seeing this once immensely powerful man so humbled had been cathartic in itself. The proceedings were broadcast from loudspeakers to a crowd outside the courthouse, and on the radio to a fixated national audience. The case was quite well prepared: tapes and transcripts of Karamira's bloodthirsty propaganda speeches were brought in as evidence, and witnesses and survivors of his numerous crimes described how he had rallied the masses to kill and ordered the massacre of his next-door neighbors. When Karamira took the stand, he denounced his trial as a charade and the government as illegitimate, because Hutu Power was excluded from the ruling coalition, and he denied that Tutsis had been systematically exterminated in 1994. "I am accused of genocide," he said, "but what does that mean?" He remained defiant even when he said, "If my death will bring reconciliation, if my death will make some people happy, then I'm not afraid to die."

I HAD WANTED to be in Rwanda for Karamira's trial, but it was over in three days, and I arrived two weeks later, just after he was sentenced to death. More trials were scheduled, of course, but none in Kigali, and I was advised against traveling outside the city. Around the same time that the trials had begun, bands of ex-FAR and *interahamwe*—many of them just returned from Zaire—had resumed their terror campaign. Tutsis were the primary victims, but Hutus who were known to have behaved humanely toward Tutsis in 1994, or who cooperated with the new government, were also targeted. The mood of tentative relief that had attended the breakup of the camps quickly ebbed, and Rwandans were beginning to wonder whether their country hadn't been invaded after all.

In January, in the northwestern province of Ruhengeri, three Spanish aid workers and a Canadian priest were shot to death—the first killings of Westerners since the genocide. The government blamed Hutu insurgents for these murders, but no conclusive investigations were ever conducted. Then, in early February, three Rwandans and two international field workers from the UN Human Rights mission were massacred in an ambush staged by *interahamwe* in the southwestern province of Cyangugu. The UN team had been on its way to a meeting, organized by the government, to urge villagers to resist the pressure to collaborate with *génocidaires*. One of the dead Rwandans was a genocide survivor, and one of the internationals was a Cambodian survivor of Pol Pot's killing fields. The Cambodian's head had been completely removed from his body. After that, most of Rwanda was treated as a "no-go" zone by foreigners.

Rwandans, too, advised me against travel. Even when I wanted to go back to Taba—just a half hour's drive south from Kigali along good roads—to see what had become of Laurencie Nyirabeza and the killer Jean Girumuhatse, I was told that nobody would hesitate to call me a fool if I got killed. The night before I flew into Kigali, a minibus taxi had been stopped by a tree placed across the main road twenty miles north of the city. The vehicle was quickly surrounded by armed men, who made the passengers get out and separate—Tutsis here, Hutus there—then opened fire on the Tutsis, killing many of them. At a bar in Kigali, I listened to a mixed group of Hutus and Tutsis discussing the incident. What seemed to disturb them most was that none of the Hutu minibus passengers, all of whom were left unharmed, had voluntarily come forward to identify themselves and report the attack.

Similar acts of terror continued, on an almost daily basis, throughout 1997 and the early months of 1998. In a good week, *only* one or two people might be killed, and in some weeks hundreds were killed. On at least half a dozen occasions, bands of more than a thousand well-coordinated Hutu Power fighters engaged the RPA in pitched battles for several days before retreating and melting back into the villages of the northwest, where they made their bases. As in the old UN border camps, the *génocidaires* lived indistinguishably intermingled with civilians, and thousands of unarmed Hutus were reported killed by RPA troops. The RPA was sensitive enough to these charges that it arrested hundreds of its own soldiers for committing atrocities against civilians, while Hutu Power's policy was to slaughter civilians who failed to join them in committing atrocities.

That was the choice in Rwanda's new-old war. In their wake the *génocidaires* left leaflets, warning that those who resisted them would be decapitated. Other leaflets told Tutsis, "You will all perish," and, "Good-bye! Your days are numbered." Hutus, for their part, were called upon, in the spirit of John Hanning Speke's Hamitic hypothesis, to drive all Tutsis "back to Abyssinia," and advised, "Whoever collaborates with the enemy, works for him, or gives him information, is also the enemy. We will systematically eliminate them."

One day, I stopped by the Justice Ministry to see Gerald Gahima. "How's justice?" I asked. He shook his head. For months, government ministers had been traveling around the country, from prison to prison, distributing copies of the special genocide law, and explaining its offer of sentence reductions for the vast majority of prisoners, if they wished to confess. But prisoners refused to

346

come forward. "It's deliberate sabotage," Gahima said. "Their leaders have them brainwashed. They still wish to maintain that there was no genocide in this country, when the fact of the matter is the genocide is still going on."

I wondered if the government regretted having the people home from the camps. "Never," Gahima told me. "The international community would have kept feeding them until we were all dead. So now just some of us die. We cannot be happy. We can only fight to live in peace." He smiled, a bit wearily, and said, "We have no exit strategy."

AFTER ONLY A few days in Kigali, I experienced the sense of total exhaustion that on previous trips had taken weeks, sometimes months, to overwhelm me. I booked a seat on the next flight out, and spent my days on a friend's porch, surrounded by bird-of-paradise flowers, listening to songbirds, watching the towering clouds over the valley collide and shred, and I escaped into a hundred-year-old novel about a dentist in San Francisco. The book was *McTeague*, by Frank Norris, and its final pages told of two men, once the brotherly best of friends, who meet and fight in the alkaline desolation of a lonely desert; one kills the other, but in their struggle, the dead man has handcuffed their wrists together.

I put the book down and went to have a beer with a Rwandan friend. I told him the story I had just read, that ultimate image: one man dead, the other locked to the body—in the desert.

"But, Philip," my friend said, "let's not be idiots. Where there are handcuffs, there's a key."

I reminded him that there was no key to unlock the vast desert in which the surviving man was stranded. I used Gahima's phrase, "No exit strategy."

"Novels are nice," my friend said. "They stop." He waggled his fingers to make quotation marks in the air. "They say, 'The End.' Very nice. A marvelous invention. Here we have stories, but never 'The End.'" He drank some beer. Then he said, "I've thought a lot lately about Jack the Ripper, because the Tutsis now say, 'Jack is in.' They don't say it, but that's the thought since this return from Zaire. They don't tell you that they haven't slept all night because there are assassins in the wall. But think of what happens in the conscience of a Tutsi who expects the arrival of his killer."

I thought about it, and what came to mind was the letter that Pastor Elizaphan Ntakirutimana, the former Adventist church president of Kibuye, gave me in Laredo, Texas—the letter he had received on April 15, 1994, from the seven Tutsi pastors who were among the refugees at Mugonero hospital telling him they would be killed on the morrow, and saying, "your intervention will be highly appreciated, the same way as the Jews were saved by Esther."

Esther was the wife of Ahasuerus, a Persian emperor, whose dominion stretched from India to Ethiopia, two and a half thousand years before the massacre at Mugonero. The essence of the story is well known to readers of the Bible: how Esther marries Ahasuerus without telling him that she is an orphaned Jew, raised by her uncle, Mordechai; how Ahasuerus's chief deputy, Haman, despises Mordechai because the Jew refuses to bow down before him; how Haman persuades Ahasuerus to issue a decree calling on his subjects throughout his realm "to destroy, to slay, and to annihilate all Jews, young and old, women and children, in one day . . . and to plunder their goods"; how Esther reveals her identity to her husband, and pleads with him to spare her people; and how the wicked Haman is ultimately hanged on the very gallows he had built for Mordechai. But there is a final, less widely remembered chapter to this heartening story of genocide averted: when Ahasuerus rescinds his earlier order of extermination, Esther has him add a clause allowing Jews "to gather and defend their lives, to destroy, to slay, and to annihilate any armed force of any people or province that might attack them, with their children and women, and to plunder their goods." In all, the Bible reports, Jews and their allies slew some seventy-five thousand eight hundred "enemies" before peace was restored to the empire with a day of "feasting and gladness."

The Tutsi pastors at Mugonero would have known their Scripture. Did they, as they waited to be slaughtered, yearn not only to be spared but also to see the enemies of Rwanda's peace liquidated? The hopes for redemption that stories like Esther's have inspired among persecuted peoples invariably carry a faith in the restorative power of avenging justice. "Pharaoh's army got drownded—oh, Mary, don't you weep," recalled the old American slave song, just as Homer sang of the sack of Troy and Odysseus's slaughter of the suitors at Ithaca.

By the late twentieth century, of course, we liked to imagine that there were better ways to make righteousness prevail against the wicked in what used to be called "international society" and today goes by the more inclusive term "humanity." My friend felt that the rest of humanity had betrayed Rwanda in 1994, but he had not lost his faith in the idea of humanity.

"I think of your country," he told me. "You say all men are created equal. It's not true and you know it. It's just the only acceptable political truth. Even here in this tiny country with one language, we aren't one people, but we must pretend until we become one. That's a big problem. I know so many people who lost everyone. A young man will come to me for advice. He'll say, 'I saw one who did it. I was sixteen then, but I'm twenty now. I have a gun. Will you turn me in if I settle the matter?' I'll have to say, 'I, too, lost much family, but I didn't know them. I was in exile—in Zaire, in Burundi. Those I lost—it's a little abstract—I didn't know them, there wasn't the love.' So if this soldier asks my advice, what do I tell him? It's a terrible business. I'll take my time. I'll take him for a walk. I'll caress him to calm him. I'll try to find his superior officer and brief him, and say, 'Watch this little one.' But seriously, eh? This isn't going away in one year or two years or five years or ten years—this horror that we saw. It's intrinsic."

I didn't say anything, and after a while my friend said, "We better find the keys to those handcuffs."

IN MID-DECEMBER OF 1997, Secretary of State Madeleine Albright delivered a speech to the Organization of African Unity in Addis Ababa in which she said, "We, the international community, should have been more active in the early stages of the atrocities in Rwanda in 1994, and called them what they were— genocide." Albright, who would be making a brief visit to Rwanda during her tour of Africa, also condemned the use of humanitarian aid "to sustain armed camps or to support genocidal killers." Simple words—but politicians tend to dislike having to say such things; that same month, in New York, I heard a senior emissary of the UNHCR sum up the experience of the Hutu Power controlled camps in Zaire with the formulation, "Yes, mistakes were made, but we are not responsible." Albright's "apology," as it came to be known, marked a significant break with the habits of shame and defensiveness that often conspired to deny the basic facts of the Rwandan genocide their rightful place in international memory.

Three months later, President Clinton followed Albright to Africa, and on March 25, 1998, he became the first Western head of state to visit Rwanda since the genocide. His stop there was brief—he never left the airport—but it was highly charged. After listening for several hours to the stories of genocide survivors, Clinton forcefully reiterated Albright's apologies for refusing to intervene during the slaughter, and for supporting the killers in the camps. "During the ninety days that began on April 6, 1994, Rwanda experienced the most intensive slaughter in this blood-filled century," Clinton said, adding, "It is important that the world know that these killings were not spontaneous or accidental

350

. . . they were most certainly not the result of ancient tribal struggles. . . . These events grew from a policy aimed at the systematic destruction of a people." And this mattered not only to Rwanda but also to the world, he explained, because "each bloodletting hastens the next, and as the value of human life is degraded and violence becomes tolerated, the unimaginable becomes more conceivable."

Clinton's regrets about the past were more convincing than his assurances for the future. When he said, "Never again must we be shy in the face of the evidence" of genocide, there was no reason to believe that the world was a safer place than it had been in April of 1994. If Rwanda's experience could be said to carry any lessons for the world, it was that endangered peoples who depend on the international community for physical protection stand defenseless. On the morning of Albright's visit to Rwanda in December, Hutu Power terrorists, shouting "Kill the cockroaches," had hacked, bludgeoned, and shot to death more than three hundred Tutsis at an encampment in the northwest, and in the days before Clinton's arrival in Kigali, as many as fifty Tutsis were killed in similar massacres. Against such a backdrop, Clinton's pledge to "work as partners with Rwanda to end this violence" sounded deliberately vague.

Still, in Rwanda, where expectations of the great powers had been bitterly diminished to very nearly zero, Clinton's account of the political organization of the genocide and his praise for the government's "efforts to create a single nation in which all citizens can live freely and securely" were understood as the sharpest international rebuke yet to the ongoing bid by the *génocidaires* to equate ethnicity with politics and to prove that equation by murder. It was a measure of Rwanda's sense of isolation that his remarks were heralded as extraordinary. After all, Clinton was simply proclaiming the obvious. But he had been under no political pressure to pay attention to Rwanda; he might more easily have continued to ignore the place and said nothing. Instead, hav-

ing chosen to sit out the genocide, he was making what was—
even at so late a date—a dramatic intervention in the war about
the genocide. As the voice of the greatest power on earth, he had
come to Kigali to set the record straight.

"It was very startling to us," a Hutu friend told me over the
phone from Kigali. "Here was a politician who had nothing at
stake, and who told the truth at his own expense." And a Tutsi I
called told me, "What he said to us is that we are not just forgotten
savages. Maybe you have to live somewhere far away like the
White House to see Rwanda like that. Life here remains terrible.
But your Mr. Clinton made us feel less alone." He laughed. "It
should be surprising that somebody who didn't really seem to
mind seeing your people get killed can make you feel like that.
But it's hard to surprise a Rwandan anymore."

I CANNOT COUNT the times, since I first began visiting
Rwanda three years ago, that I've been asked, "Is there any hope
for that place?" In response, I like to quote the hotel manager
Paul Rusesabagina. When he told me that the genocide had left
him "disappointed," Paul added, "With my countrymen—
Rwandans—you never know what they will become tomorrow."
Although he didn't mean it that way, this struck me as one of the
most optimistic things a Rwandan could say after the genocide,
not unlike General Kagame's claim that people "can be made bad,
and they can be taught to be good."

But hope is a force more easy to name and declare one's al-
legiance to than to enact. So I'll leave you to decide if there is
hope for Rwanda with one more story. On April 30, 1997—almost
a year ago as I write—Rwandan television showed footage of a
man who confessed to having been among a party of *génocidaires*
who had killed seventeen schoolgirls and a sixty-two-year-old Belgian nun at a boarding school in Gisenyi two nights earlier. It was
the second such attack on a school in a month; the first time,
sixteen students were killed and twenty injured in Kibuye.

The prisoner on television explained that the massacre was part of a Hutu Power "liberation" campaign. His band of a hundred fifty militants was composed largely of ex-FAR and *interahamwe*. During their attack on the school in Gisenyi, as in the earlier attack on the school in Kibuye, the students, teenage girls who had been roused from their sleep, were ordered to separate themselves—Hutus from Tutsis. But the students had refused. At both schools, the girls said they were simply Rwandans, so they were beaten and shot indiscriminately.

Rwandans have no need—no room in their corpse-crowded imaginations—for more martyrs. None of us does. But mightn't we all take some courage from the example of those brave Hutu girls who could have chosen to live, but chose instead to call themselves Rwandans?

May 1995–April 1998

353

ACKNOWLEDGMENTS

I am indebted above all to the hundreds of Rwandans in all walks of private and public life who generously entrusted me with their stories.

To supplement my own reporting, I consulted a great variety of writings on Rwanda, published and unpublished. I wish to acknowledge the authors of some of the standard works, representing diverse perspectives, which helped to inform me: Colette Braeckmann, Jean-Pierre Chrétien, Alain Destexhe, Alison des Forges, André Guichaoua, René Lemarchand, Louis de Lacger, Catherine Newbury, Rakiya Omaar, Gérard Prunier, and Filip Reyntjens. I'm also grateful for the United Nations IRIN electronic news bulletins.

My reporting from Rwanda first appeared in *The New Yorker*, and the support of its editors has been essential in writing this book. I am especially grateful to Tina Brown for her unflagging commitment to this distant and difficult story, to Bill Buford, who first sent me to Rwanda, and to my superb editor, Jeffrey Frank, whose advice, friendship, and sanity have buoyed me through my work. Jennifer Bluestein, Jessica Green, and Valerie Steiker helped with research and as anchors during my long absences from home; Henry Finder, William Finnegan, and David Remnick gave good counsel; John Dorfman, Ted Katauskas, and Liesl Schillinger in the fact-checking department, along with Eleanor Gould and an army of back-up readers, saved me from many errors and infelicities.

Many thanks to the editors of *The New York Review of Books, Transition, DoubleTake, The New York Times Magazine* and its Op-Ed Page, for publishing pieces of my work from central Africa. And special thanks to Seth Lipsky, at *The Forward*, who first put me to work as a reporter.

Many thanks to Elisabeth Sifton, my editor at Farrar, Straus and Giroux. Her intelligence, humor, and rigor—always invigorating—make it an honor to work with her.

Many thanks for the kindness and guidance of Sarah Chalfant at the Wylie Agency, whose commitment has been a boon to my writing life. And thanks also to Chris Calhoun for his dedication and friendship at the outset.

Many thanks to the Corporation of Yaddo, where part of this book was written; to the echoing green foundation and The United States Institute for Peace, for essential financial support; and to The World Policy Institute for institutional support.

Many thanks for the generous hospitality in Kigali of Richard Danziger, Aline Ndenzako and their daughter Daisy, and of Peter Whaley, Kate Crawford and their daughter Susan. On the road in Rwanda and Zaire, Alison Campbell, Thierry Cruvelier, and Annick van Lookeren Campagne were great company. At home, in New York, Vijay Balakrishnan provided a crucial pillar of friendship and a sharp ear for work in progress. I am especially fortunate to have wise parents, Jacqueline and Victor Gourevitch, and a true brother, Marc, who are my most demanding and rewarding readers, great companions, and a constant stimulus. I also thank my grandmother, Anna Moisievna Gourevitch; my memory of the stories she told me presides over this book. Finally, Elizabeth Rubin, by her example, her intelligence and her pluck, her wit and her warmth, has inspired and sustained me throughout this work. For her company, from near and from far, I am truly grateful.